BRACKLEY
THROUGH TIME

Trevor Davies

AMBERLEY PUBLISHING

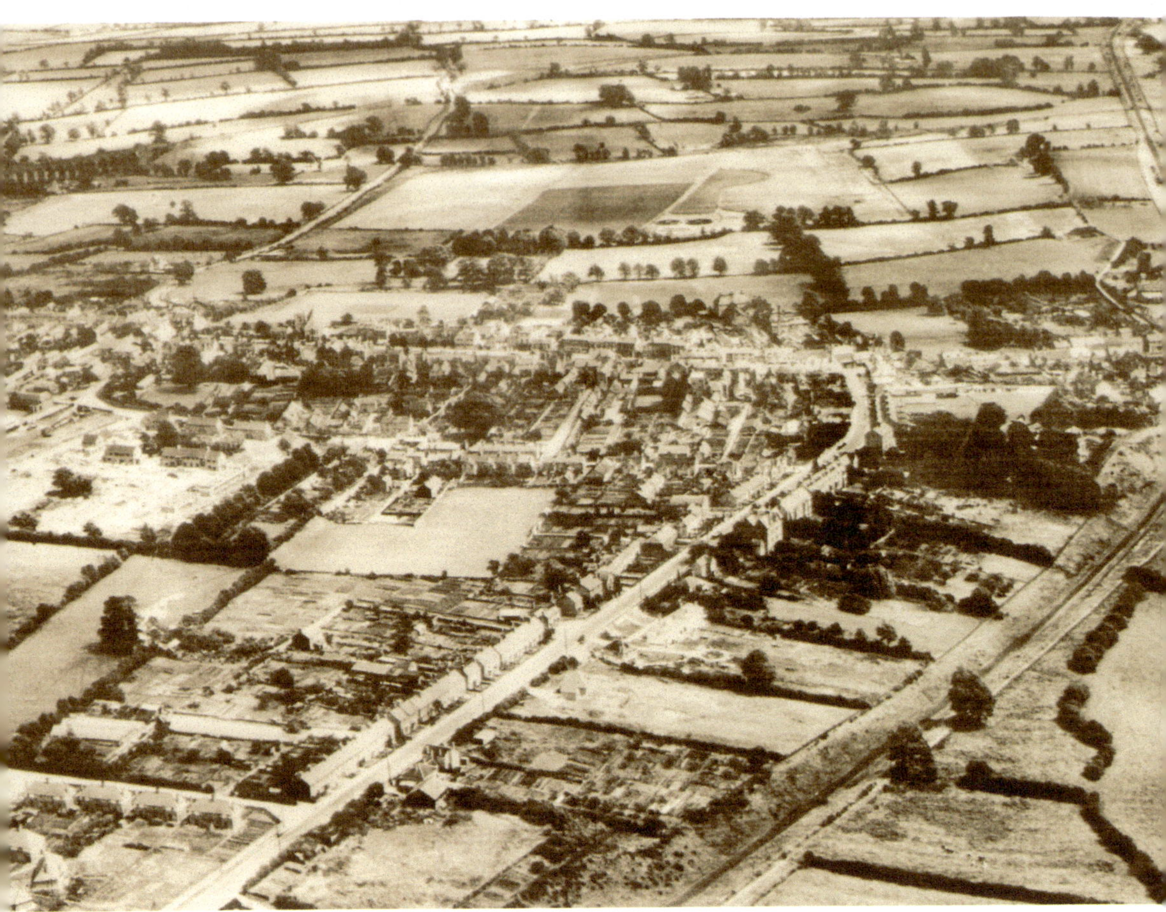

Aerial Map of Brackley Before Modern Developments

First published 2014

Amberley Publishing
The Hill, Stroud, Gloucestershire, GL5 4EP
www.amberley-books.com

ISBN 978 1 4456 1893 7 (print)
ISBN 978 1 4456 1905 7(ebook)

British Library Cataloguing in Publication Data.
A catalogue record for this book is available from the British Library.

Typesetting by Amberley Publishing.
Printed in Great Britain.

Introduction

The High Street today is nearly a mile in length and extends from the southern bypass roundabout (near Tesco supermarket), up the hill and through the town until it meets the northern part of the bypass at the BP petrol station roundabout. It contains many good quality houses, mostly built of stone. Large, modern estates have developed over the last fifty years and will continue to be developed in the foreseeable future. The chief industries in the Middle Ages were wool, lace and agriculture, while today Brackley is the home of many food, racing, chemical and finance industries. There are currently three main industrial/commercial estates in the town.

Today, the town is set in the heart of an area of major economic growth, with associated commercial and residential properties and infrastructure being created. Major expansion is taking place in Milton Keynes, Bicester and Banbury. Road connections between Brackley, local towns and the North and South of England are generally excellent. The town today is conveniently located for the A43 dual carriageway, allowing easy access to the M40 and M1 motorways. The road system is probably down to the Romans consolidating their conquest of the country and establishing a network of roads for communication and supply purposes. Watling Street runs quite close to Brackley. Railway services can be found in Banbury, Bicester and Milton Keynes.

The accepted theory about the origin of the name of Brackley is that it is derived from the legacy of a man called Bracca, who lived between AD 550 and 650. He owned a 'ley', or clearing, and founded a small village, which became known as Braccaley, consequently evolving into Brackley. Secondly, generations of Brackley people believed that it derived its name from the Anglo-Saxon *Bracken*, meaning 'fern', which was present in large amounts in the neighbourhood, but apparently the area was forested, not heathland. 'Brackley' is also a Germanic word, so it could be that its roots are down to the Saxon invaders.

The town has royal connections and was the site of an important meeting between the barons and representatives of the King in 1215, the year of Magna Carta. King John and the barons were apparently planning to sign Magna Carta at Brackley Castle, but eventually did so at Runnymede.

The site of a castle built by one of the Norman barons is still called Castle Hill. They wanted to get from Oxford to Northampton as quickly and safely as possible, so they built one of their motte-and-bailey castles to protect their ford and new road from hostile Saxon peasants. Samuel Clarke, an eminent Orientalist and one of the co-adjutors of Bishop Walton in publishing the Polyglot Bible, was born here in 1623. Dr Bathurst, Bishop of Norwich, who died in 1837, was also a native. Brackley gives the title of Viscount to the Earl of Ellesmere.

In the 1860s, Brackley featured in Karl Marx's famous book *Das Capital* as being one of the most downtrodden places in England for agricultural workers. The economic strength of the town has generally waxed and waned over the centuries. The thirteenth, seventeenth and nineteenth centuries were particular high points.

Local historian Professor John Clark believes that one of Brackley's most important residents, the poet Mary Leaper, was born in 1720, She is currently becoming a cult figure in the USA. She died in 1746.

The town is anxious to take advantage of the new economic strength associated with the surrounding area, and a series of new developments are shortly to commence, including new housing developments, a supermarket, new medical services and a full upgrade of the town hall. South Northamptonshire Council has been working with the town council and local community to put Brackley on a footing to find a new era of prosperity and well-being.

The community of Brackley has a strong and resilient heart, with many residents having family connections for many decades, even centuries. It has many successful and long-standing community organisations providing for a wide variety of different ages and interests. For example, Brackley organises wonderful annual festivals: the Carnival, music festival, beer festival, wine festival, food festival, Festival of Motorcycling, Soapbox Derby and others. Brackley's association with music goes back a long way, and the town is particularly renowned for its brass band and music festival. Sometime in the 1890s, Sir John Stainer conducted a performance of *The Crucifixion* in the town. While there are those who feel that its central identity has been lacking for many years and that many recent residents of Brackley do not fully engage with the town, there is a sense that the future is altogether at least as exciting as Brackley's past; many people are working hard for a better Brackley, including the local town council, various civic groups and local businesses.

Acknowledgements

Thanks to my fellow Rotarian, Caryl Billingham, a past mayor of Brackley and fount of knowledge about the town, for her time, tolerance and patience. Thanks also to rotarians Paul Whitney and David Johnson for their insightful comments and assistance with recorded memories.

Many thanks to Revd Terry Richards for checking factual and presentational accuracy of the material, and to Rosemary Leeper for the benefit of accessing her research.

I am grateful to Steve Goulding, Irene Freeman, Alan Jukes, Carole Walton, Geoff Wilkins, Sonia Bowmar-Cothern, Samantha Saunders, Robert Franklin, Stephen Done, Doug Ryan, Anna Yates, Philip Purdie for helping me to source suitable old photographs of Brackley.

My thanks also to many people for their memories and reflections on Brackley past, present and future.

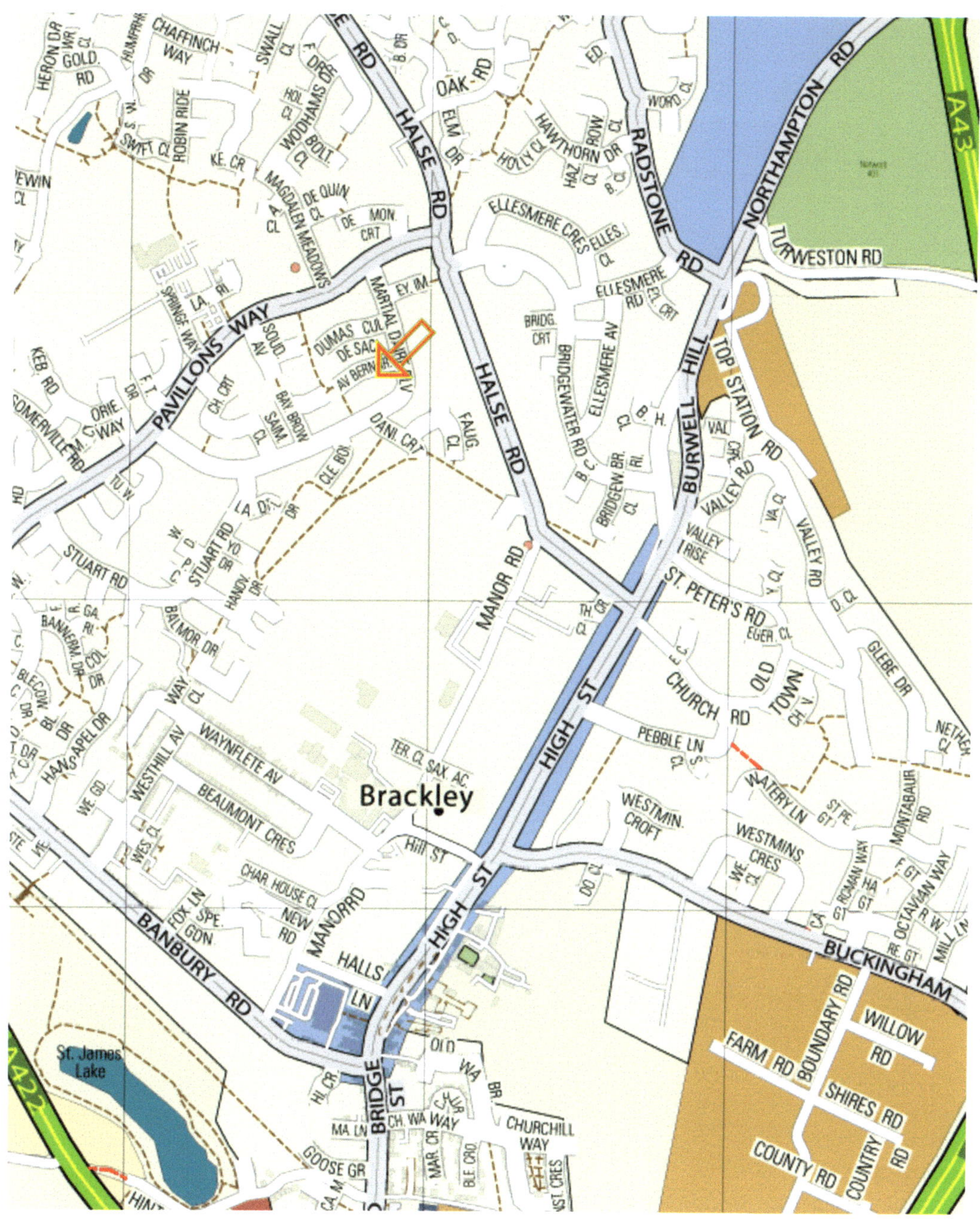

Current Street Map of Brackley

Part 1

A Journey from South to North

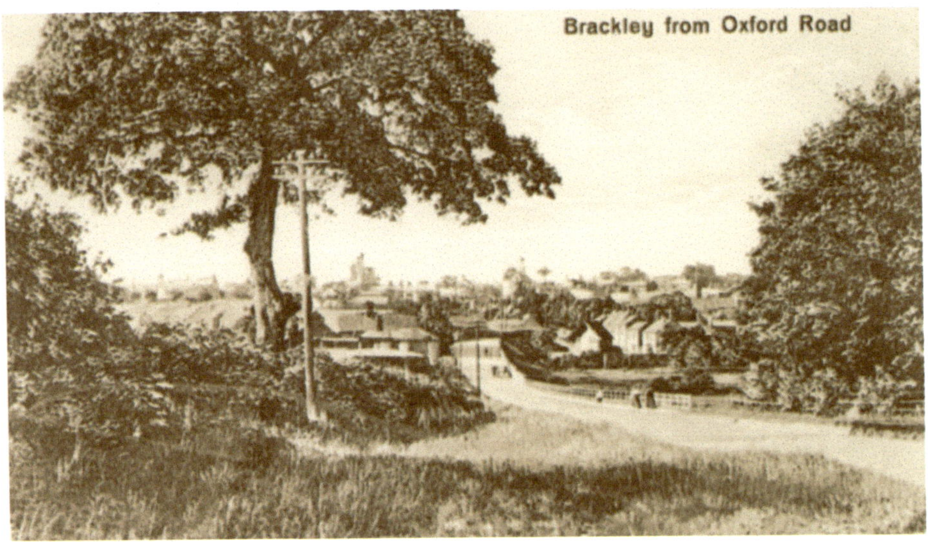

View Towards Railway Bridge Travelling North

An idyllic view of the run into Brackley at the turn of the twentieth century. The old photograph is taken from the old A43 that ran adjacent to the new southbound road (that originally ran only to 'Bottom station'). The railway ran through the foreground (*see humpback bridge*). All of the railway infrastructure was removed in the late 1960s to make way for alternative commercial developments. Now the busy A43 Brackley bypass runs from where the photograph was taken, steering the heavy traffic travelling from north to south away from the centre of Brackley.

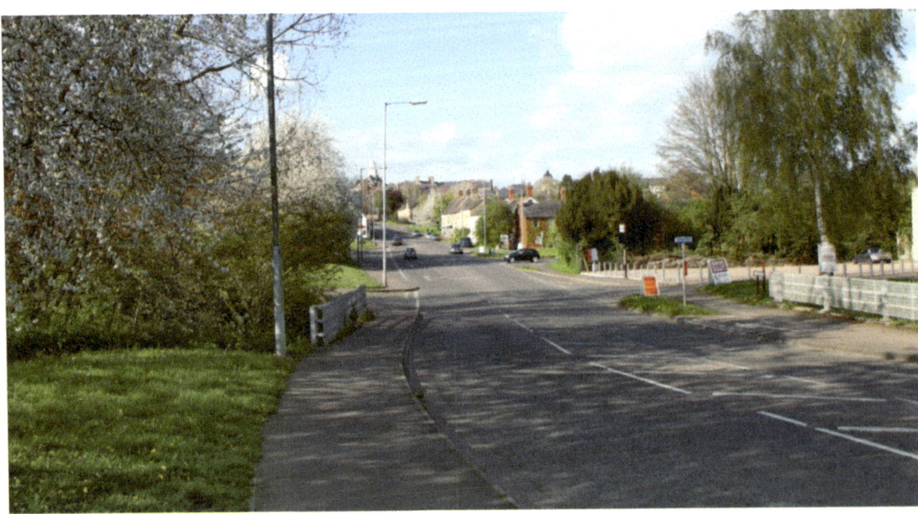

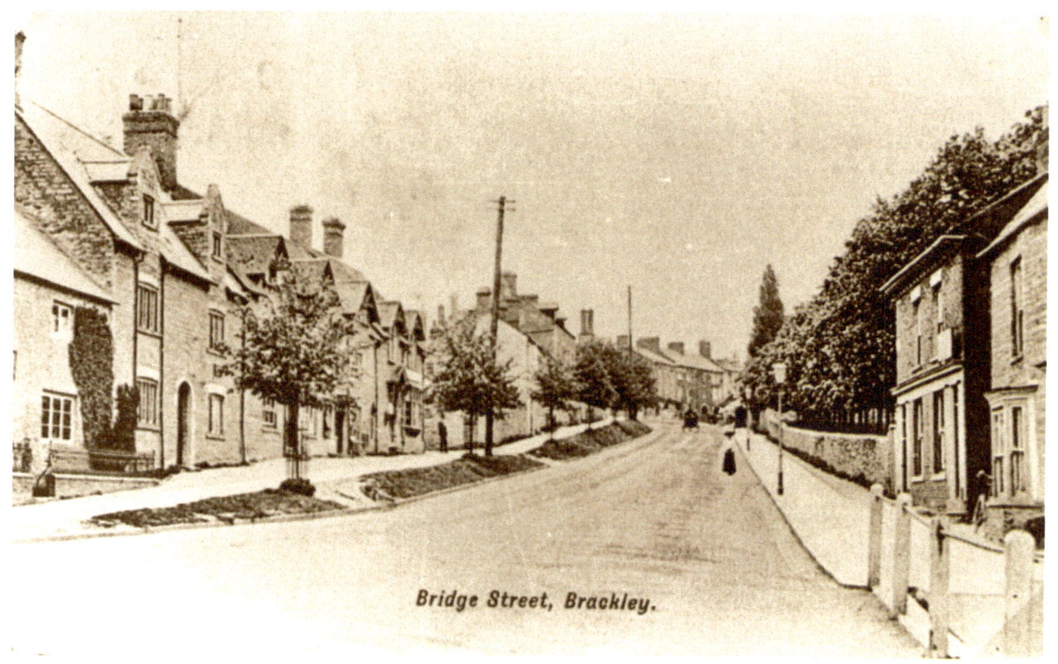

Bridge Street, 1908

Near Here, the castle church of St James used to exist near the new fire station. The church was demolished in 1836, but the remains of the gravestones can be seen in the verge opposite the fire station (*see inset*). Looking up Bridge Street from the bottom of the hill, the second cottage on the right used to be a sweet shop run by Mrs Twynham, which was then turned into a television shop. The cottage is owned by the Feoffee charity, who also now own No. 33. Cars, street furniture and road lines litter the view today.

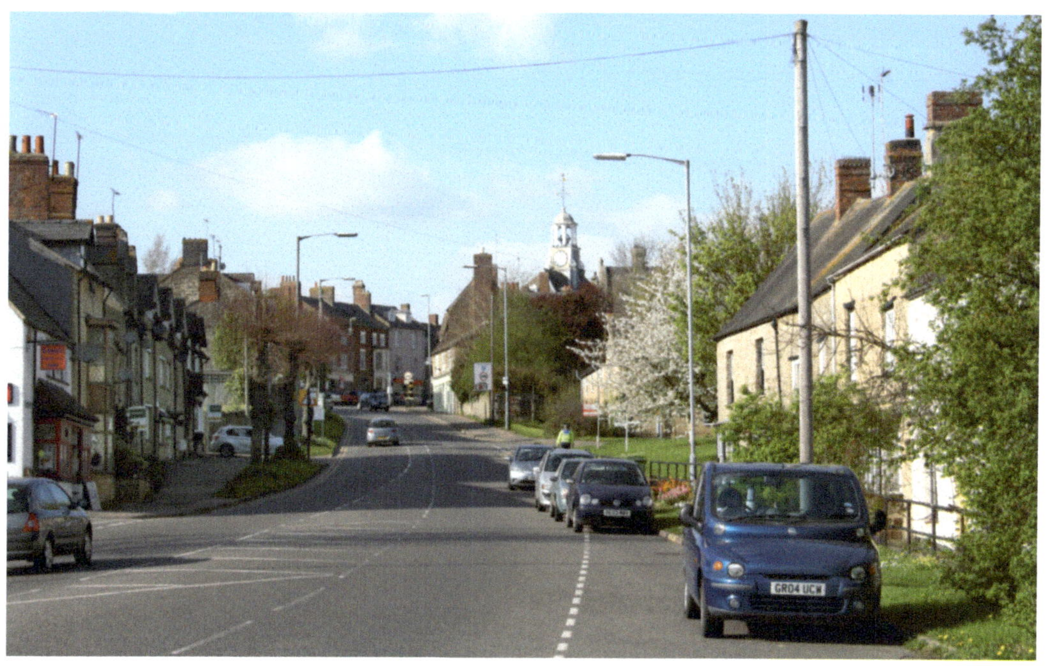

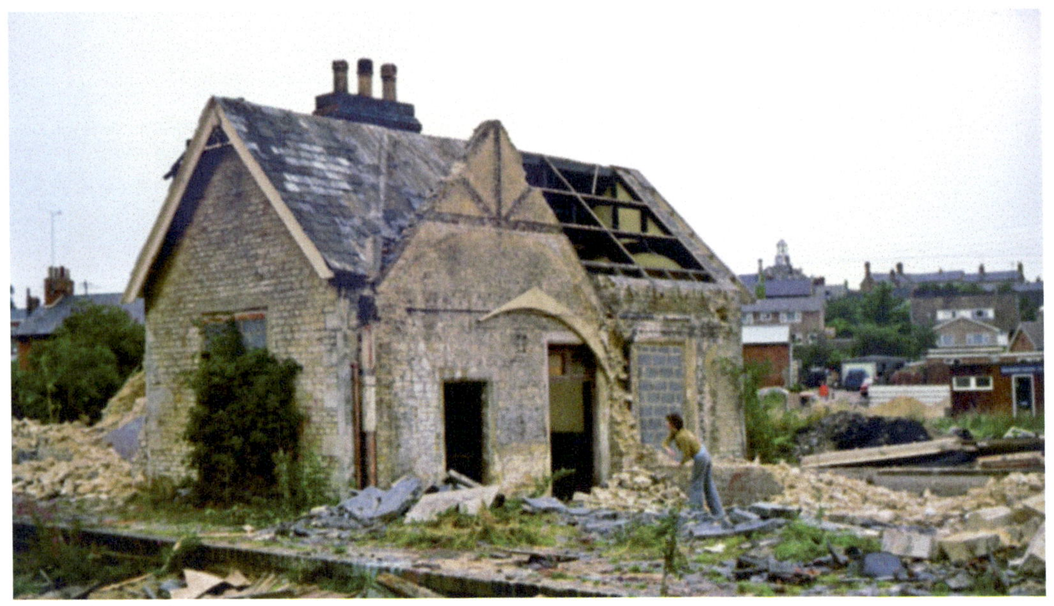

Brackley Town Station, 1976

This station would now be perfect to travel to Banbury, Buckingham or even Bletchley. Brackley was an attractive station with a building of local yellow-grey stone, situated on the St James industrial estate. This building was the old booking office/waiting room. There was quite a lot of open ground around the station itself. The station consisted of a single loop serving two platforms. The goods yard was quite small and included a cattle dock and a goods shed at right angles to the line, requiring a turntable. There was also a water tank on a single column fed by a nearby stream. The Locomotive public house was always in its current position on the other side of the road, and the Hinton Road was realigned after the bridge over the railway was taken away and the A43 straightened. Previously, you drove over the humpbacked bridge and then turned directly right into Hinton Road.

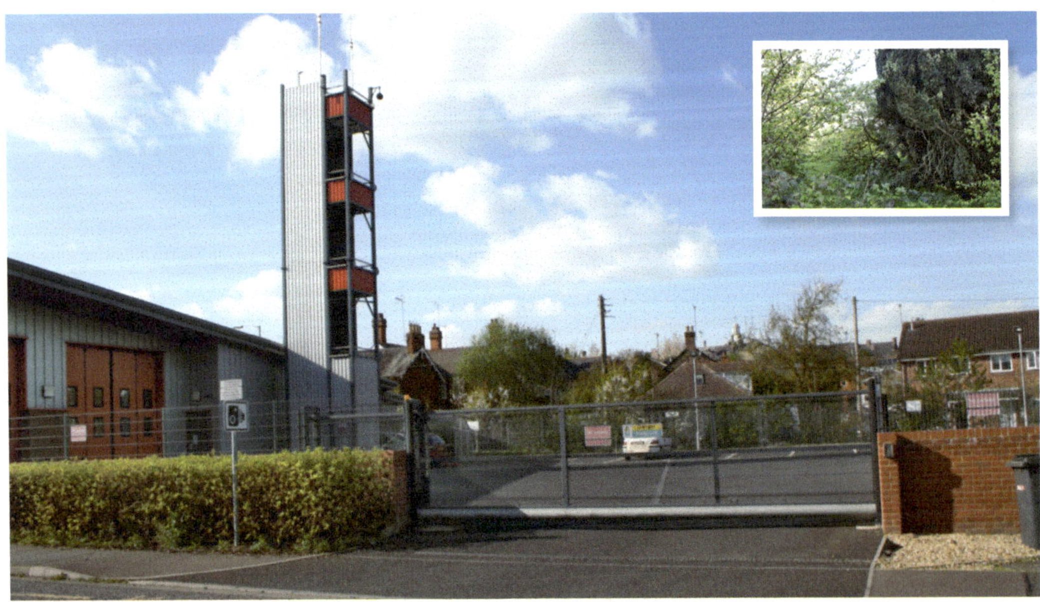

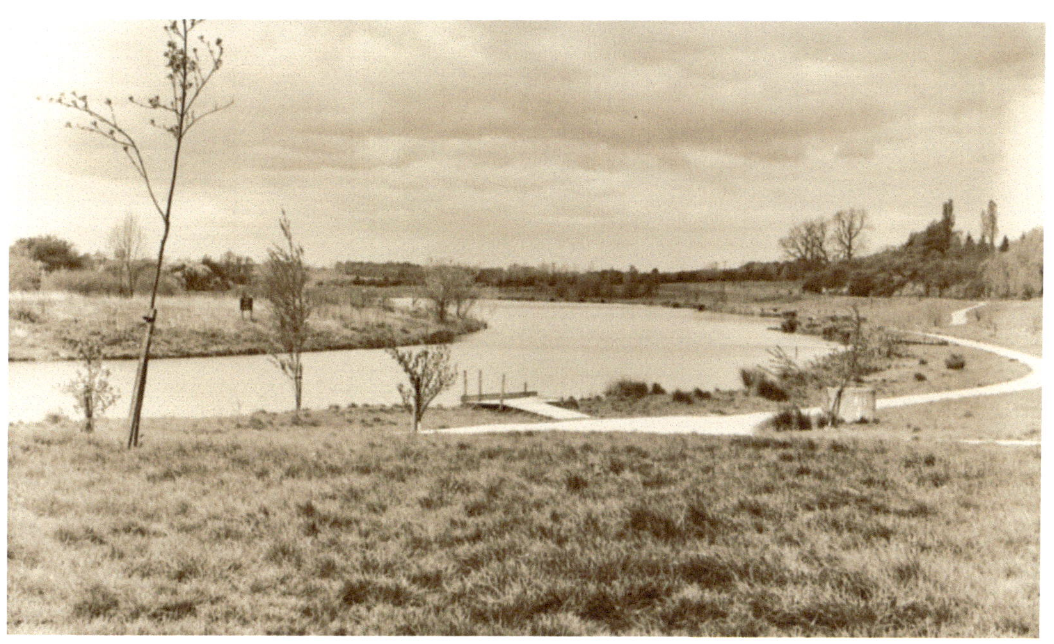

St James Lake, *c.* 1980

The lake is thought to have been created on or around the site of Brackley Castle, which was destroyed in 1173. Previously a fishing lake, the current lake is man made and covers approximately 3 acres. It is surrounded by parkland of around 5 acres. It was created by the Anglian Water Authority in 1977 as a balancing lake for the new residential development of Brackley. The site is tranquil and popular for family walks, waterfowl and diverse birdlife. A pocket park follows the old railway cutting running adjacent to the park. The Rotary Club of Brackley coordinated the initial planting of trees around the lake.

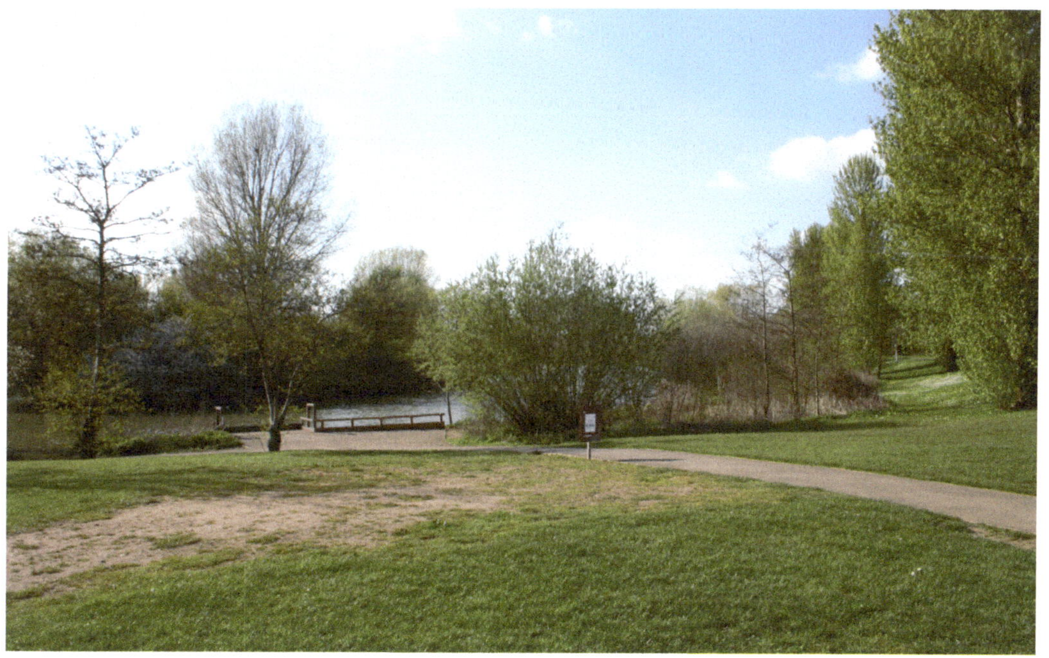

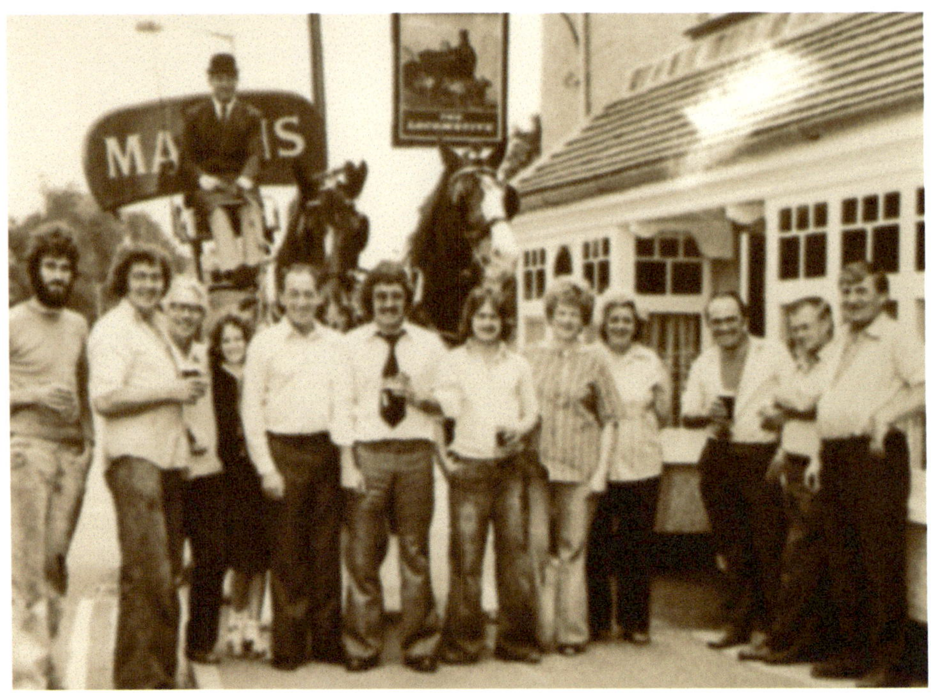

Locomotive Inn, 1950s

Illustrating the days when Brackley had a railway, photographed near the site of 'Bottom station'. The Locomotive was always a locals' pub, but at one time would also have been open to passing trade when the railways were working with commuters and visitors were travelling regularly to Brackley. Mrs Miller and George were the publicans in the 1950s. The Locomotive public house is below.

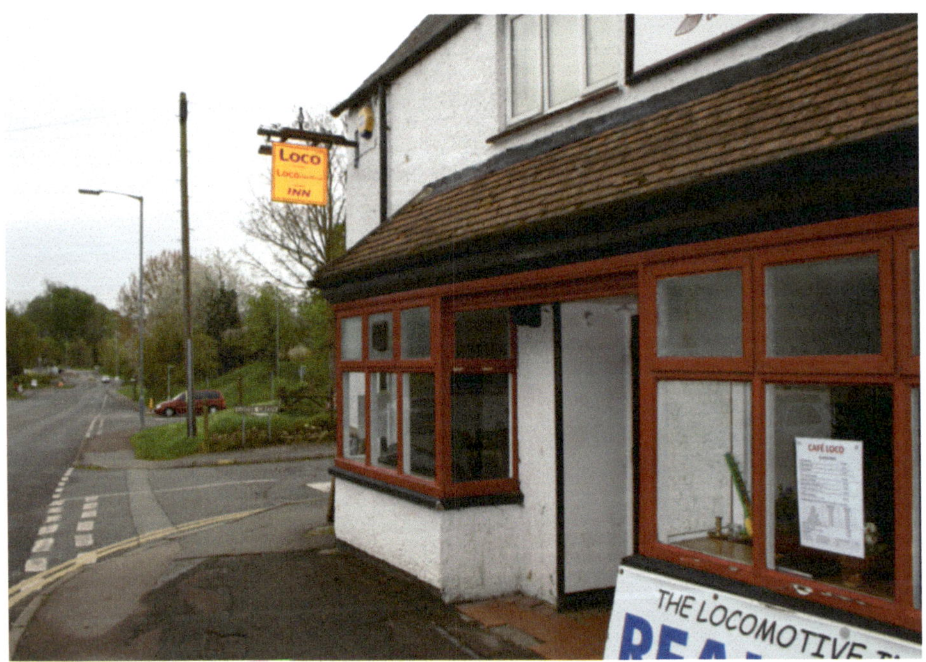

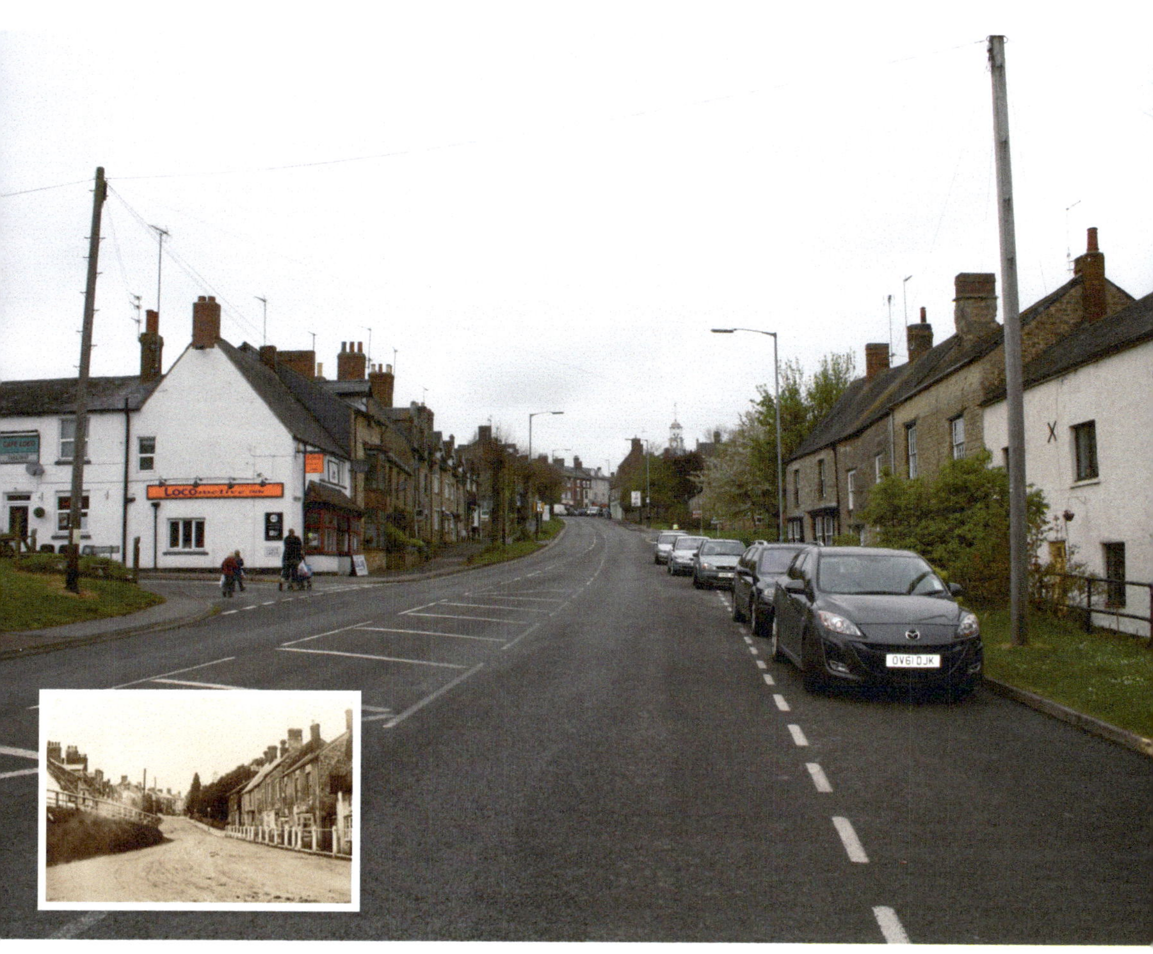

Bridge Street, *c.* 1930s

The road adjacent to the houses led directly to the bottom station and to Herrieff's Farm Road. The old main road went away to the other side of the fence on the left-hand side and over the railway bridge at the bottom. When the road was straightened to its current arrangement, the lane to the station (from which the old photograph was taken) became the highway. There was probably a pub or a hotel near No. 36 or No. 38.

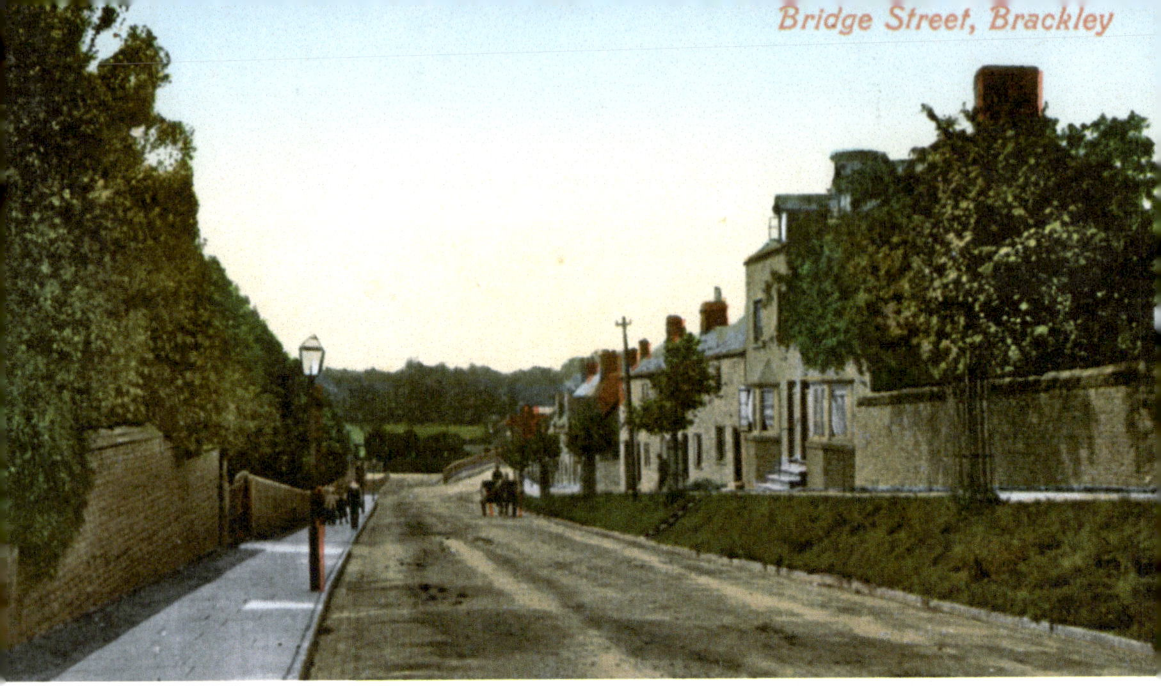

Bridge Street, *c.* 1900

Looking south towards the bridge, near to what is now the Mercedes Petronas entrance. Behind the wall on the left is a Victorian Gothic building that became a nursing home. Previously, it was owned by a Rotarian dentist, Colin Miller, a past mayor of Brackley. Behind the building is now a modern twentieth-century residential estate. Individual cottages and houses line the hill. On the right behind the wall was the garden of Brown's Central Stores. At the bottom of the hill and over the bridge, the countryside began with expansive fields developed in the 1960s. A gasometer and gasworks also stood on this site prior to development.

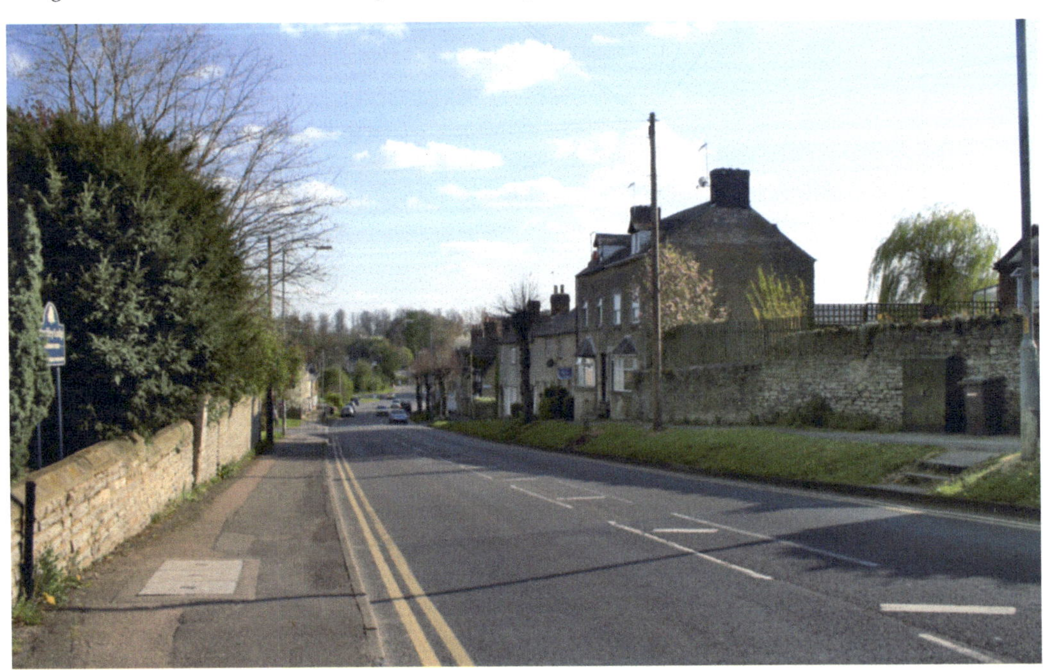

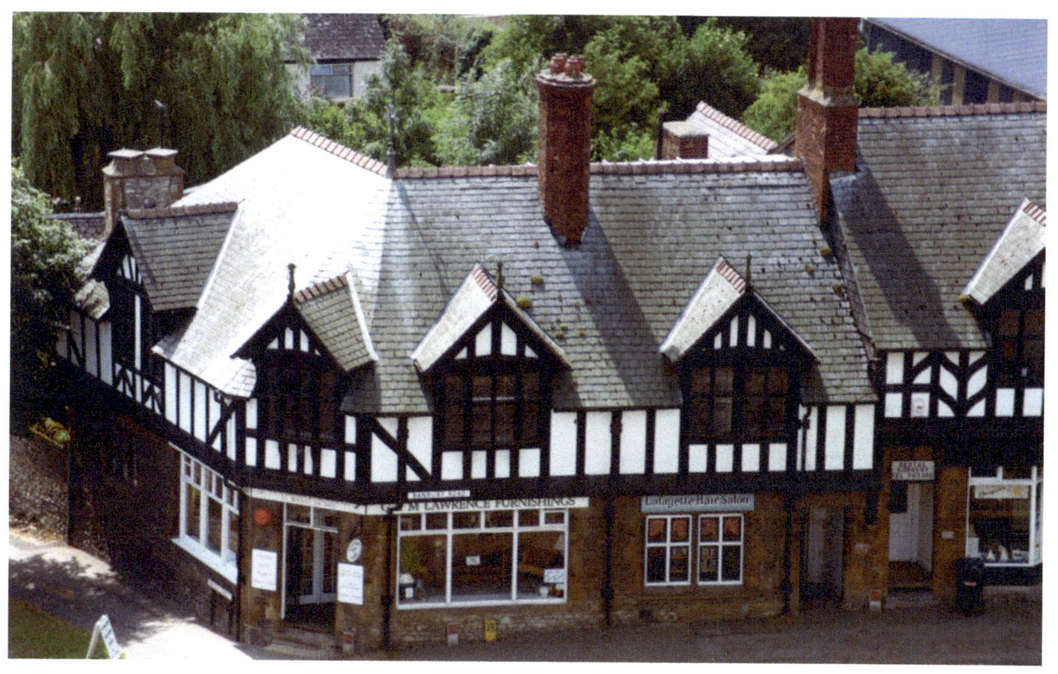

Junction of Bridge Street and Banbury Road, 1994

The photograph above shows the shop at the junction of Bridge Street and the Banbury Road in 1994. The character of the Banbury Road was shaped by the Victorian expansion of Brackley. It is a timber-framed building that gives real character to this part of the town. G&M Lawrence Furnishing occupied the premises for many years until 2005, followed by the RSPCA. The optician's and Baileys Solicitors' have been neighbours on the Banbury Road for some time.

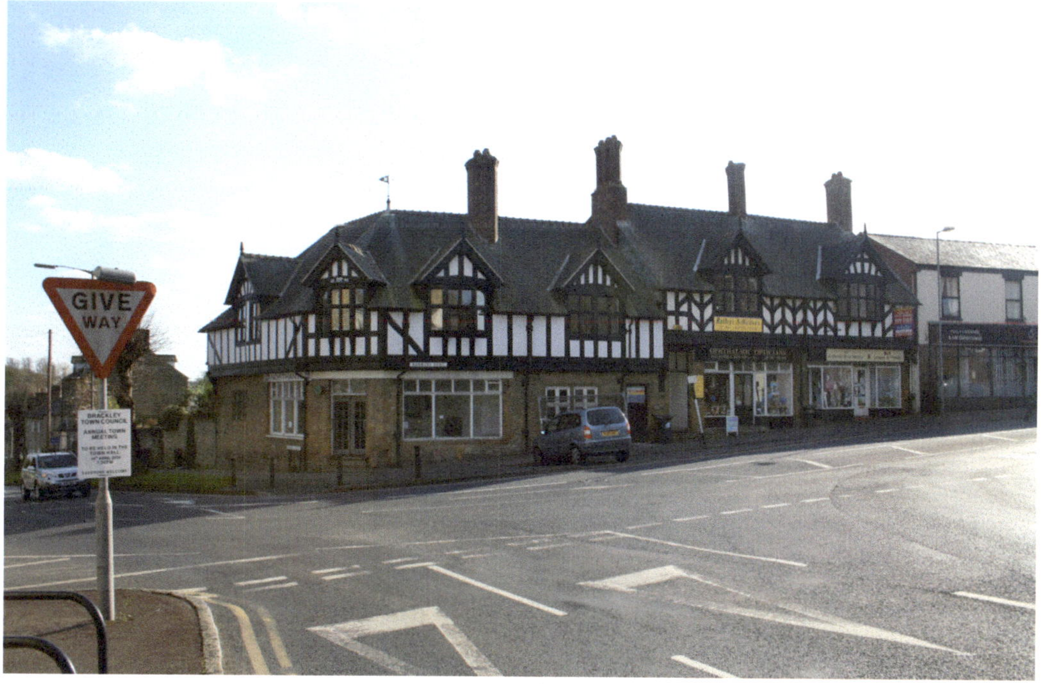

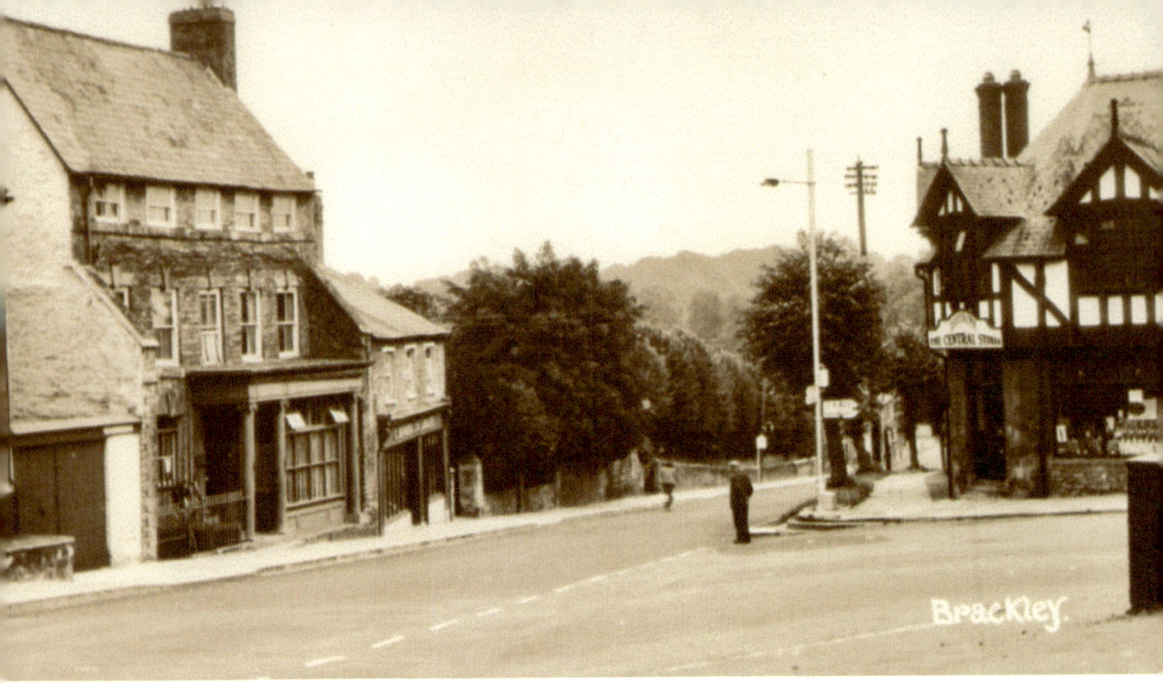

Top of Bridge Street, 1812

Buildings along Bridge Street are generally made of stone with slate roofs. Many have small timber casement windows, with long wooden lintels reflecting the building tradition at the time. In the photograph shown, the occupier was F. Allen, tobacconist and confectioner. Now it is known as the Green Room café, a pleasant meeting centre for coffees and light snacks to watch the world go by. Prior to that, it was a hairdressing salon – Andrea and Achille. At one stage in its history, it was a saddler's, and after that it was Kieldson and August Accountant's. In the 1950s, the building was owned by Mr Delves.

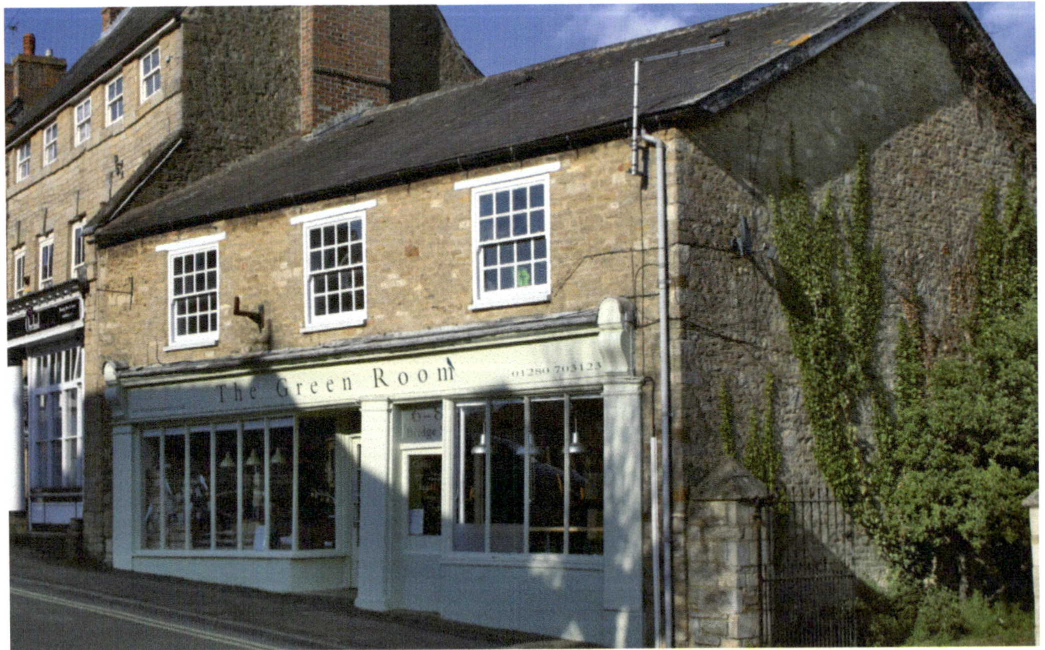

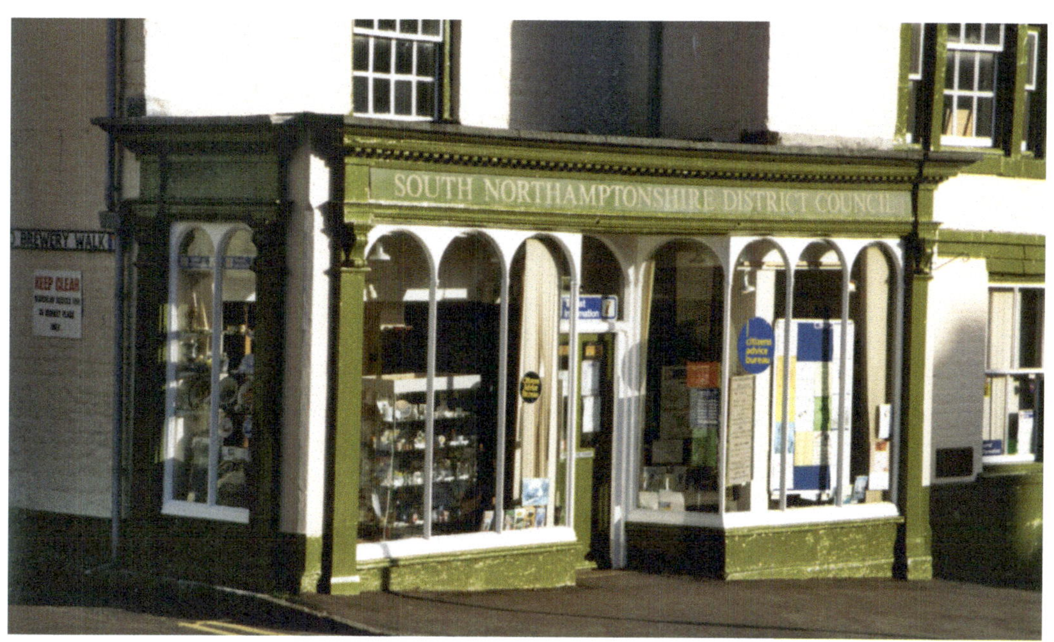

Bridge Street

Bridge Street forms part of the original thirteenth-century planned town. Most of the buildings along the street are from the eighteenth century or earlier. This building is characterful in the way it links to the next building over the archway. The Hopcroft and Norris brewery was once situated through the archway. The building shown was used by South Northamptonshire as a tourist office in the 1990s, where tourists and locals could obtain tickets and information for local events and activities and materials to help access the beautiful surrounding area to Brackley. It was Vyle & Co. gents' outfitters in the 1960s. Bronnley's had a shop and office when the outfitters closed, until SNC took the premises over. It is now a dental practice called Orchid's.

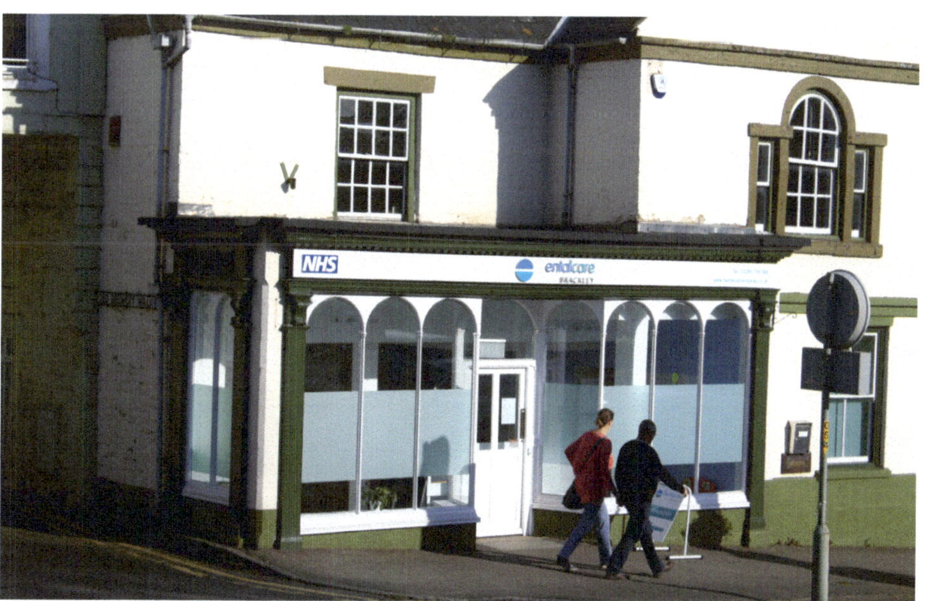

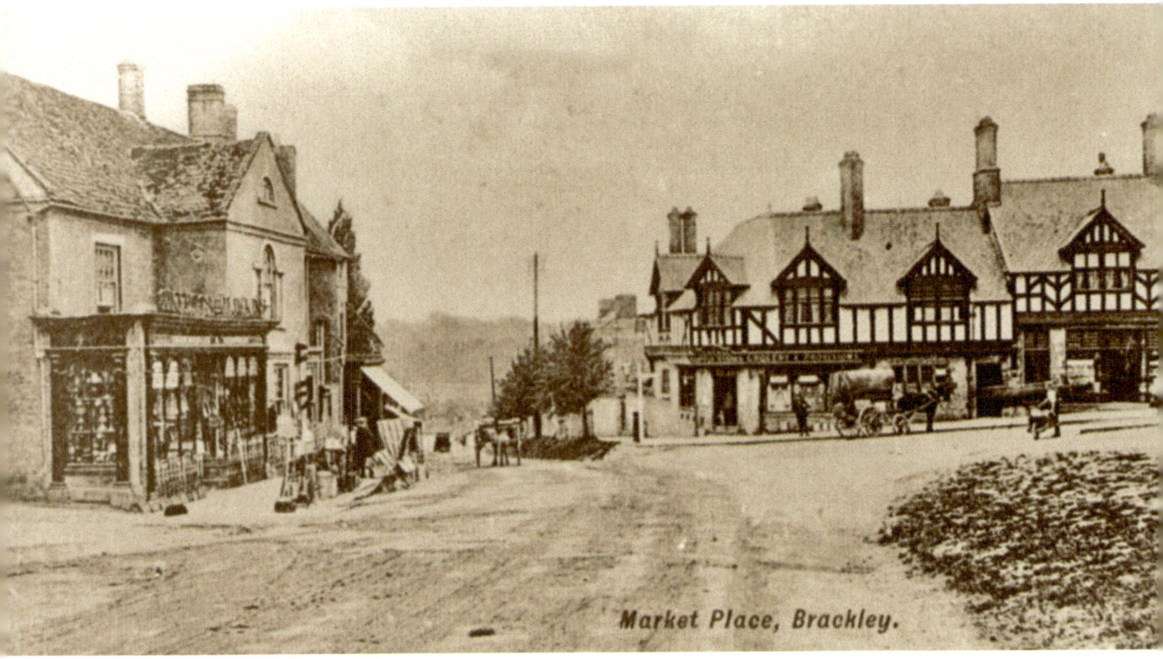

Market Place, Brackley.

Bridge Street, 1908

Taken from below the town hall. How calm and unhurried the scene was in 1908, unrecognisable today with the absence of the now busy junction between High Street, Bridge Street and Banbury Road: horses, carts and wagons. Note the hardware store on the left. Bridge Street connected the castle site, which guarded the river crossing at the town's southern boundary, with the market place. Many of the cottages along Bridge Street would have originally been thatched but are now converted to slate roofs.

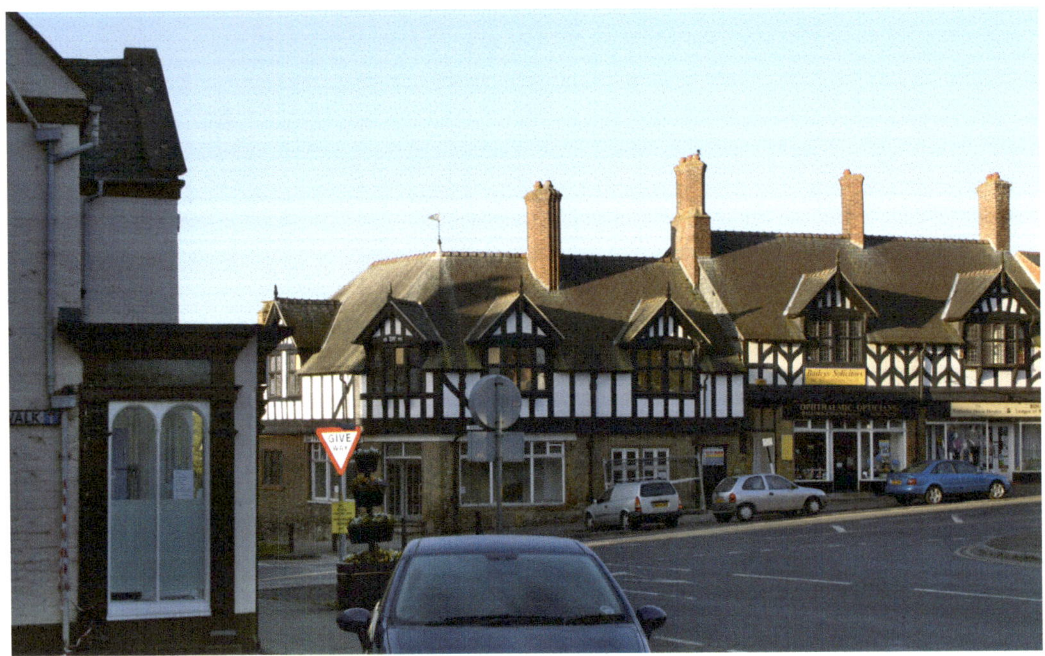

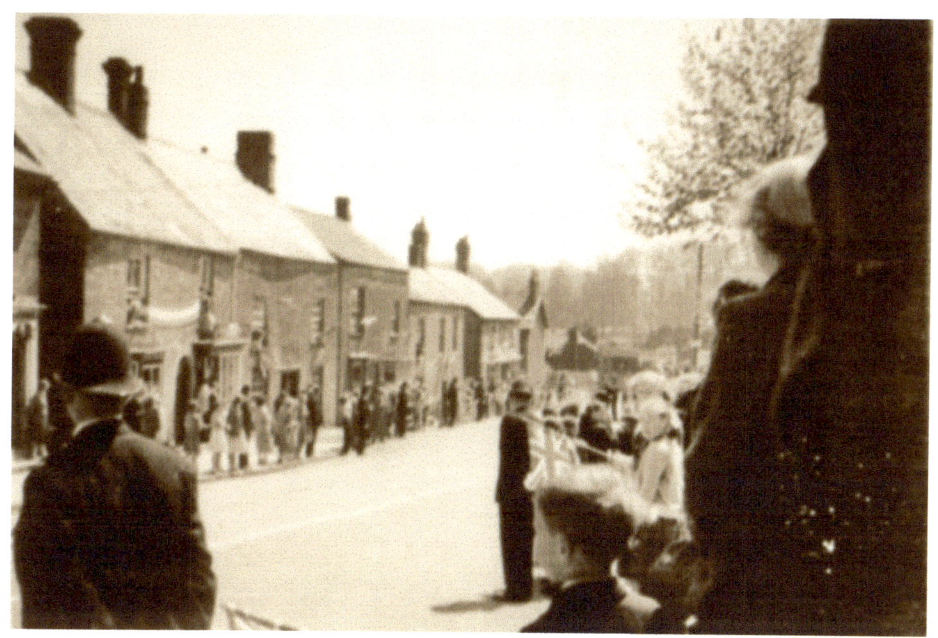

King George VI Passed Through Brackley

On 13 May 1950, King George VI, Queen Elizabeth (Queen Mother) and Princess Margaret arrived at Brackley station en route to the first official British Grand Prix held at Silverstone. At the last minute, it was discovered that the platform would be too low for the royal train's exit door, so an old wooden ammunition box had to be found and upended next to the door. They were then driven up through the town.

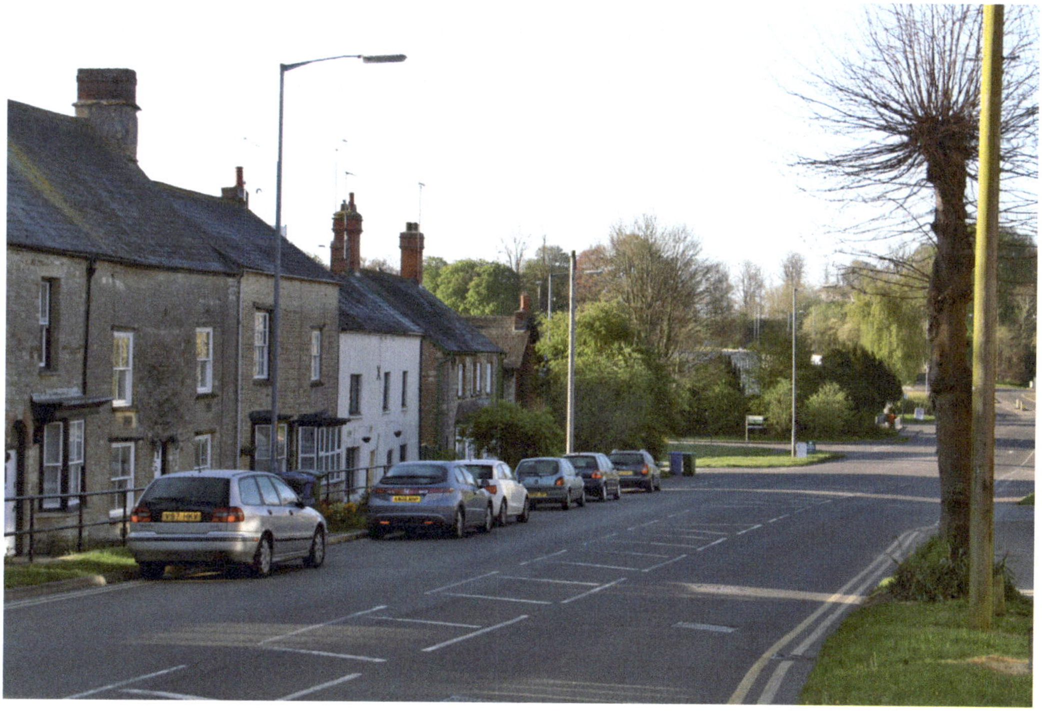

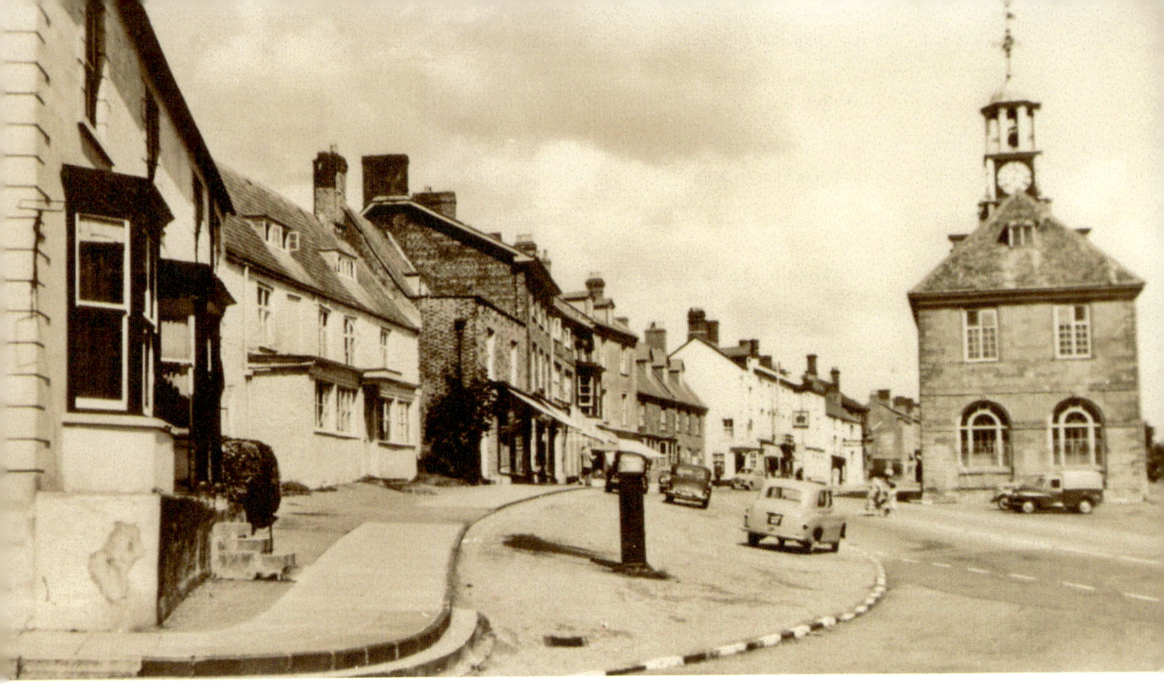

Market Square

Facing north towards Market Square, *c.* 1950s. Walter Johnson lived in the Temperance Hotel (second building on left). He was the last Freeman of the Borough of Brackley, and had previously served as mayor in the 1930s/1940s. Johnson Avenue was named after him in the 1950s. Next door up was L. J. Buthers (underwear, ladies clothes, children's clothes); followed by a drycleaner's (Ridgeways); a shoe shop (MacGees); The Private Hotel (No. 12 High Street), which became a florist's and is now a betting shop; then Barnes and Lanham (more recently Barnes and Campling).

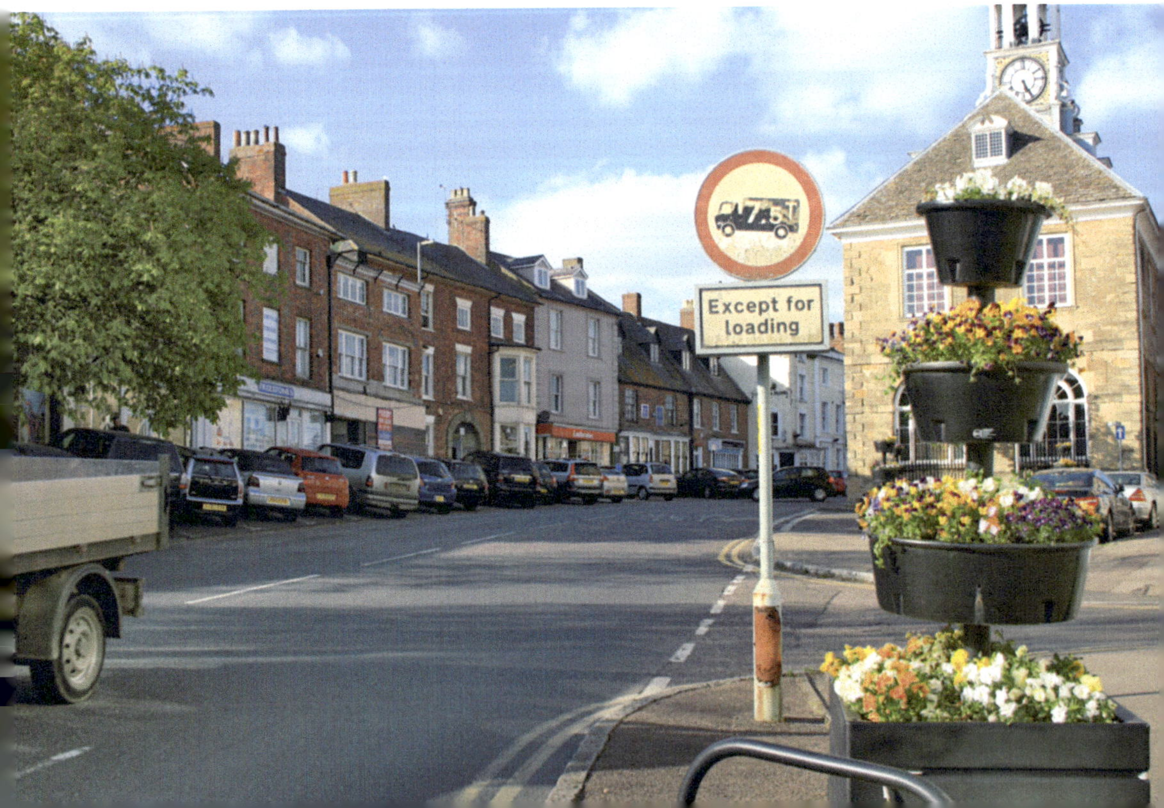

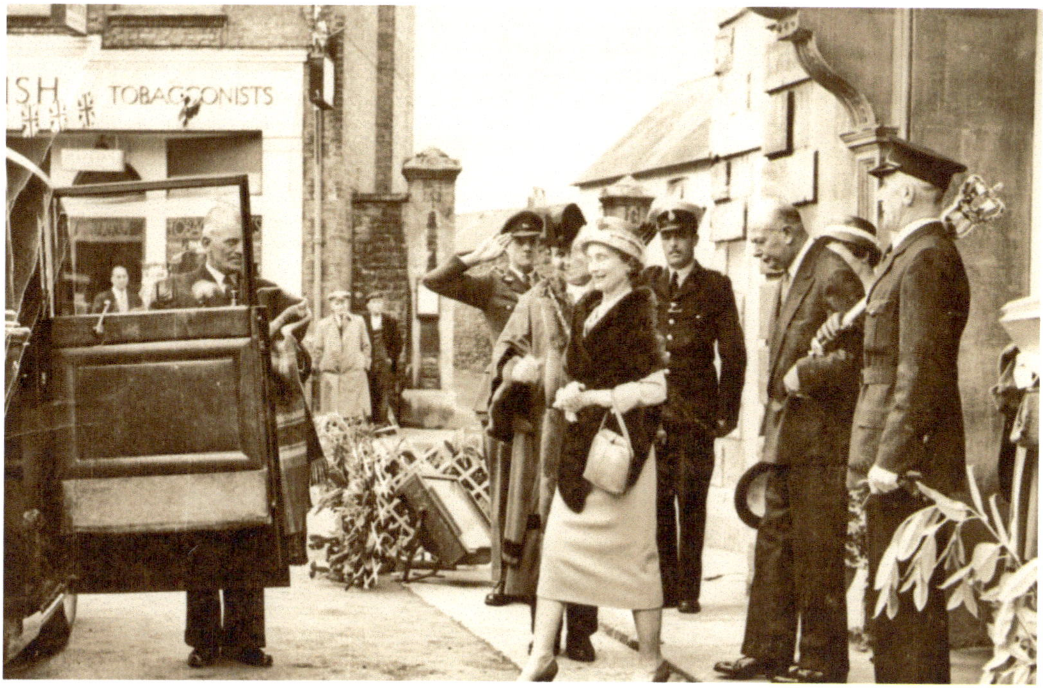

Charter Celebrations

A major event in the history of Brackley was the Charter Celebration in 1960, the 700th anniversary of the Borough of Brackley (the town lost its borough status in 1974). Cllr Miller was Town Mayor and the borough council gave a luncheon in honour of Their Royal Highnesses, The Duke and Duchess of Gloucester. The macebearer was Harry Edwards. Celebrations lasted from 21 May until 4 June that year.

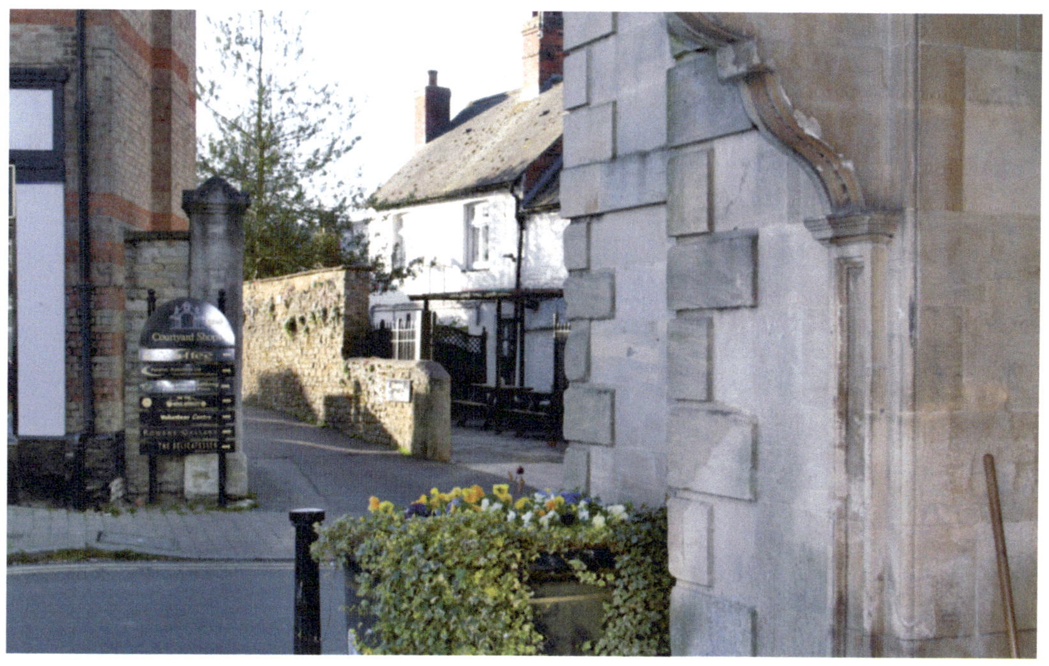

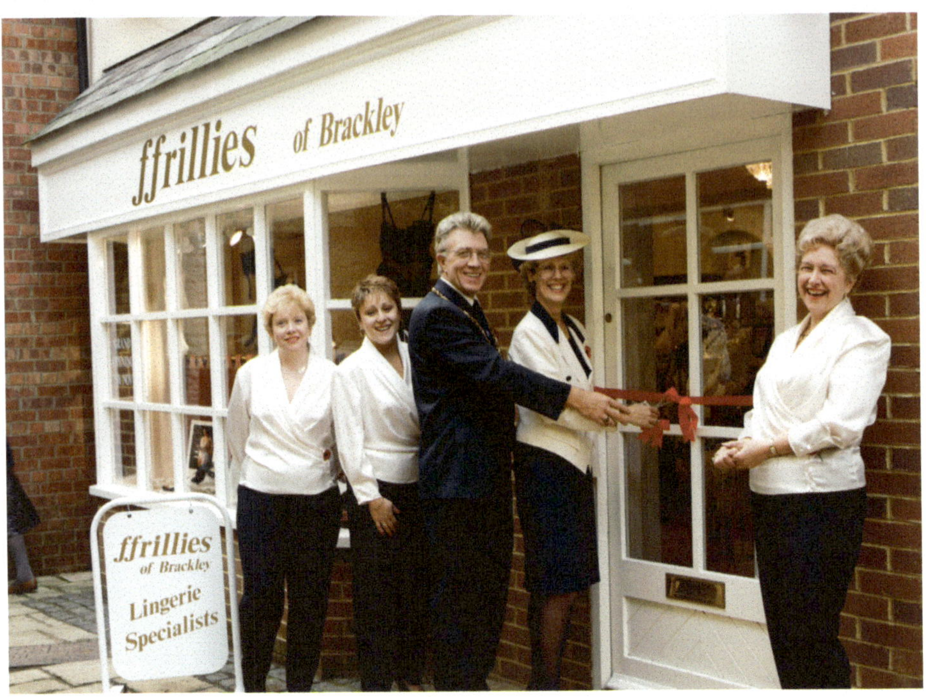

Frillies' of Brackley, 1992

Frillies' was a ladies' underwear shop in Draymans Walk, now Defern Beauty Salon, a colourful addition to the range of retail outlets in Brackley and opened by Mayor Trevor and Heather Gregory (*seen above*). The town had a long line of mayors, perhaps extending back to the early fourteenth century. Draymans Walk now hosts a restaurant, the band club and a tattoo shop, among others.

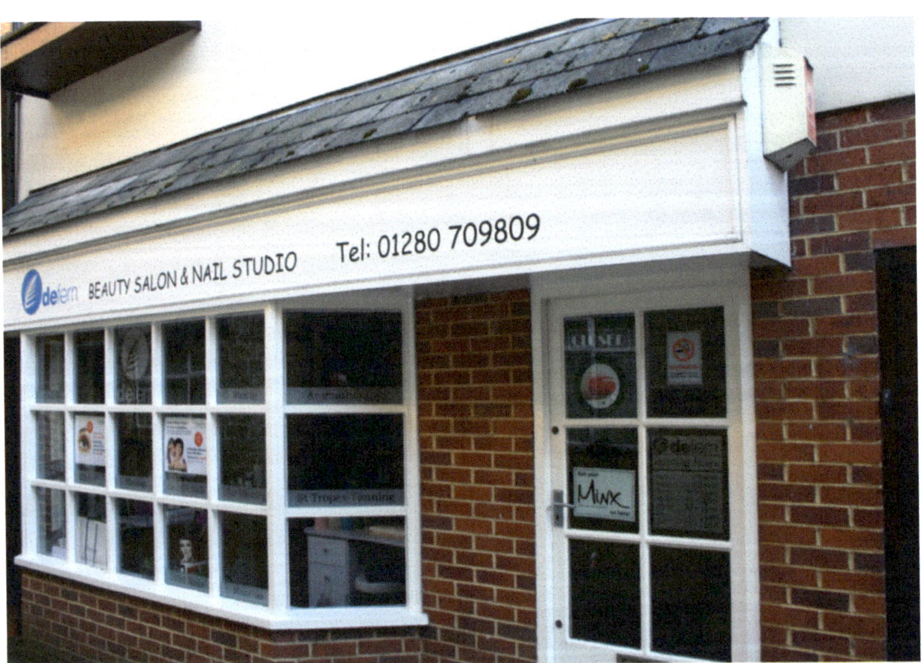

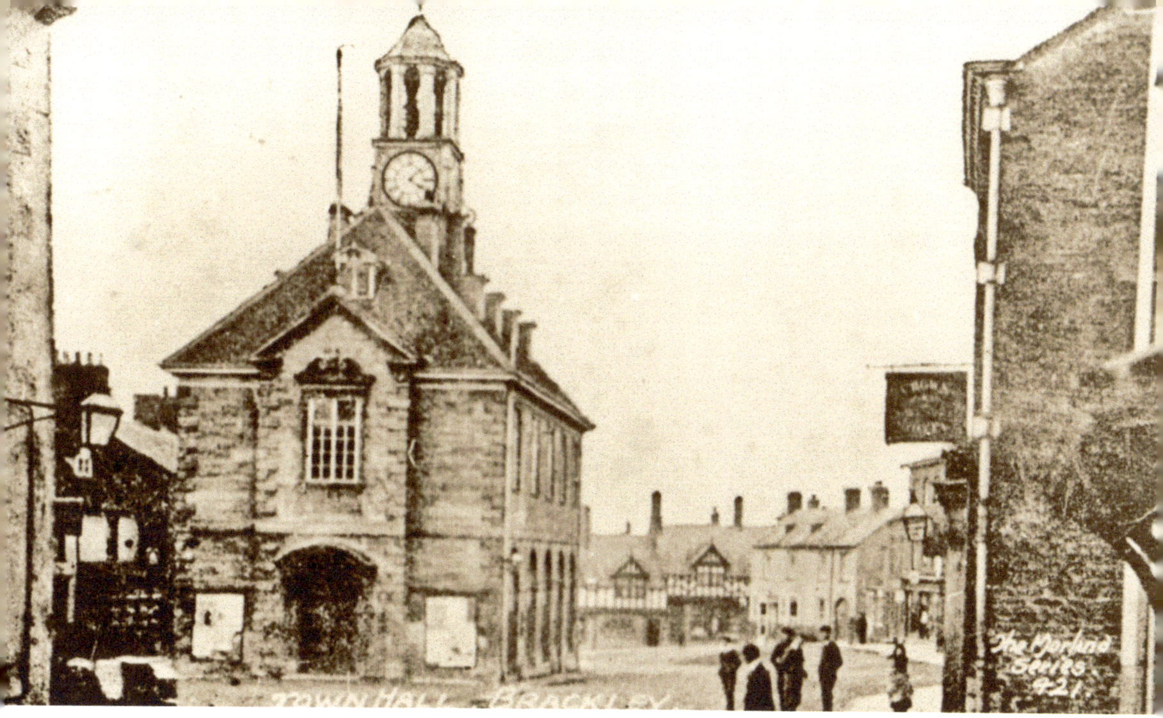

Brackley Town Hall, 1905

The town hall is Georgian and was built in 1706 by the Egerton family (4th Earl of Bridgewater) at a cost of £2,000. He subsequently sold it to the borough council for 1*s* (5p in today's money). Originally, the ground floor had open sides to allow market trading in local commodities, such as wool, and then, in the nineteenth century, corn. The upstairs of the building was, and still is, used for council meetings, political dinners, election meetings, country balls and dances. The manorial court first met in the new building in September 1707 and all the burgesses, together with the mayor and the alderman were expected to be present, all being announced by the town crier. All town officers attended, including the three constables; the inspector of rawhide skins; the examiners and sellers of leather; the ale tasters; the bread weighers; the clerks of the market; the bellman and the crier. Planning is currently taking place for improvements and renovation of the hall.

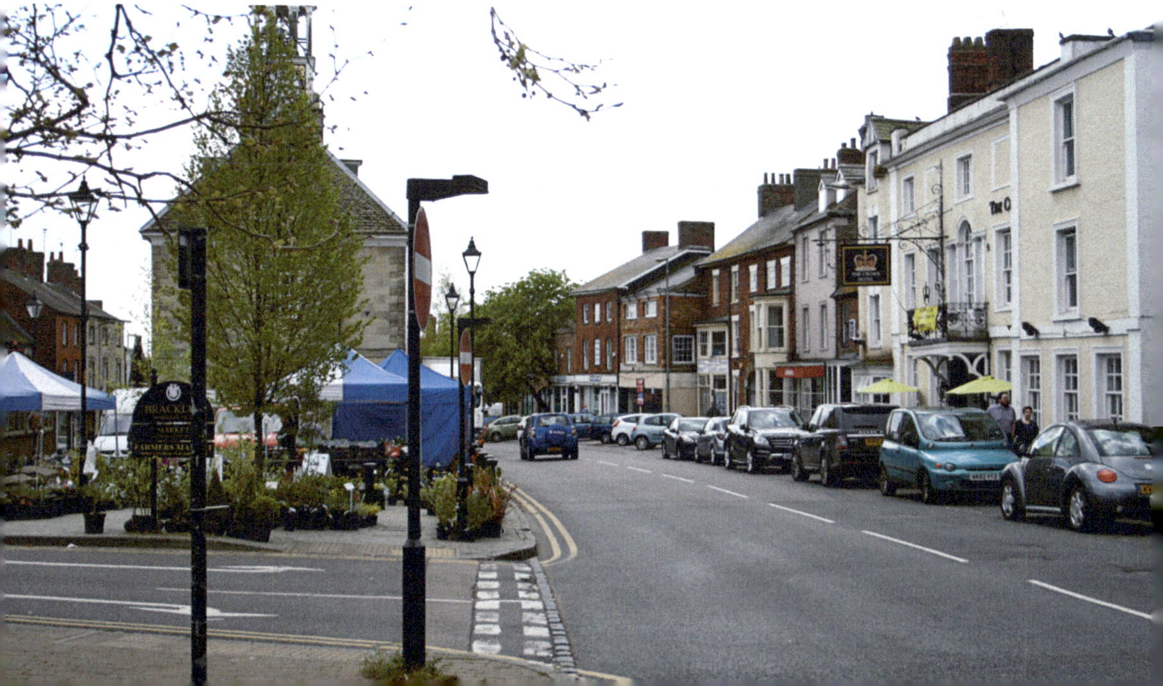

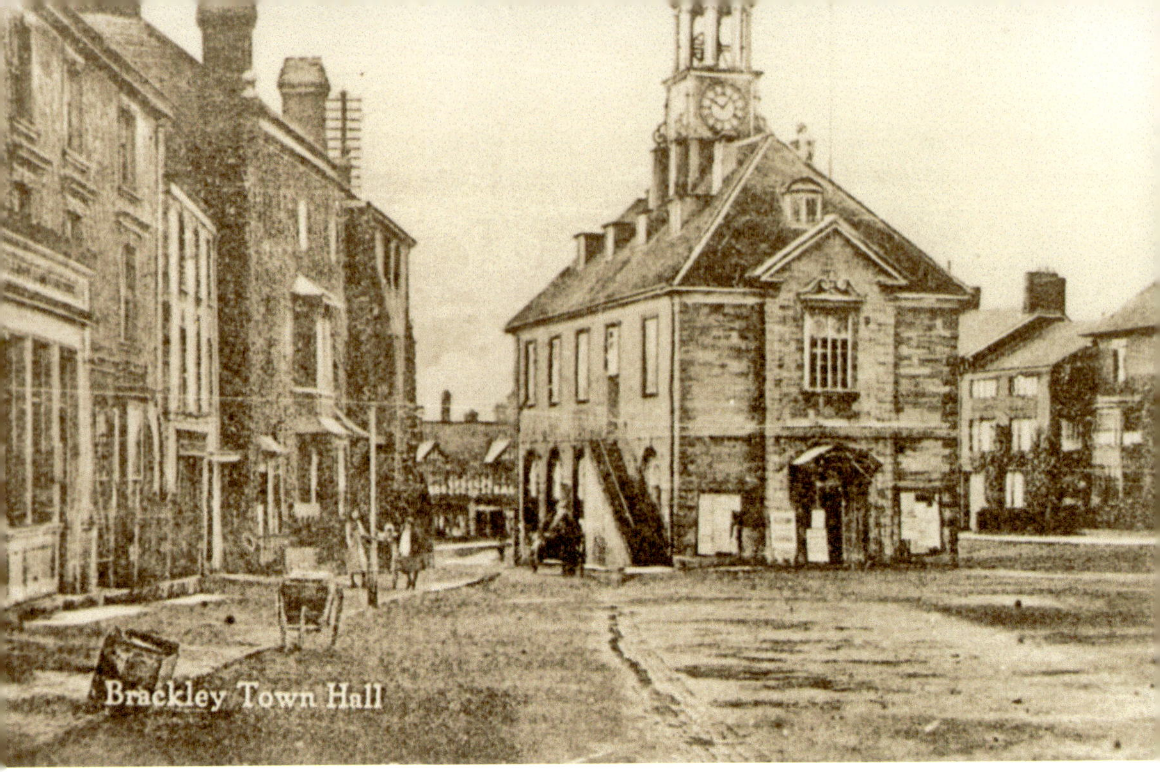

Brackley Town Hall

Brackley Town Hall, c. 1905

Facing north travelling towards the market square from Bridge Street, we are now familiar with parking bays on the left side of the street. The Market Square and Bridge Street feature a number of other early eighteenth-century houses and inns, mostly of brick and, in several cases, combining red and blue bricks in a chequered pattern. Below, the second building on the bottom left used to be a Temperance Hotel.

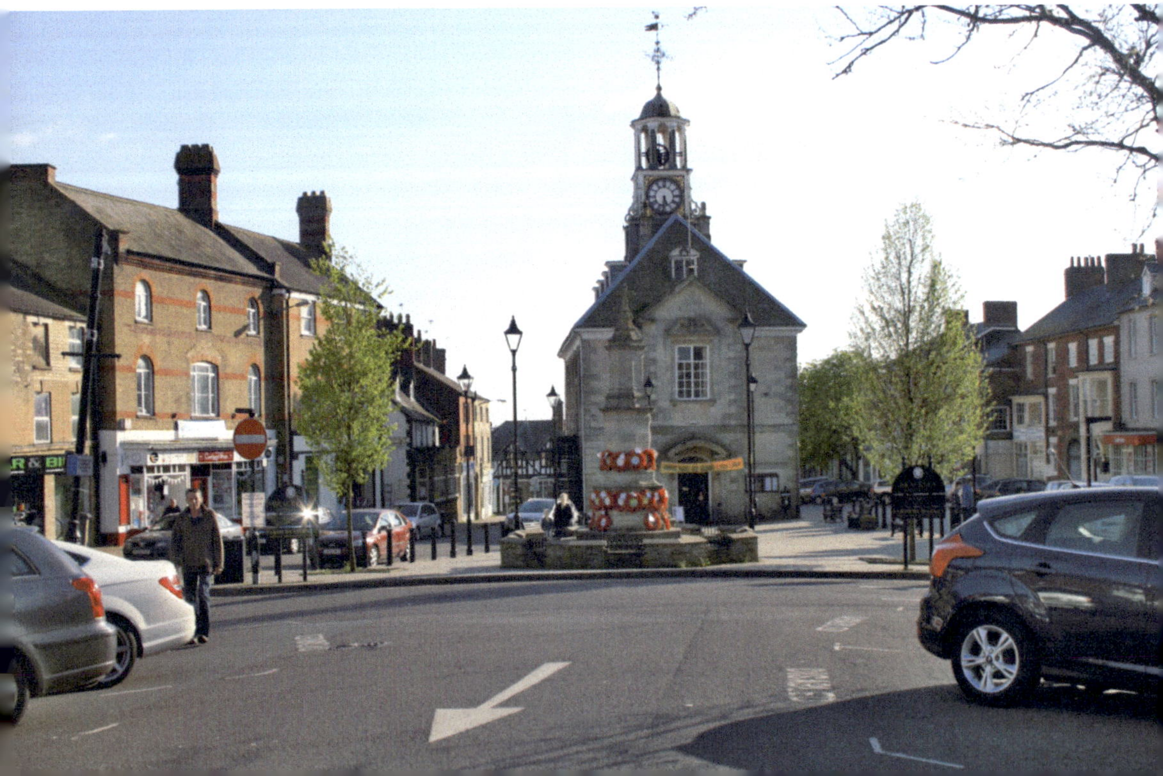

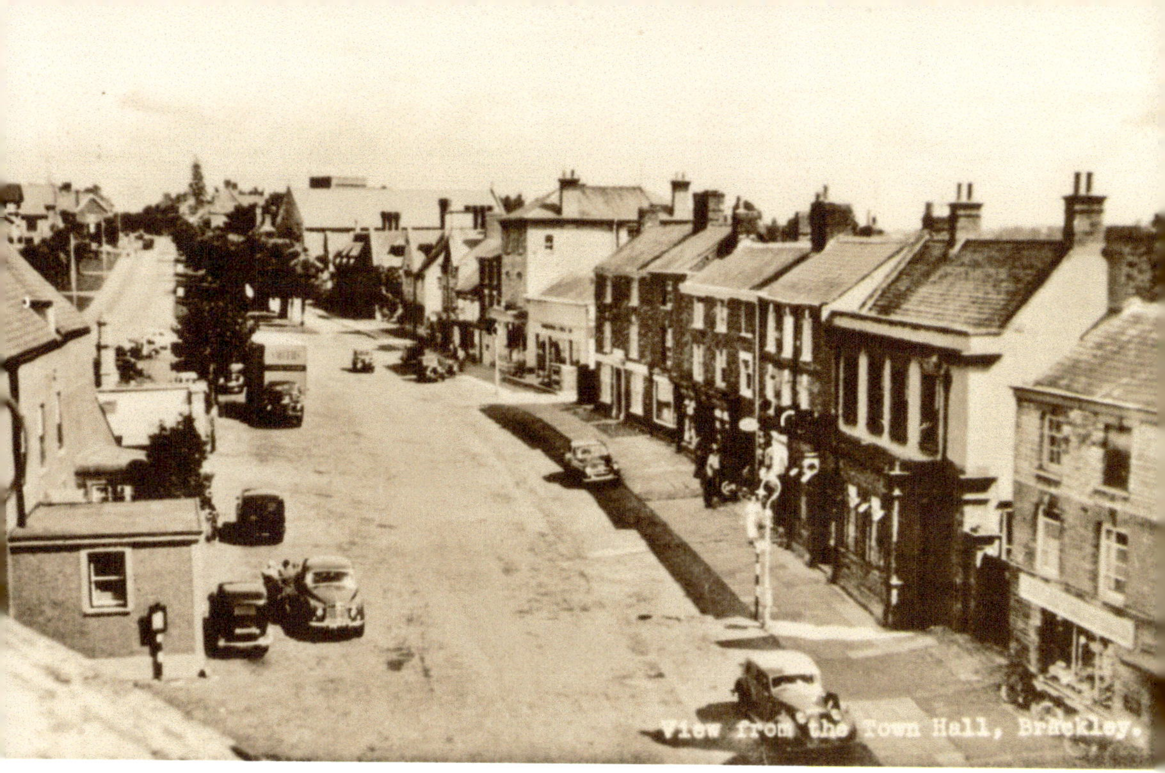

View Towards Magdalen College, *c.* 1950s

A surprising view of what is now the Market Square across the Piazza from the town hall (east side on the right). Notice the building on the right, which was a chemist. In the twentieth century, Boots the Chemist (previously Patterson's) was situated on the market place and was open until 1951. However, it was pulled down in 1961, leaving a much more open space as part of the central Market Square.

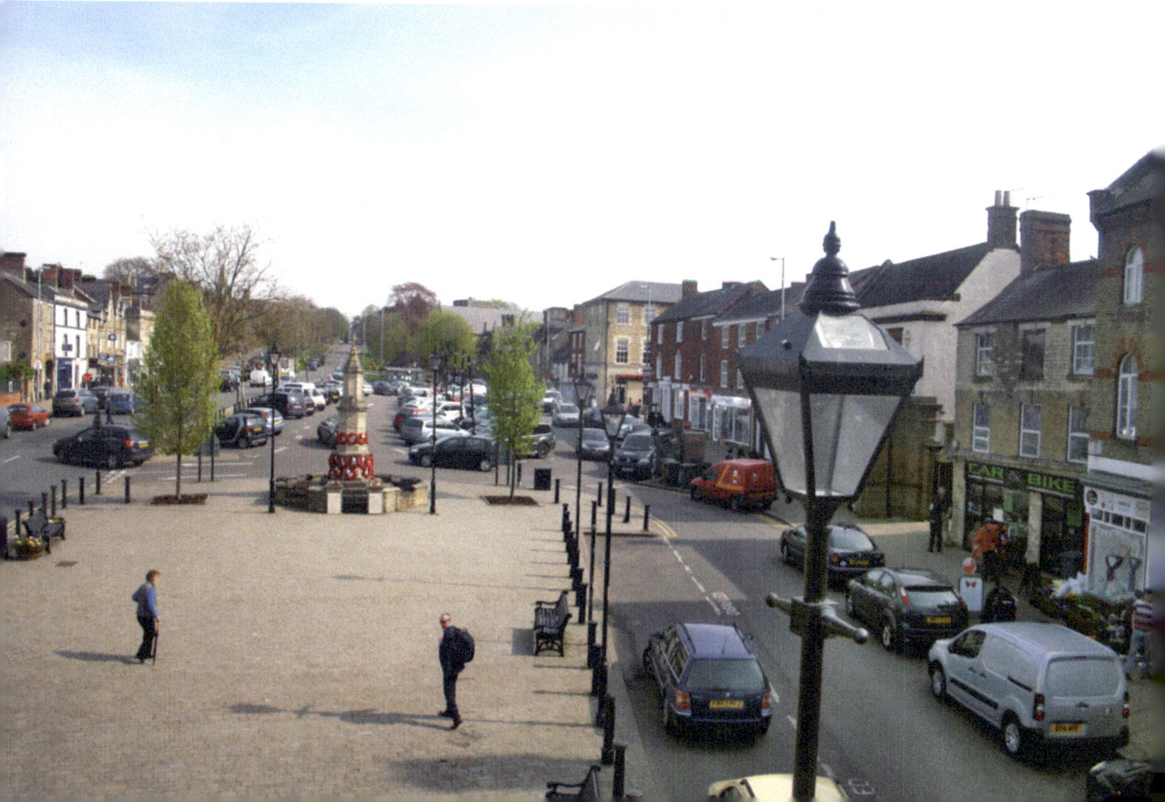

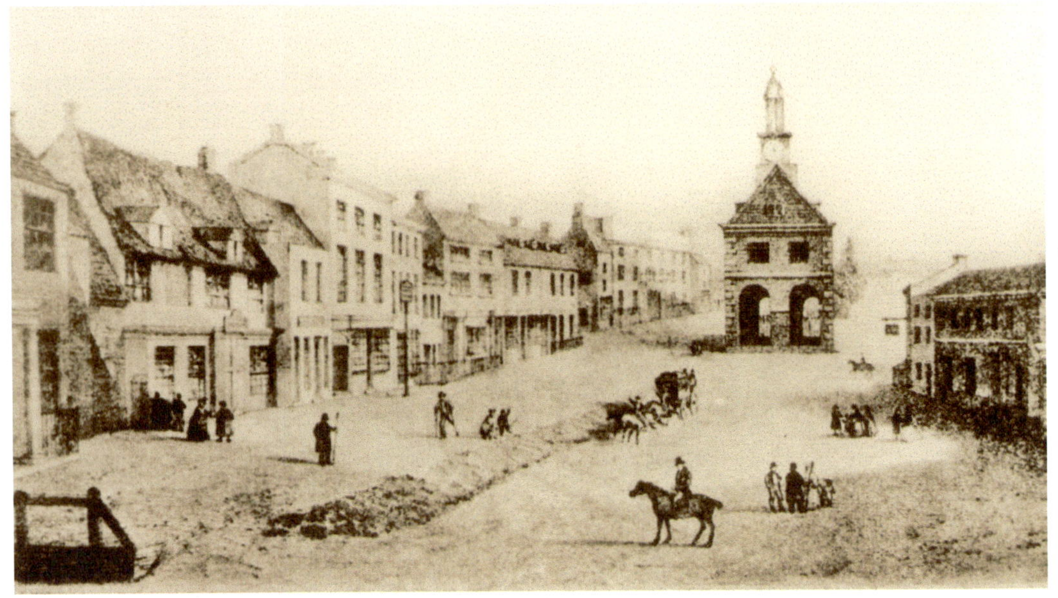

Late Nineteenth Century

The Market Square has always been the beating heart of Brackley, from the days when farmers from surrounding villages brought their animals to trade. The market's origins date back to the early 1700s, when it was considered an important centre where the town crier announced any news or information. Although its form has changed over the years, it is still a meeting place for many people. The square is enclosed by a beautiful tree-lined avenue and overlooked by the iconic town hall. Today, it is the centre of trade and commerce for the town, with a varied selection of traders, including retail and restaurants. It remains a meeting and social place for residents, hosting national and local celebrations. Market day is on Fridays, with farmers markets held once a month on Saturdays. May Day celebrations on 1 May each year are held, with local Morris men performing at 5.30 a.m.; breakfast (and beer) are served to all.

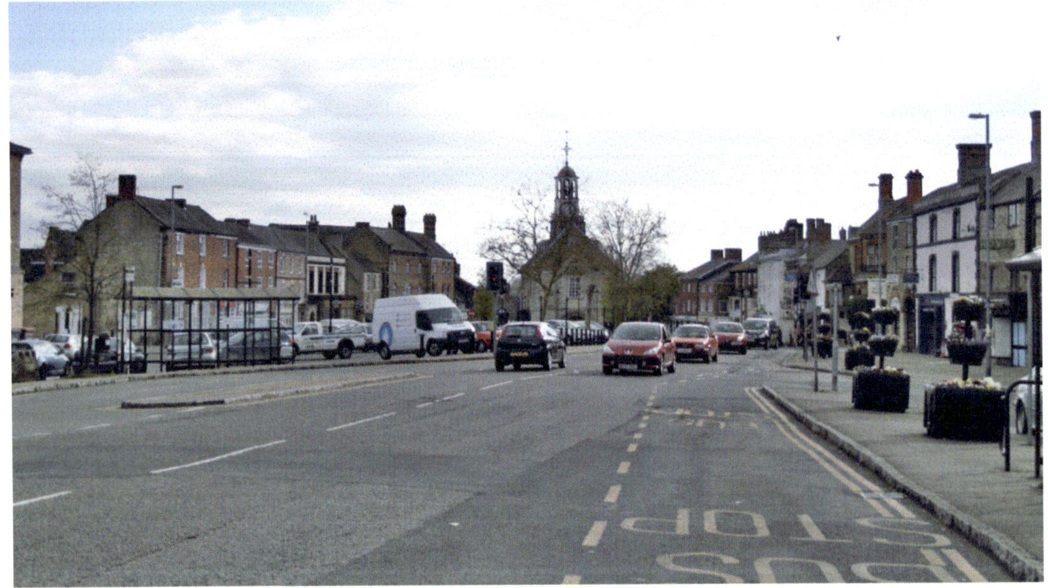

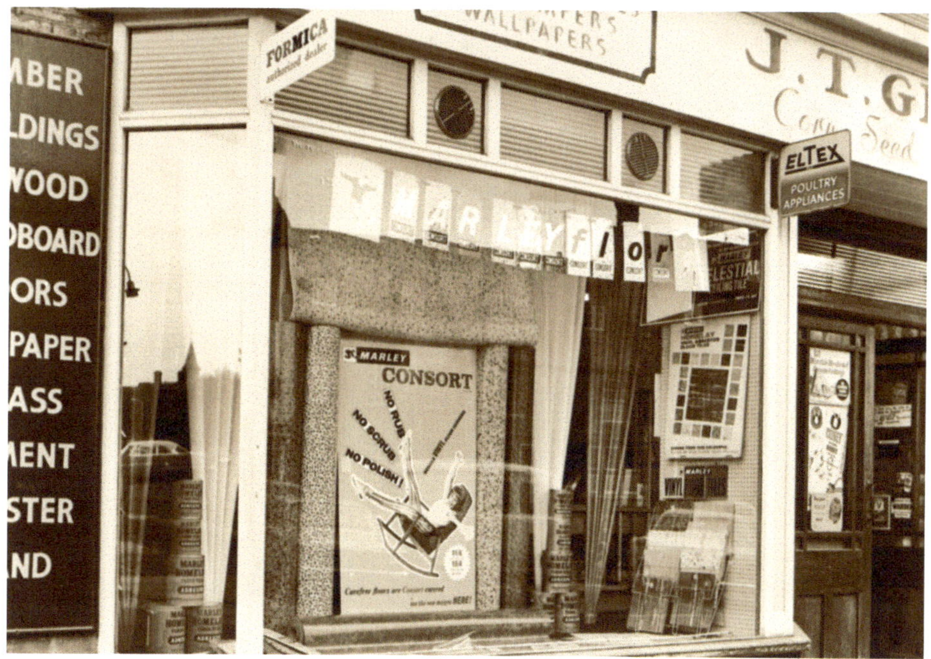

J. T. Shop Window, *c.* 1970s

This was once J. T. Green & Son, ironmonger's and hardware at No. 15 Market Place, subsequently taken over by Carpenter's in the same guise. Gordon Bradshaw had the newsagent's at No. 13 Market Place (formerly owned by Caryl Billingham's family), and effectively moved to larger premises next door. This became Bradshaw's (Brad's) and subsequently the Courtyard Mews. Brad's shop (No. 15) was the place where you could buy anything in the grocery, drinks and newsagent's lines. It was well used by the community. Now the Courtyard Mews exists at the site, a labyrinth of boutique traders, including Lilli Mae's and Rowans Gallery. Behind the mews is the Courtyard, with a coffee shop and Clayson's Deli.

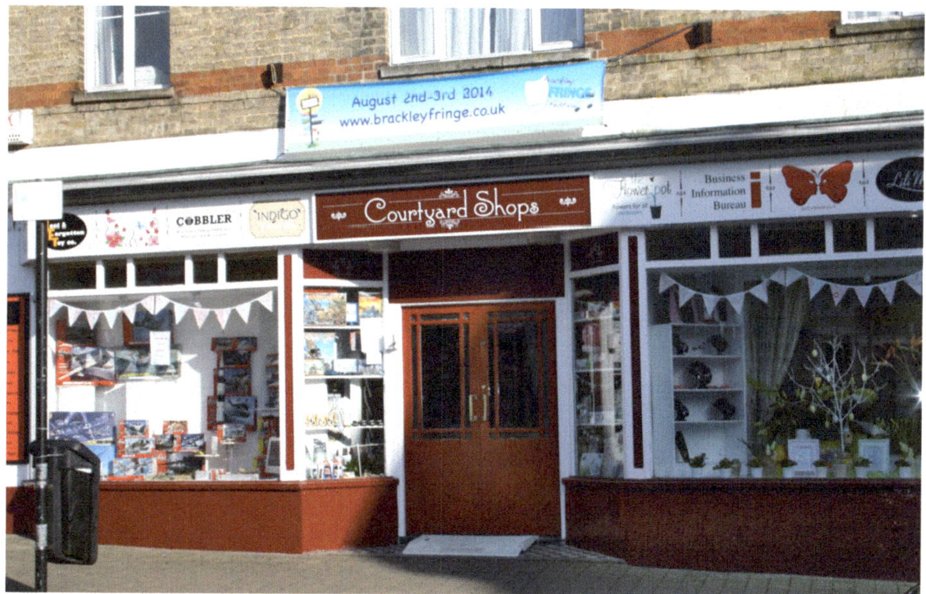

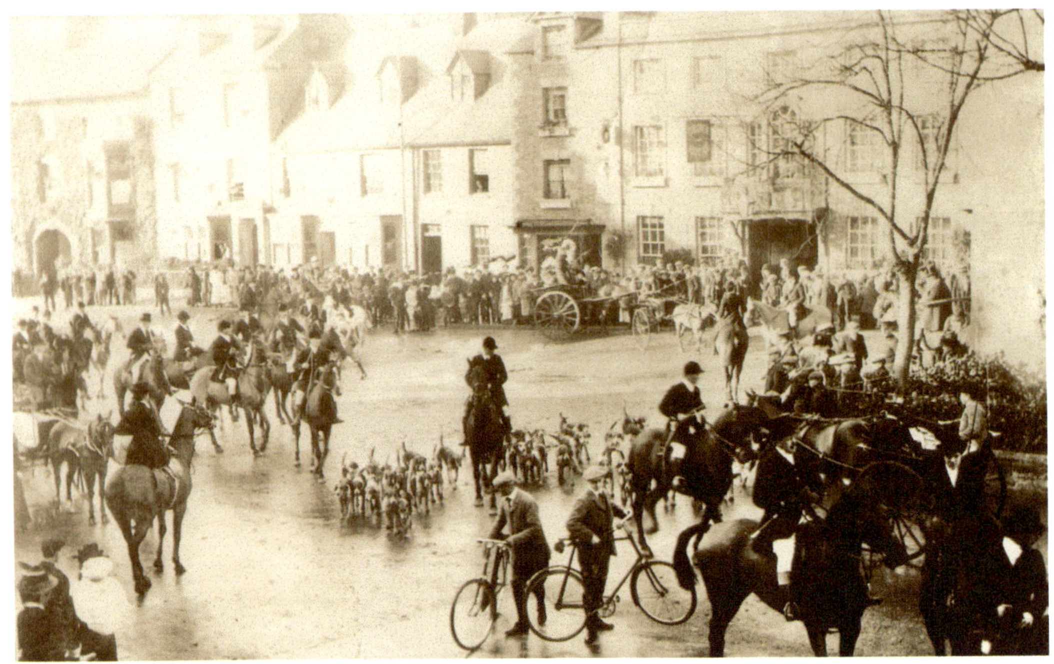

Grafton Hunt, Market Square, *c.* 1900s

The Grafton Hunt met regularly in the square around 2–3 times a year until the early 1960s, often with many onlookers. The Grafton Hunt was named after its founder, the Duke of Grafton. With the exception of a brief interlude from 1842 to 1861, when the hounds passed into the hands of a relative, Lord Southampton, the name of the pack has remained unchanged. The 7th Duke gave the hounds to the country and they are now owned by trustees. The bloodlines of the present pack can be traced back to the original hounds. Outside the Crown Hotel, note the Edwardian hats on the left.

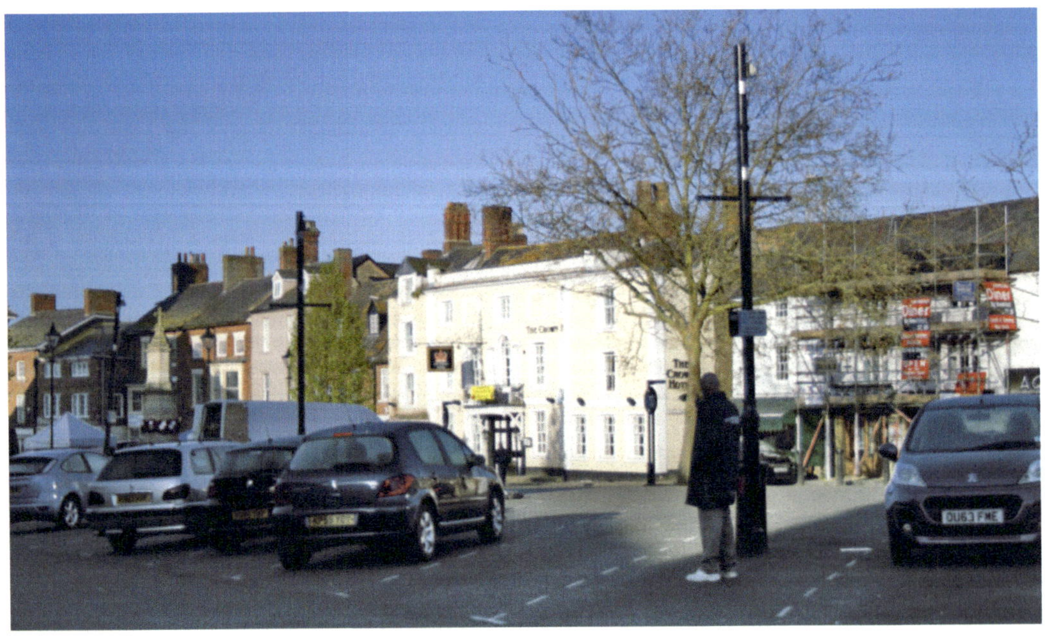

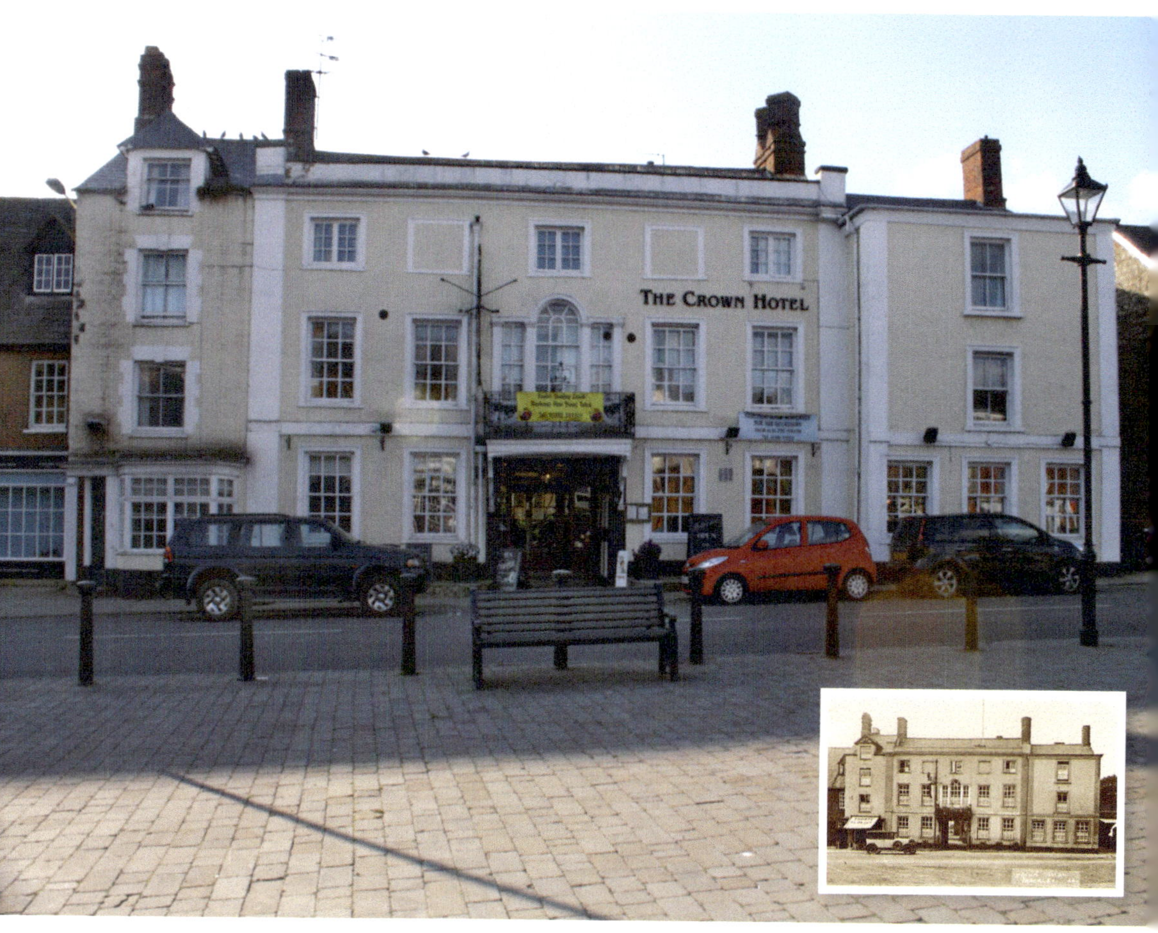

Crown Hotel, 1922

The Crown Hotel has changed hands several times in recent decades and is currently the town's only hotel. It was built in the sixteenth century as a coaching inn, and in August 1649 it was the cause of a major fire, in which fourteen apartments at the back of the inn were destroyed. The main damage was caused when the fire spread to the chandler's shop in Halls Lane and £200 worth of tallow exploded. The inn was repaired, and in 1680 it cost £35 to renew the lease for the inn and some surrounding farmland. By 1729, Magdalen College was charging £127 for the lease, but they had to drop the price to £95 in 1737. By now, the Crown had by now become an important coaching inn. To the left was Thorpe's florist (originally part of the hotel), followed by a betting shop then Taylors Estate Agent's.

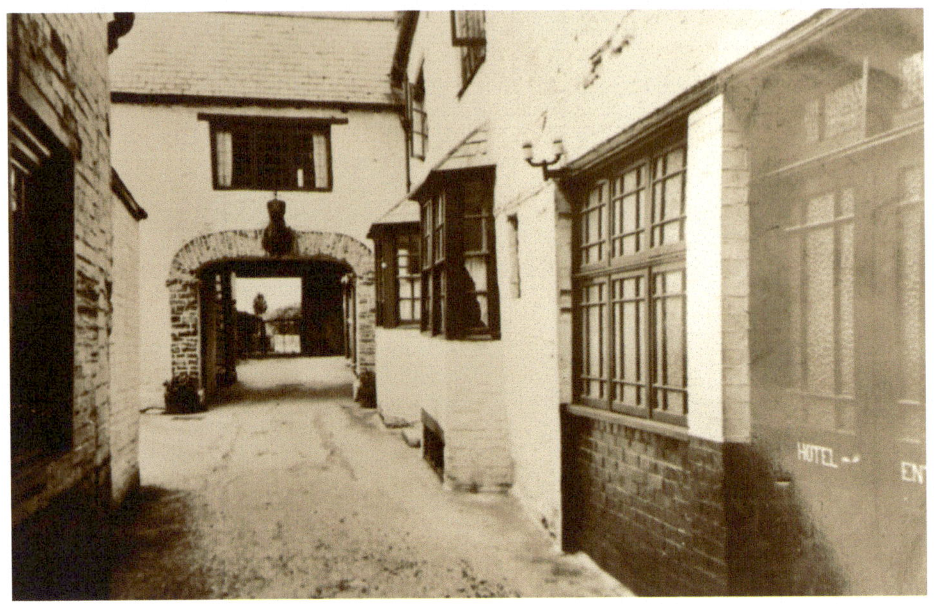

Crown Hotel Entrance, *c.* 1900s

The picture is through the main doors, and the double doors on the right are where the reception is now. Going through to the back, the arch leads to what was the stables, now the function room. The groom's living quarters are now staff quarters. The car park to the Crown is accessed to the rear of the hotel (currently through the Waitrose car park and near the Antiques Cellar). Irene Freeman remembers the days when you had to be 'posh' to go in the Crown; the less well-heeled used the Red Lion. It was known as a 'horsey place', true to its traditions as a coaching inn. There was a sadler's situated at the top of Bridge Street, and stabling was opposite in Halls Lane. Many American servicemen and some of their families stayed there in late 1950s and early '60s.

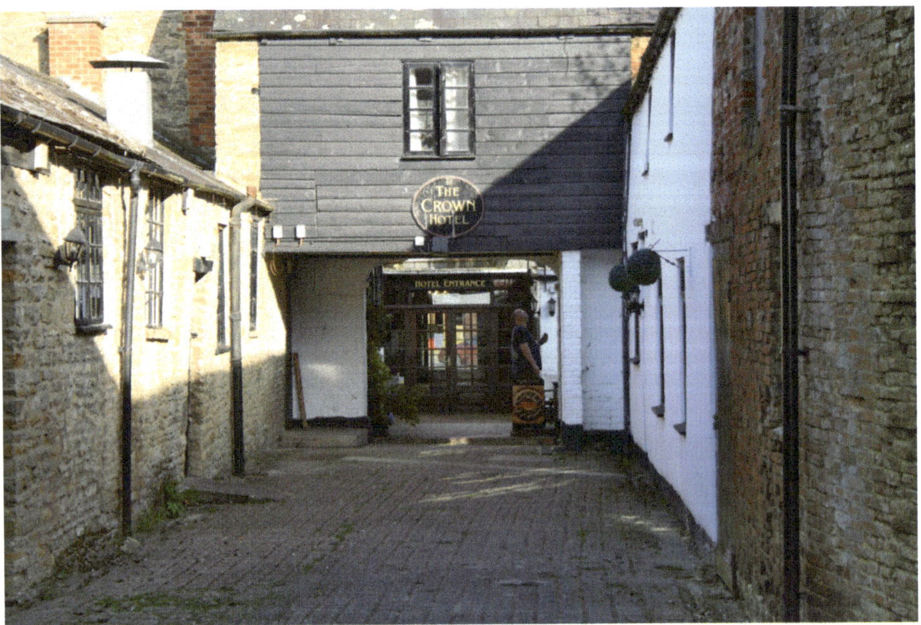

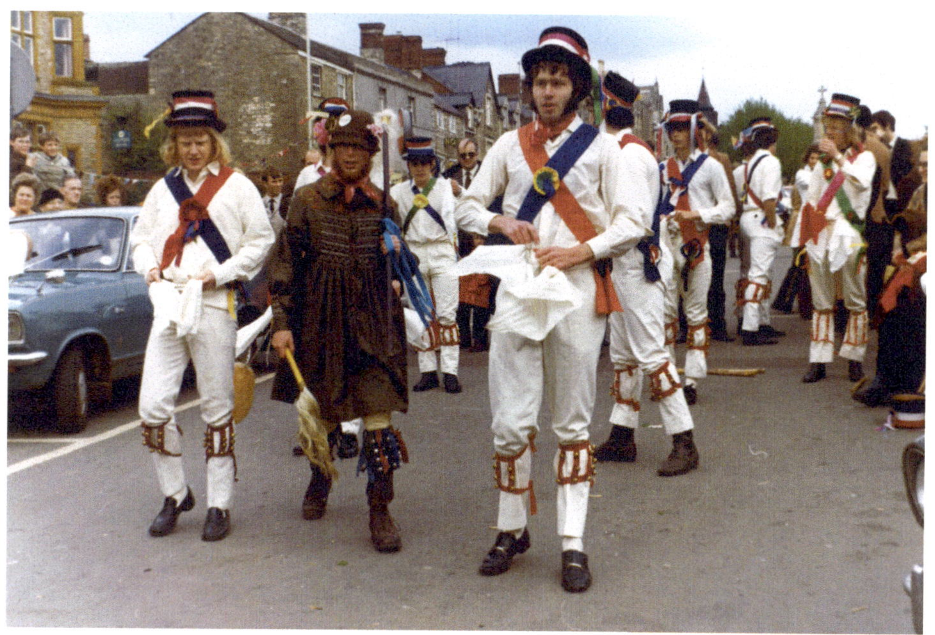

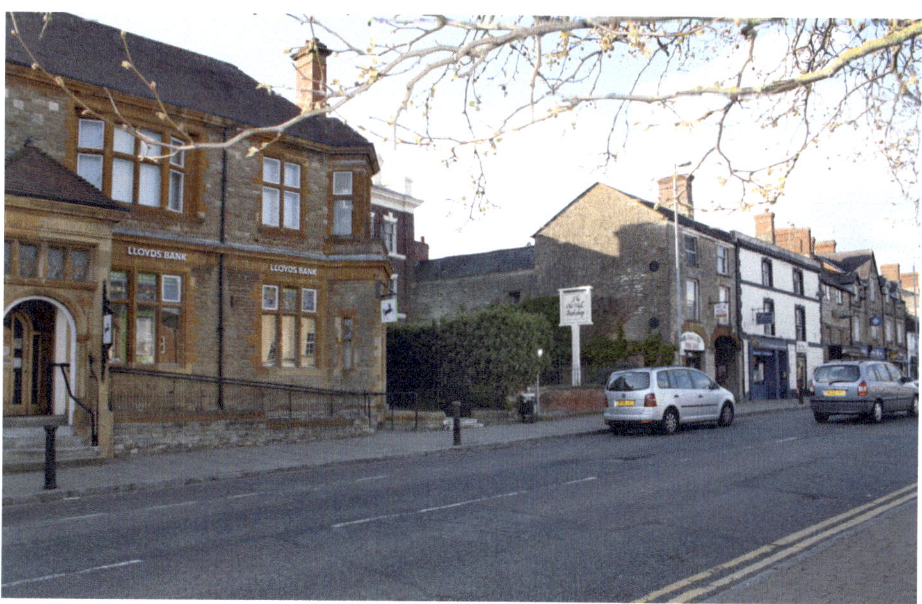

Brackley Morris Men, *c.* 1970

Brackley Morris men in front of Old Hall Bookshop and Lloyds bank building. Brackley is one of only ten sides listed by the Morris ring as 'traditional'. Its history is known to extend back to the early 1700s, and there's a strong local belief that the Morris men were associated with the presentation of an engraved solid silver communion paten dated 1623. Today, it is still going strong and appears on key dates in Brackley and surrounding villages. A man called Thomas Curtis called it the 'Metropolis of Morris Dancing'. The Grade II listed building of the Old Hall Bookshop can be seen in the top left-hand corner of the photograph, set back from the main building line. They have been selling new, secondhand and rare books since 1977.

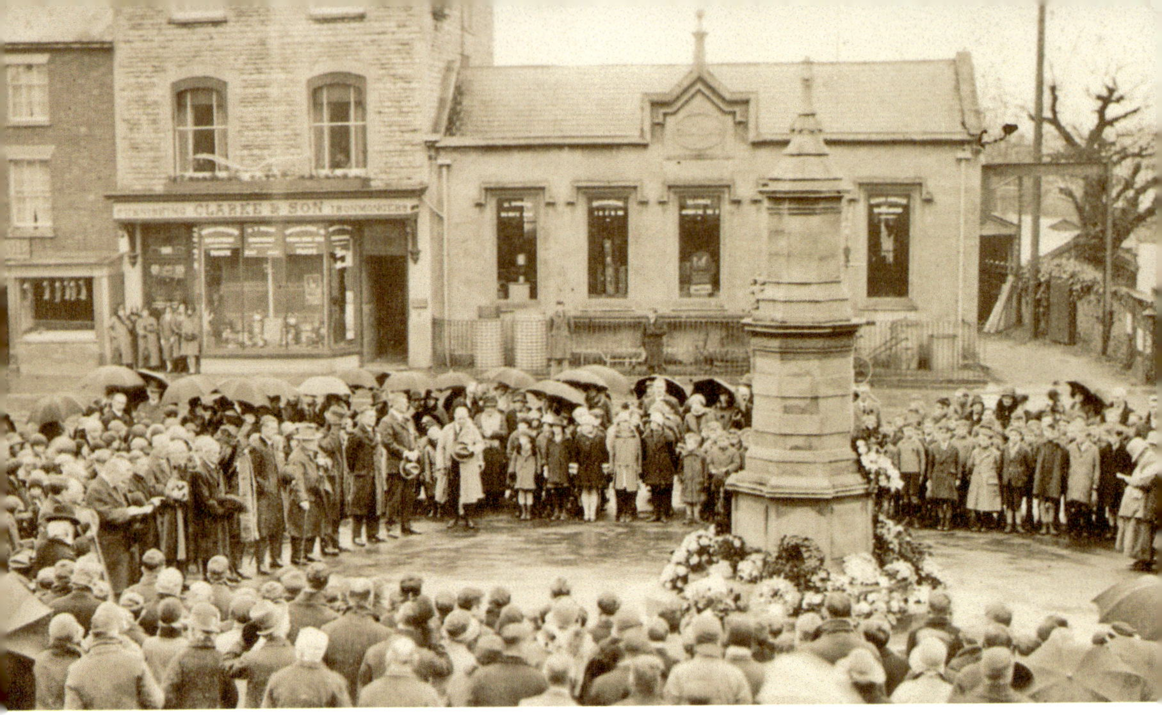

Remembrance Day, 1969

An annual Remembrance Day parade has taken place in Brackley since the end of the First World War, when they began across the country. This memorial commemorates the residents of Brackley who were killed or went missing in the First World War (sixty-eight names) and the Second World War (fifteen names). Many such memorials were erected after the First World War. After the Second World War, the names of those who died in conflict were also added to the memorial. In front of the town council offices in the High Street, names are listed by the year of death with name and regiment. Around the bottom is a list of all the places that battles in which they fought. The Second World War fallen are on two plaques either side at the front. Clark's ironmonger's, now Costa coffee, was next door to the library. Mr Clark was a once mayor of the town.

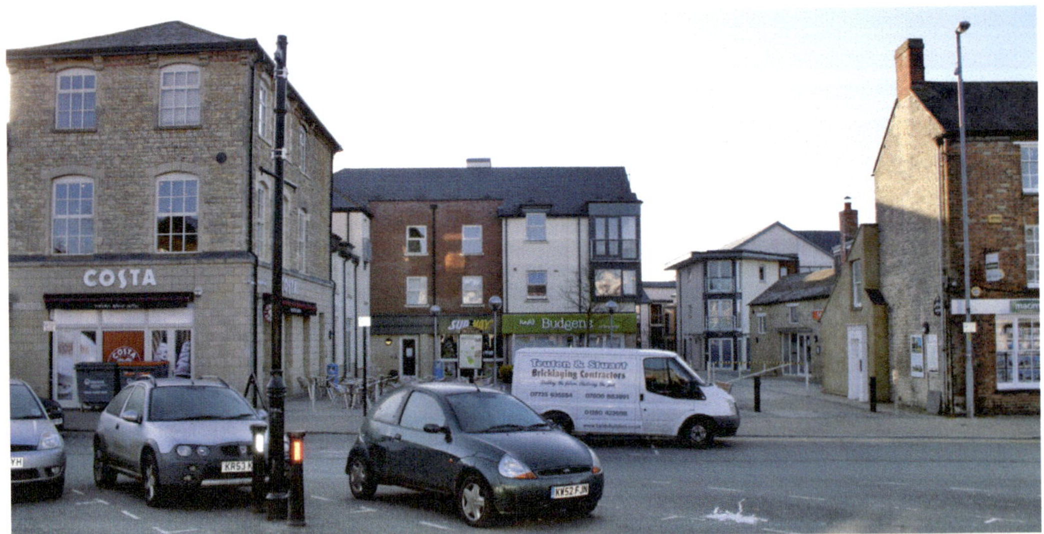

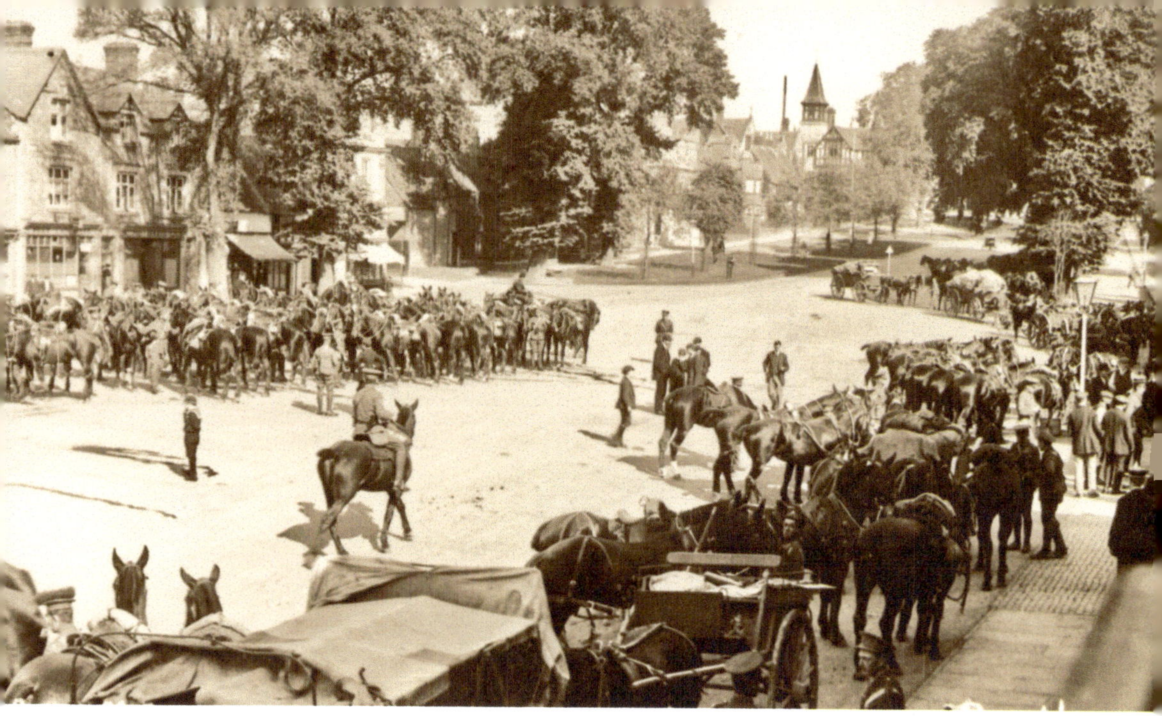

Army Manoeuvres, 1913

A common sight in the period. The 1st Northamptonshire Yeomanry (TA) had a base in Brackley. Its regimental headquarters and 'A' Sqn were based at Northampton, 'B' Sqn at Daventry and 'C' Sqn at Brackley. On mobilisation in August 1914, the 1st Northamptonshire Yeomanry was attached to the part of the First Mounted Division of the Eastern Mounted Brigade. They have the Freedom of Brackley, which means that they have permission to march through town with bayonets fixed. Brackley was the only town to allow this except Northampton. There was also a territorial and drill hall in Brackley.

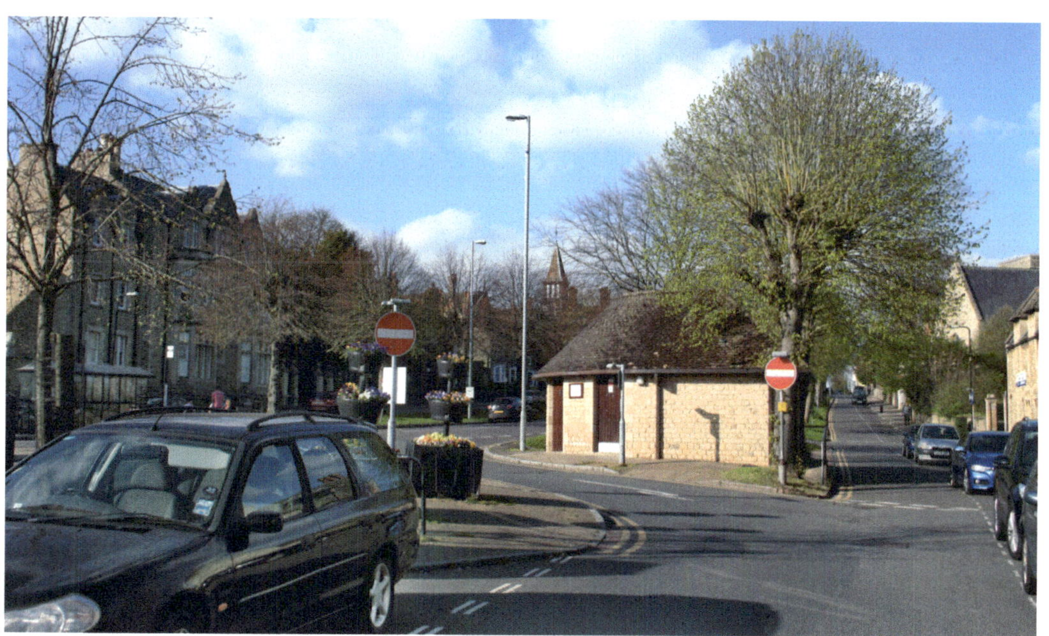

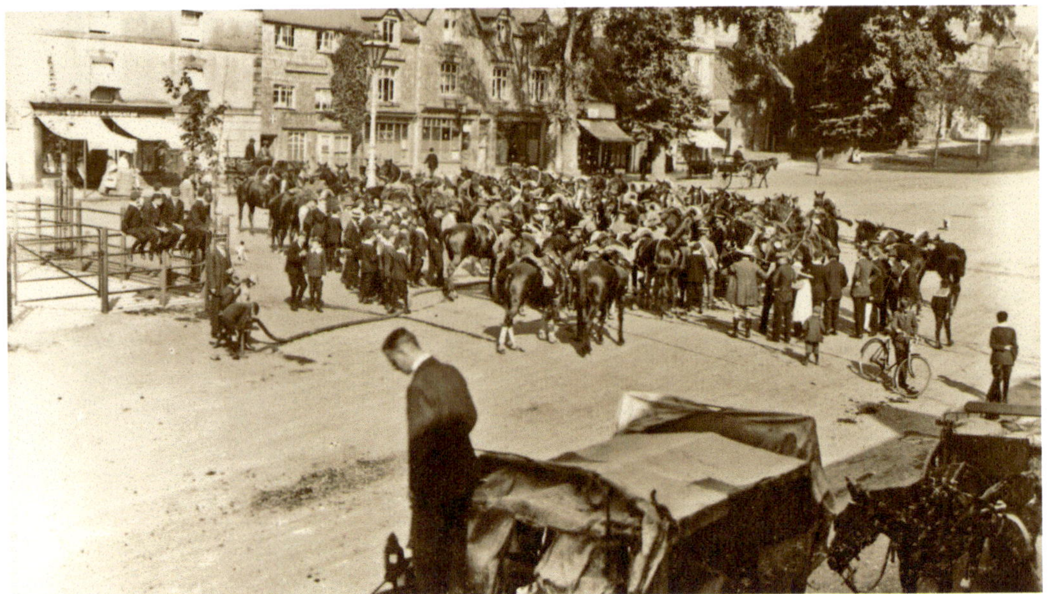

Army Manoeuvres, 1913

In this photograph of the manoeuvres, notice the permanently constructed animal pens for the town market. The current Boots the Chemist is in the background, which was the site of the old post office. The manoeuvres of 1913 across the country excited much attention, both locally and nationally. King George V and Queen Mary attended, along with Winston Churchill, then First Lord of the Admiralty, and Baden-Powell. There were military observers from most of the major European powers, along with representatives from the colonies. *The Times* described these exercises as essentially a practice of command function in an expeditionary force of four infantry and one cavalry divisions. Some 50,000 men and 25,000 horses had been brought into north Buckinghamshire and south Northamptonshire, where they were dispersed for three weeks of training before being assembled to form the two forces that engaged each other over five days from 22 September. The exercises of 1912 and 1913 played their part in preventing German dominance in Europe.

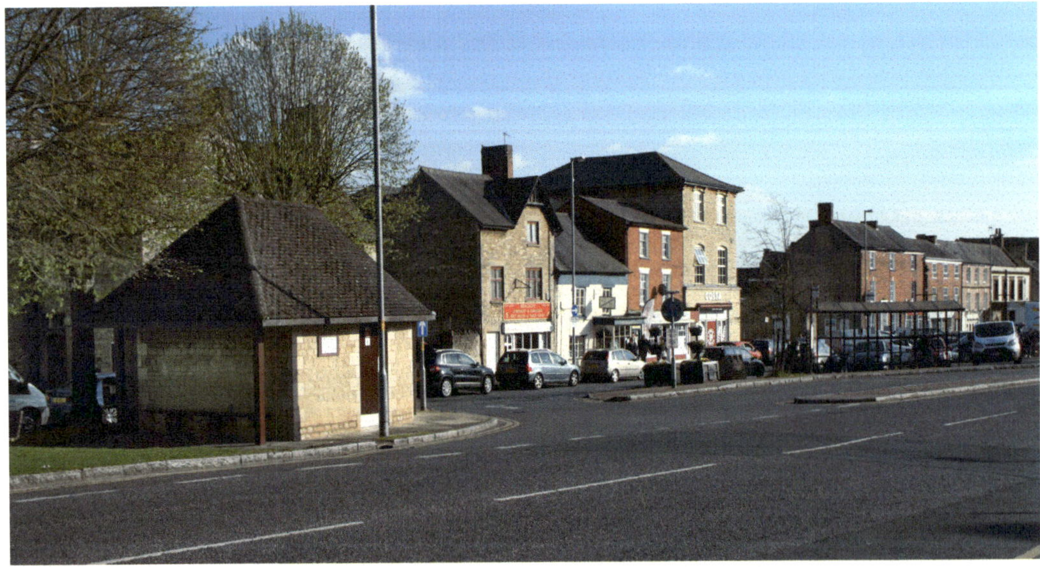

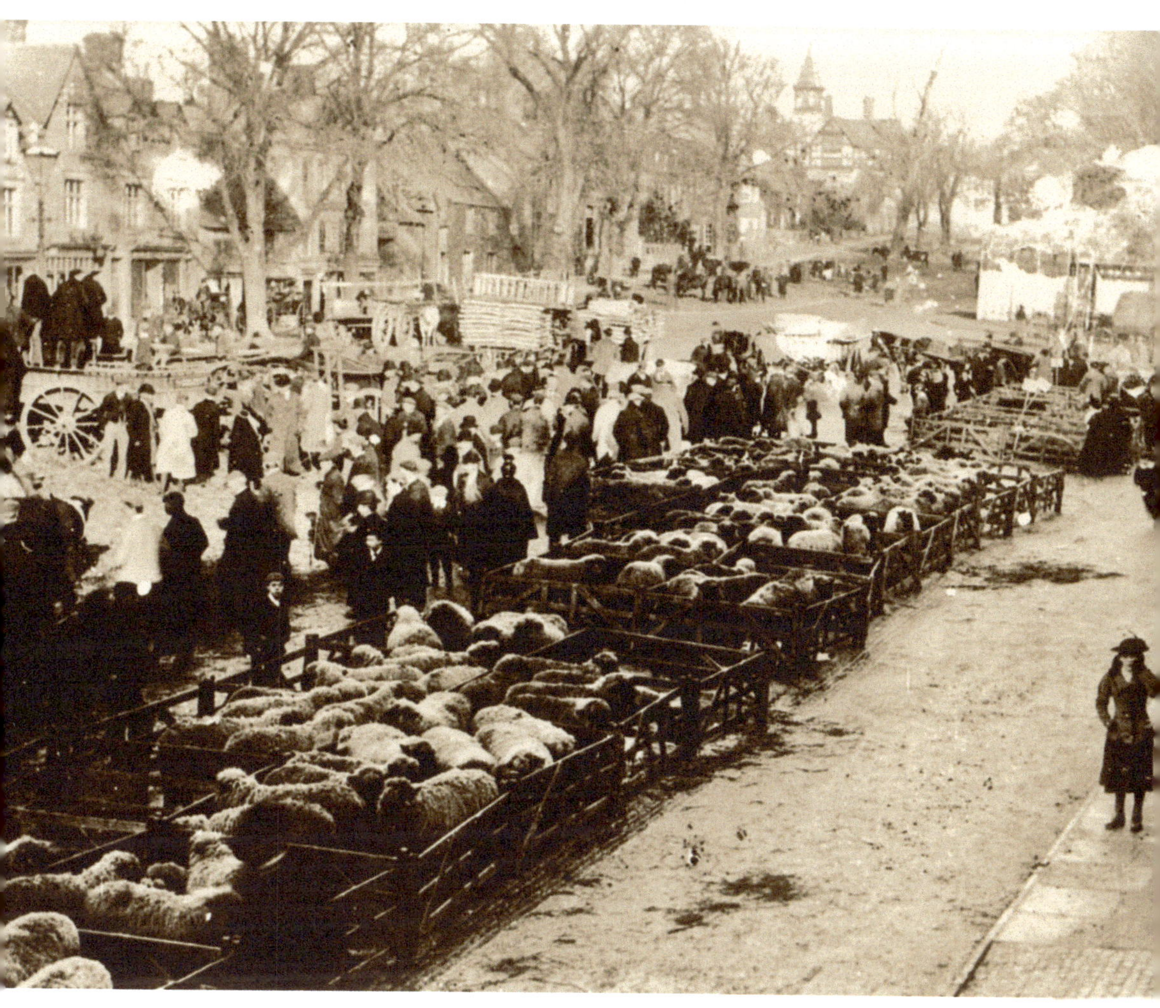

Brackley Cattle Market, Late Nineteenth Century

Note the horses grazing on the green. There are no vehicles – a far cry from more recent days when the main A43 was the main thoroughfare to the north and traffic, including HGVs, thundered through the town. Since the opening of the bypass, the traffic is considerably reduced. The market used to be on Wednesdays. The fairs were principally for horses, horned-cattle, and sheep, and took place on the Wednesday after 25 February, the second Wednesday in April, the Wednesday after 22 June, the Wednesday after 11 October (a statute-fair), and 11 December, which is a great fair for cattle and wearing apparel. The animal market finished in the early 1960s when agricultural practices were changing. In the 1980s, the Market Square was typically full of parked cars, but at night it was a lorry park so the drivers could rest. Nowadays, the market takes place on the Piazza outside the town hall and the parking area always seems full of parked cars.

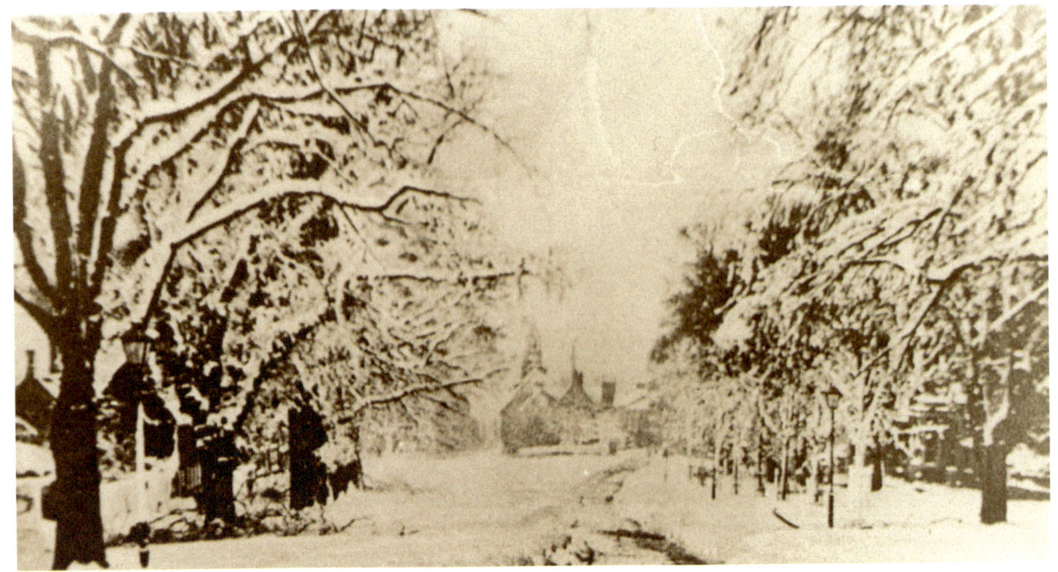

Towards the Town Hall and High Street, 1905

A winter scene looking south towards the Market Place and town hall. In addition to the Crown Hotel on the Market Place, the Red Lion (next to the town hall) was also a seventeenth-century coaching inn. It was one of the more important inns of the town, and in 1883 an auction was held there to sell off parts of a mill in Syresham. But it was the Reindeer Inn, now Barclays bank, that was the first in Brackley in 1789 to have a daily coach service to London. Road improvements during this time were funded through tolls at turnpikes. Gems, Autosave and Courtyard Mews are current retailers housed in the buildings on the left of the photograph. Caryl Billingham bought Gems (ground floor) and had to lower the floor. Walter Parish (Carol's grandfather) previously had two shops, including Gems (No. 13). It was the only example of art deco in the High Street.

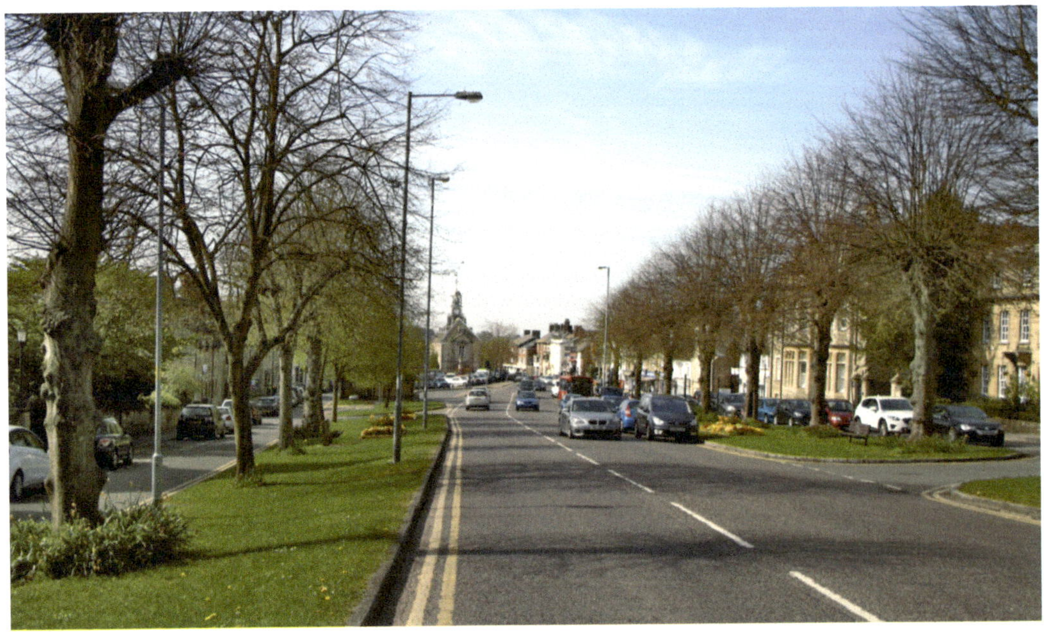

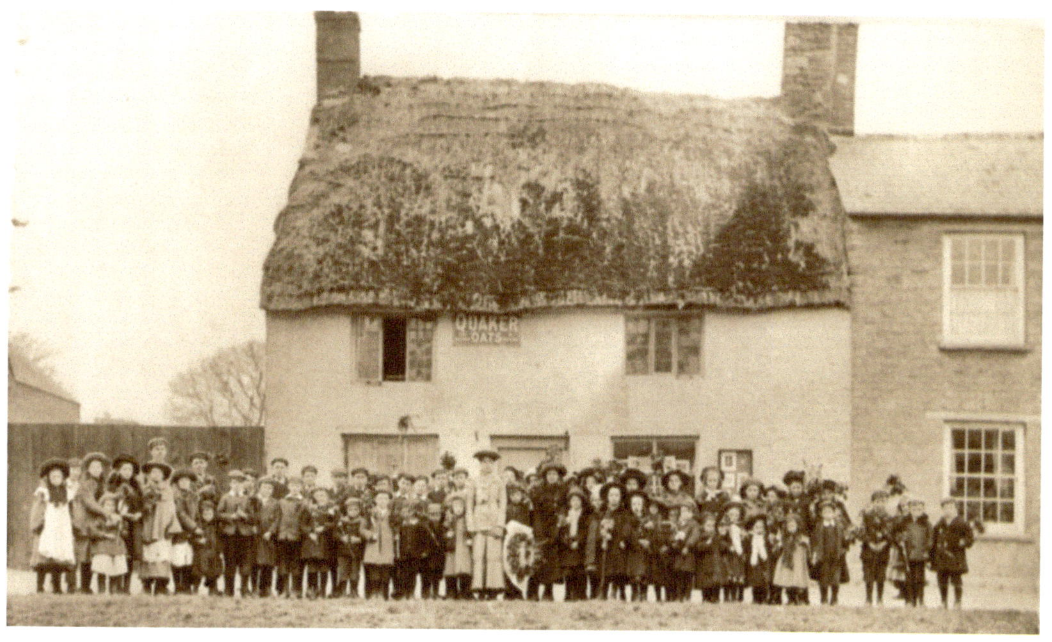

May Morning at Brackley, 1904

A wonderful early photograph of the original post office. As recorded in the UK Genealogy archives, 'The town has a head post and telegraph office, has two banks, a police station with a magistrates' room, some good inns, a cottage hospital, and a workhouse, with accommodation for 200 inmates.' The Post Office in the UK has gone through significant reorganisation since this photograph was taken, when mail came into Brackley Central by train and was distributed to the residents. Telegraphs and telephones were managed by the Post Office, along with the long-forgotten telegrams. Nowadays, the post office is further up the High Street past the traffic lights, and the sorting office is on the opposite side of the road.

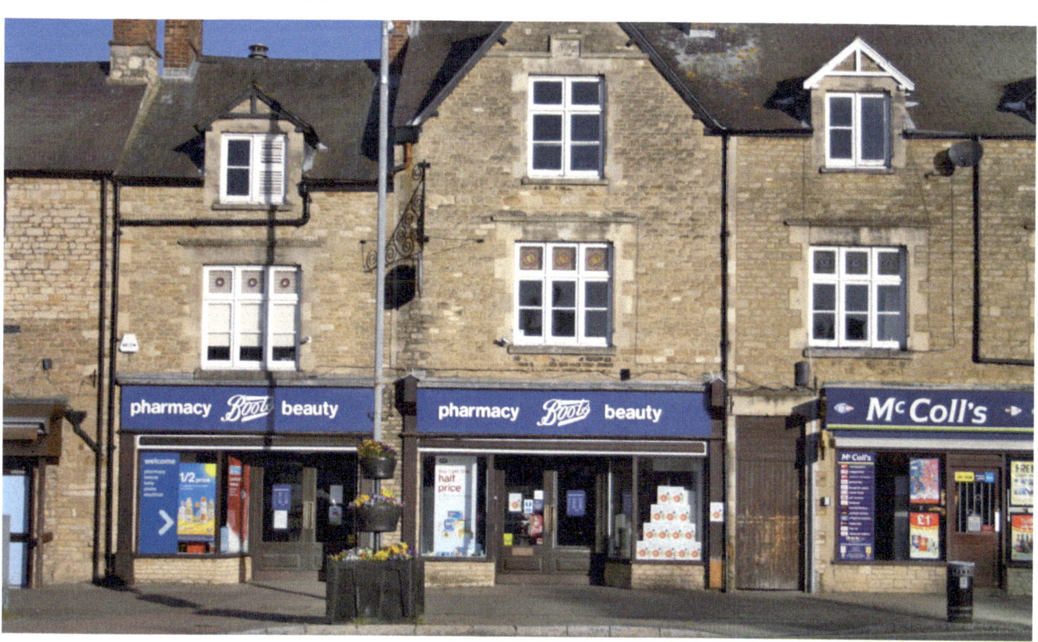

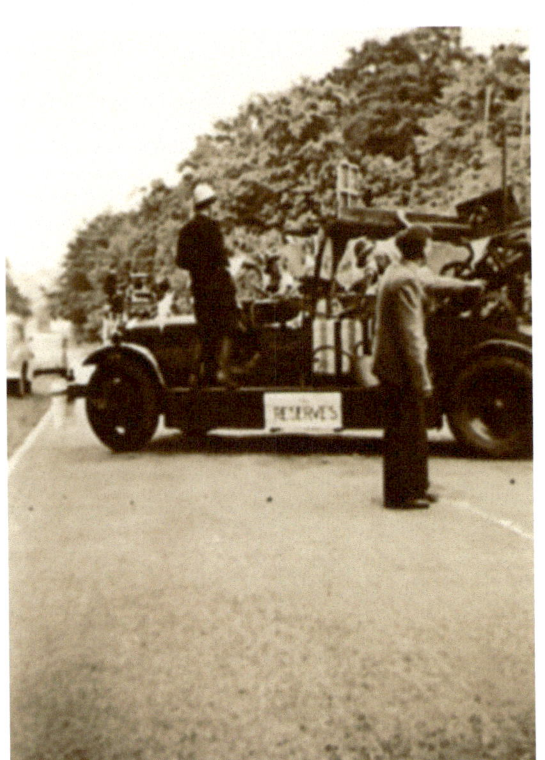

J&C Motors, 1953

A fire engine, part of the Coronation Day celebrations. J&C Motors ran a garage in the High Street until the 1980s; they were located at the back of No. 100 High Street. It was owned by Messrs Jefford and Caffyn, hence the name. Their elder daughter, Sue, married Robin Faccenda, which is who established Faccenda Chickens in 1962, today a renowned brand. With its proximity to Silverstone, Brackley is known as a racing town and has housed many companies linked with the motorsport industry. Currently, Mercedes Petronas is enjoying much success with drivers Lewis Hamilton and Nico Rosberg. Brawn GP, Honda, British American Racing and Tyrrell have operated in the town, and Force India F1 operates a wind tunnel on the former site of the north railway station. J&C Motors moved to Burwell Hill and became Burwell Hill Garage (where Jarvis Court now stands).

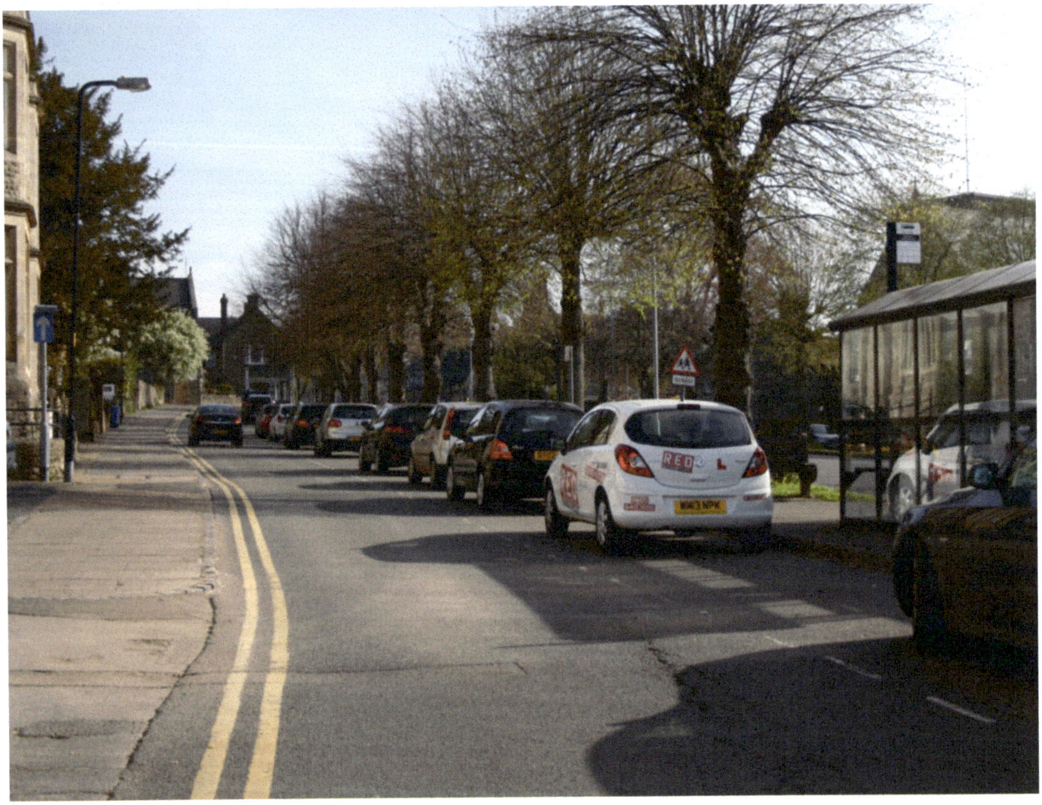

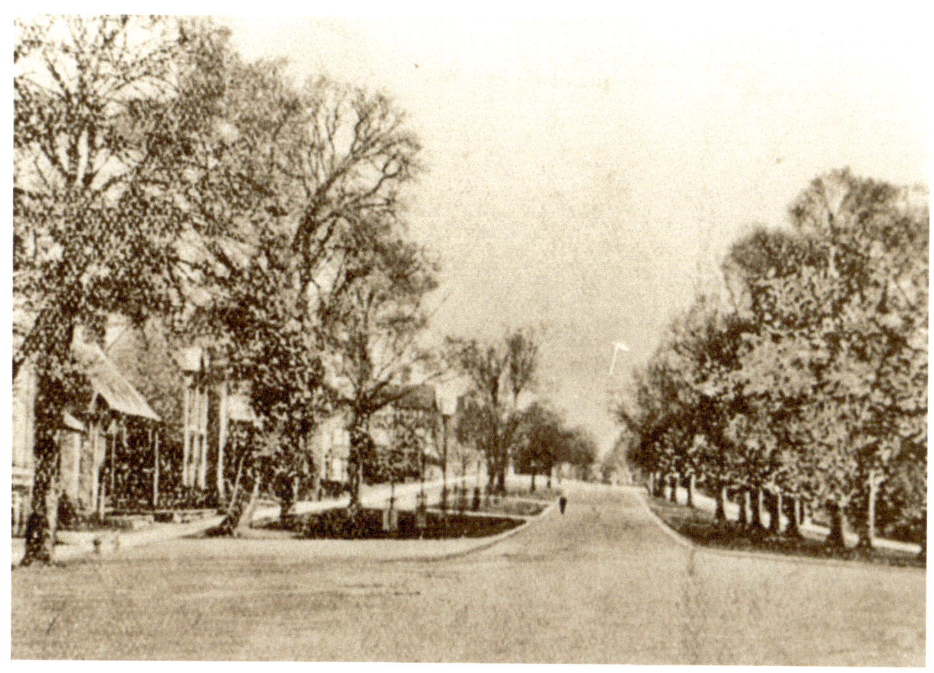

Looking North from Market Place, 1904

The High Street has always boasted a beautiful tree-lined boulevard looking north towards the Bell Tower. The width of the verges has changed over time to make provision for parking cars, but the trees have always complemented the many architecturally magnificent houses on the west side and the beautiful St John's site of Magdalen College school on the east. Brackley House is on the bottom left. The road is narrower in the old photograph than it is now – there were two rows of trees with only a footpath on the left.

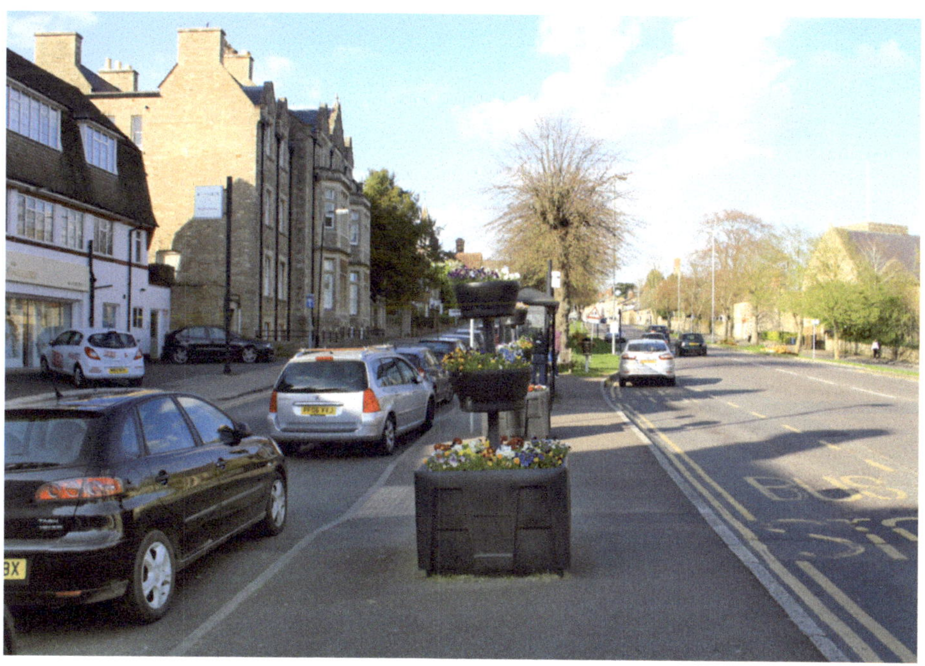

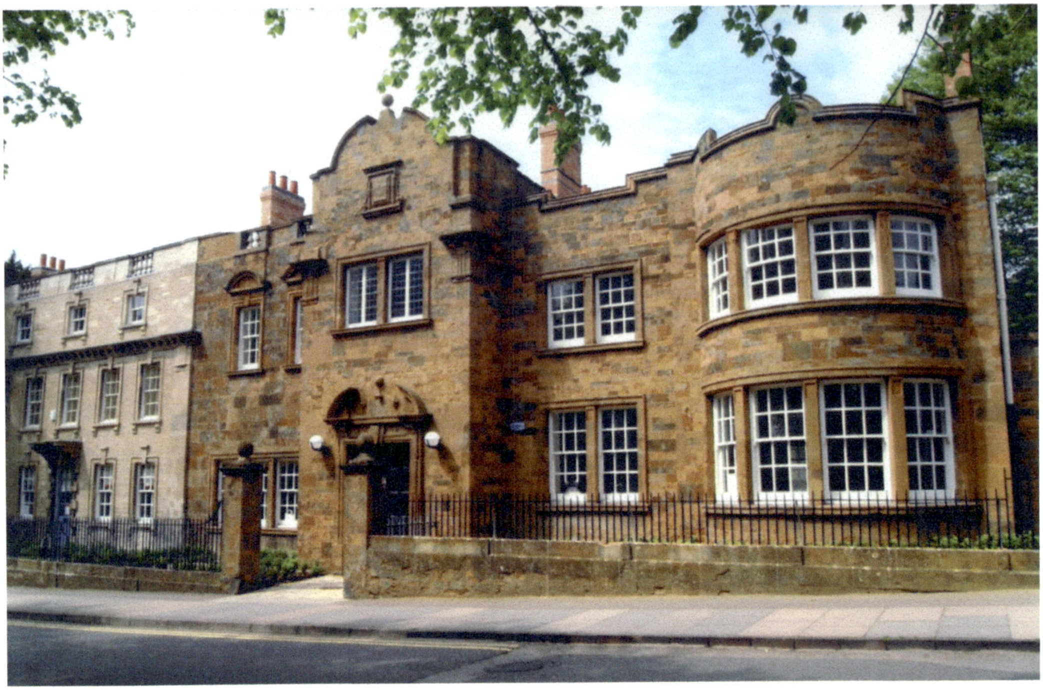

No. 4 High Street, *c.* 1980

The majority of the buildings in the Market Place are listed and many have seventeenth-century or earlier origins (often with eighteenth- or nineteenth-century façades). This building is Grade II listed. Many of the buildings, such as this one, are high quality, but some are in need of attention, particularly following the recession, with several vacant retail properties in the surrounds.

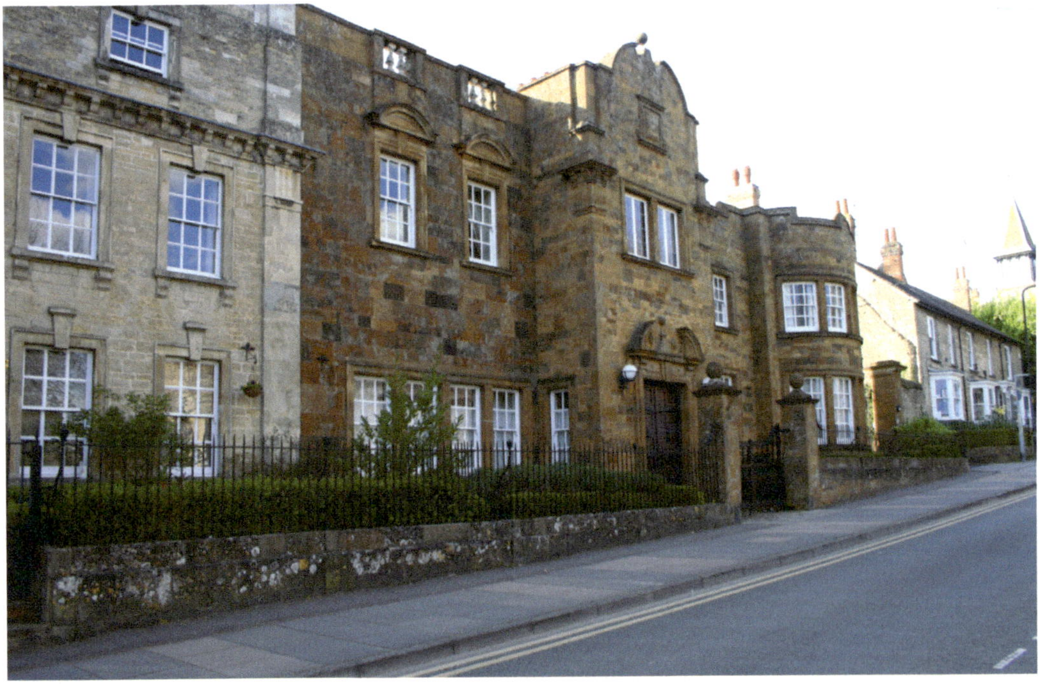

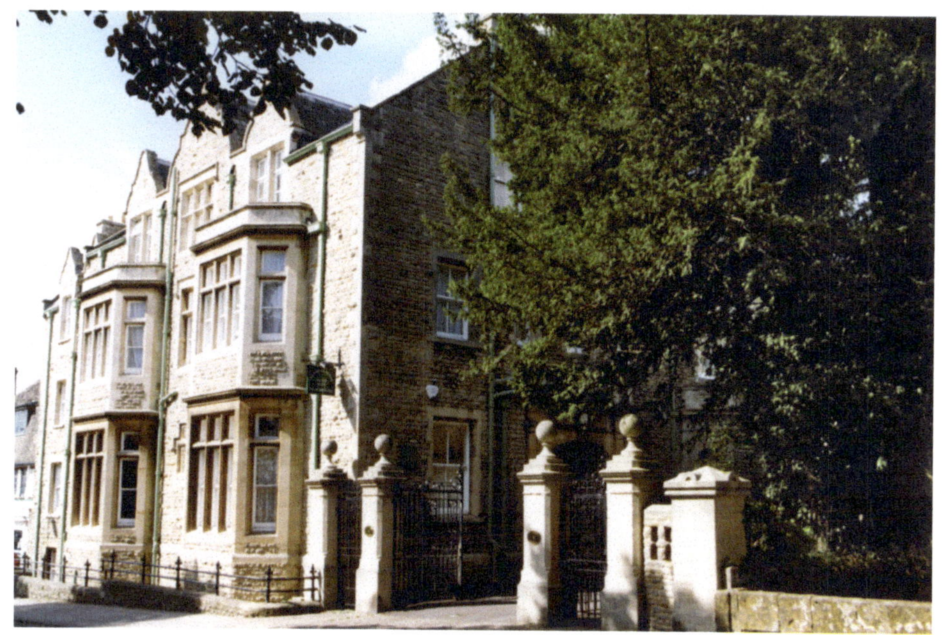

Brackley House, *c.* 1980s

Climbing the hill from the Market Place towards the Bell Tower, you cannot fail to be impressed by the new apartment block on the left-hand side just past the Hair Gallery. In a previous life, this was a retirement home, a bed and breakfast and the local registry office, until it was closed by the South Northamptonshire Council. The careers service was based there for a short while. In 1822, Col. William Cartright, second son of William Cartright of Aynho, lived in the building. He encouraged the system of enclosure for Brackley and the establishment of a system of poor relief. In 1829, the Enclosure Act for Brackley was passed. It was finally converted into apartments in the 2000s, with a house built in the back garden.

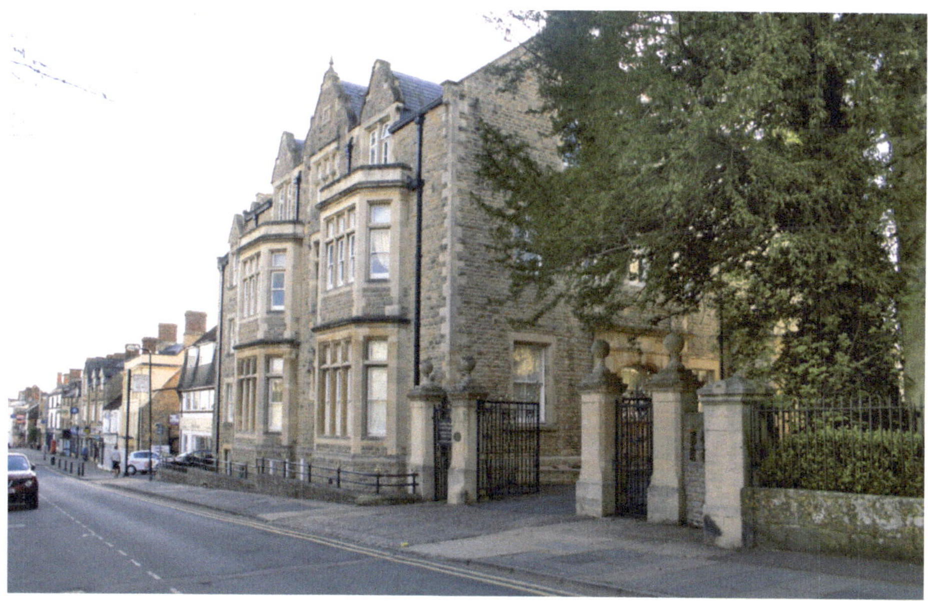

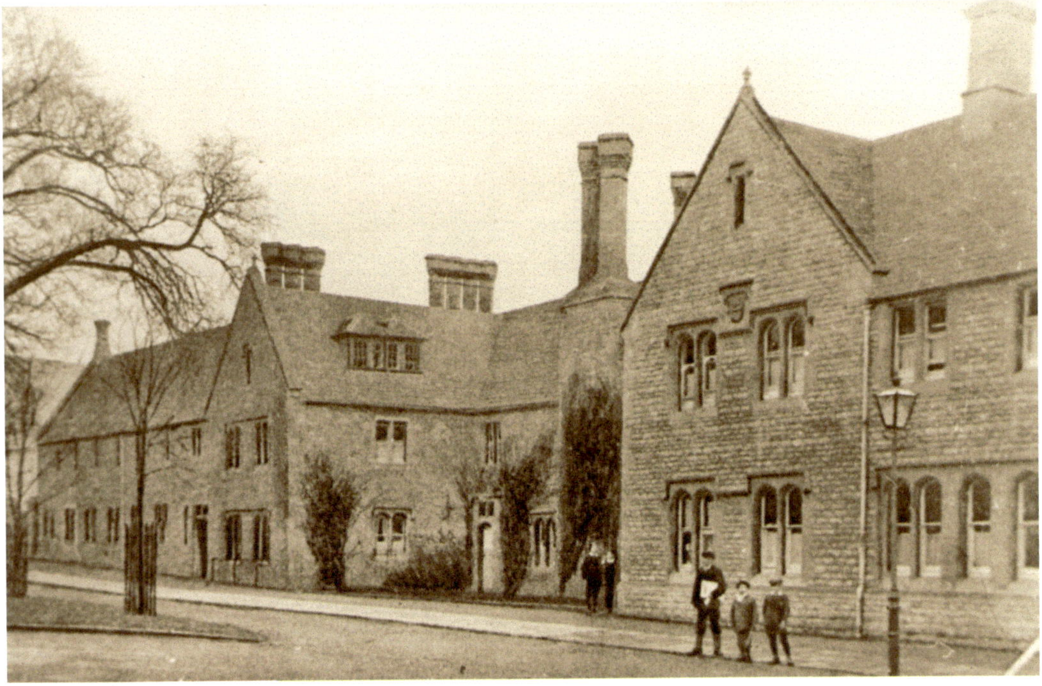

Magdalen College School (MCS)

MCS Brackley is one of three 'ancient' Magdalen College schools, the others being its sister colleges in Oxford and Waynflete, Lincolnshire. The school is currently on two sites: the former secondary modern site at Waynflete Avenue accommodates secondary schooling up to Year Eleven, after which students transfer to the St John's site (the old MCS) for most of their lessons during the sixth form.

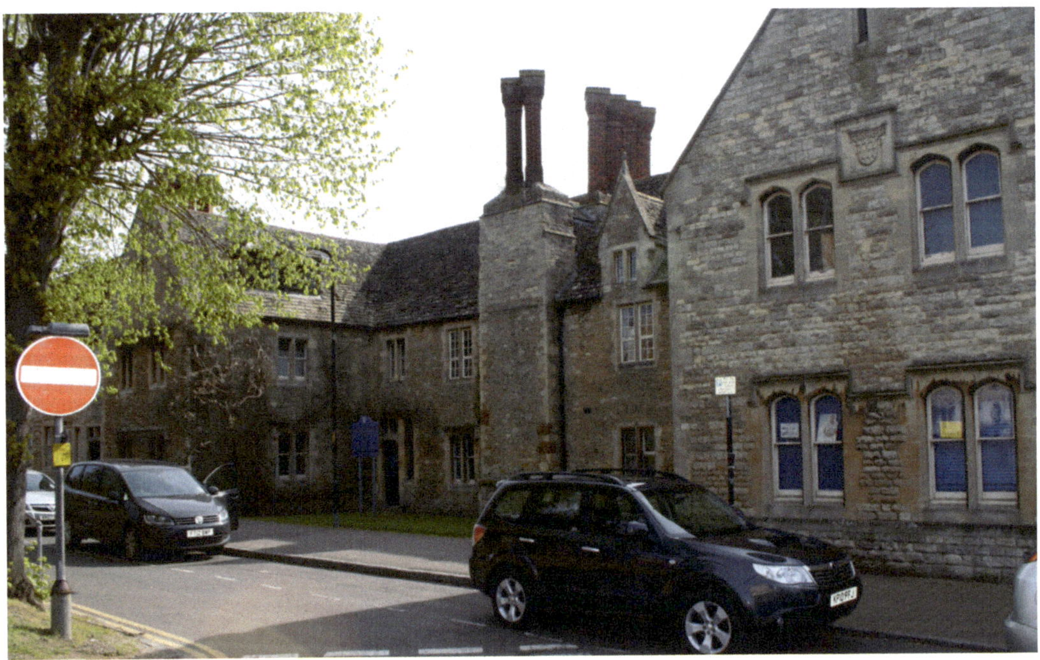

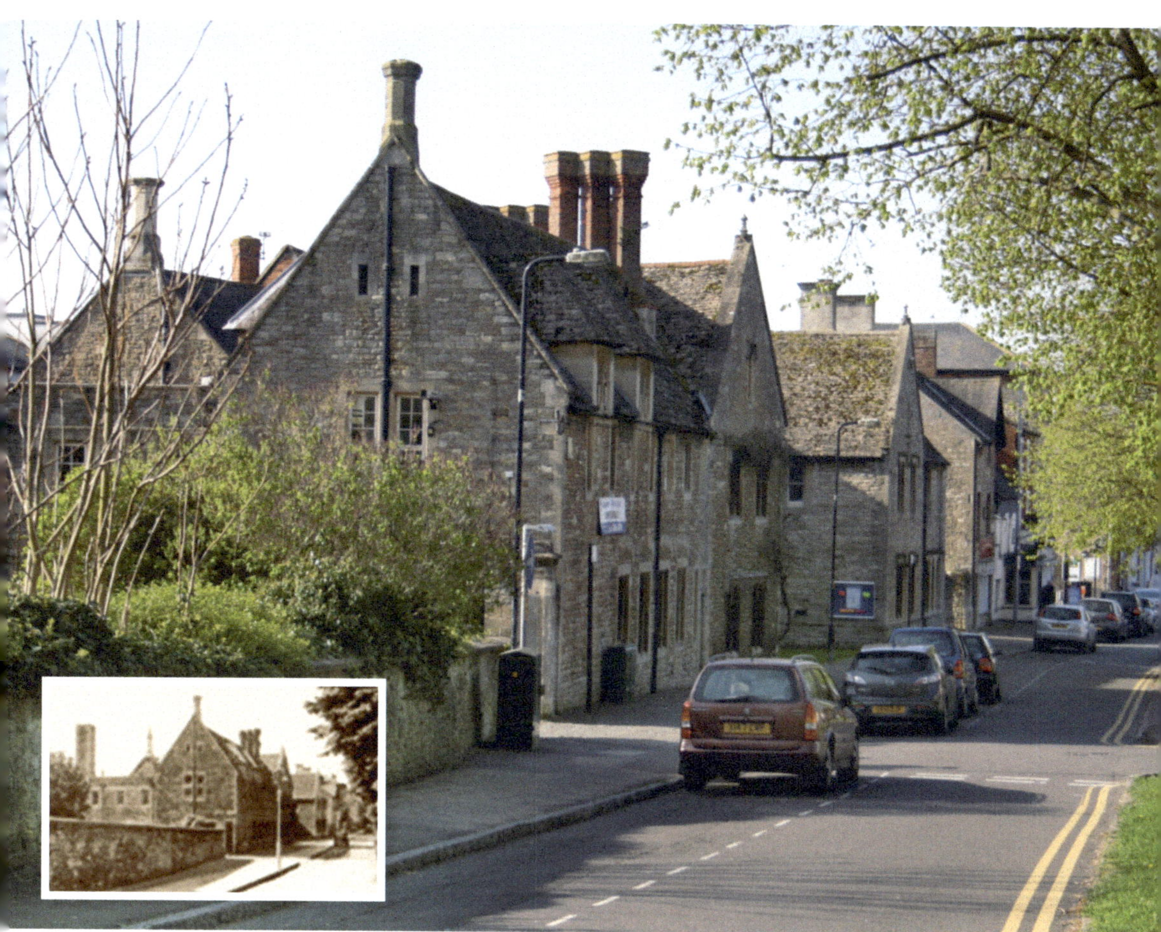

Magdalen College School, St John's Site

The original Free Grammar School was founded around the year 1447 by William of Waynflete, who endowed it for ten boys, with £13 6*s* 8*d* per annum; this sum was paid by the Society of Magdalen College, Oxford, to whom the site of the ancient hospital was granted at the time of its dissolution. In September 1973, MCS merged with the girls grammar school (Brackley High) and Brackley Secondary Modern School to form a new comprehensive school on two sites, while the girls' school was converted into the new Southfield Primary School. The oldest building on the St John's site was the master's house, now used as an examination room. There was once an underground passage that connected it to the chapel. Today, Magdalen College School is a successful voluntary controlled co-educational comprehensive school serving the eleven to eighteen age range. It converted to academy status in January 2013.

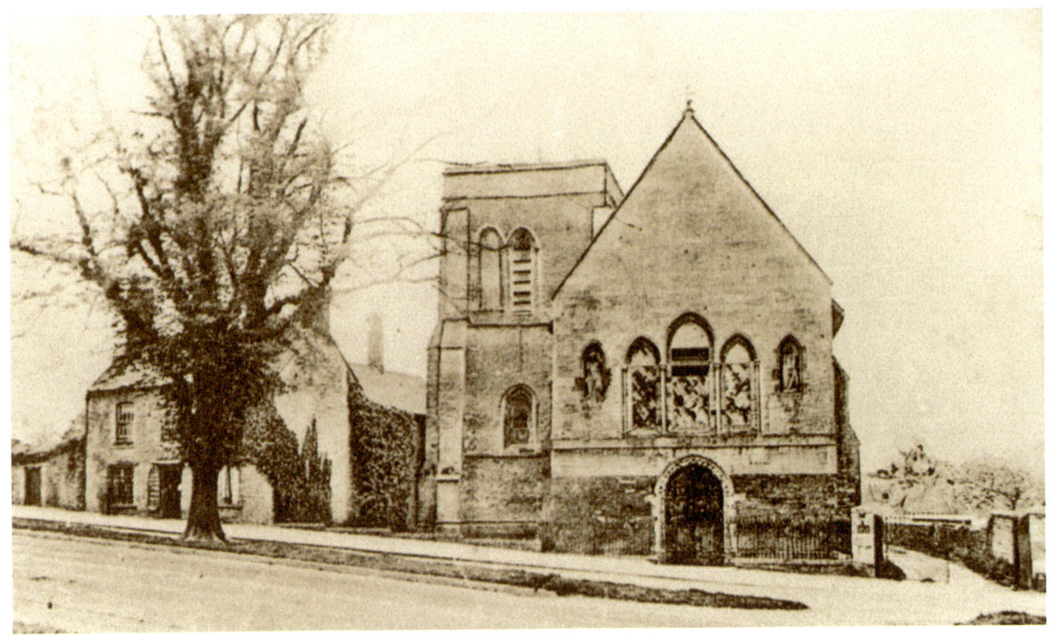

Magdalen Chapel, 1908

Formerly a chapel for the hospital of St James and St John, the earliest dateable parts are late twelfth-century, although many parts are thirteenth century. Initially, it would have had two storeys: the chapel on the ground floor and the new hospital and dormitories above. It remained a hospital for around 250 years. The chapel underwent a major restoration between 1869 and 1870 by John Buckeridge. It is constructed of stone rubble and is one of the largest and oldest school chapels still in use in England. It remains in regular use by the school, the Church of England and the local community.

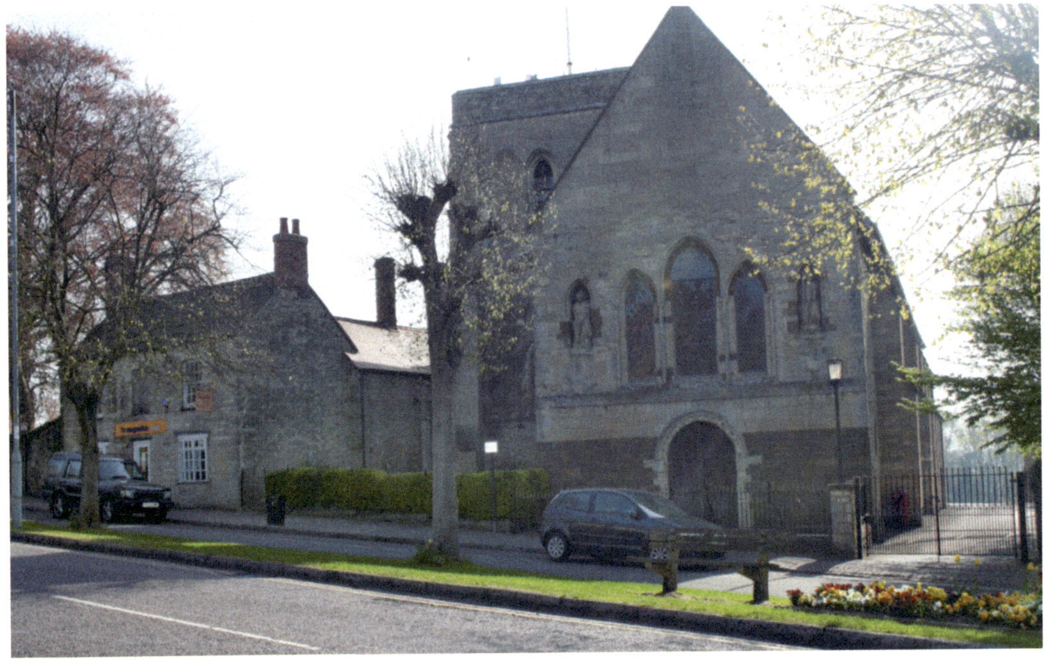

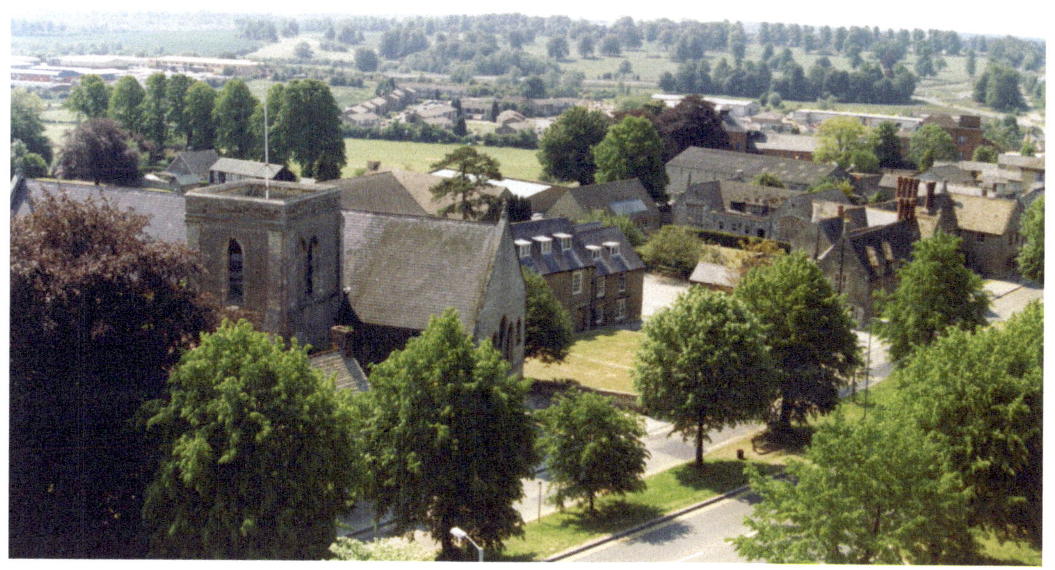

Magdalen College School From the Bell Tower, 1990

Note also the chapel in the foreground and the new apartment blocks on the former Burgess site in the background. The site now occupied by the school was originally the Hospital of St James and St John, founded around 1150 by Robert le Bossu, who also built the chapel in 1160 dedicated to St John near the hospital for the souls of his ancestors. He was the son of Robert le Beaumont, a follower of William the Conqueror, who came to England in 1066, fought at the Battle of Hastings and was allocated the area of Brackley. Very little now remains of the original hospital buildings because they were so badly looked after. In 1484, it was sold to Magdalen College, Oxford. By 1548, there was a school on the site. The school's initial purpose was to allow students of the college in Oxford to escape the plague affecting Oxford at the time.

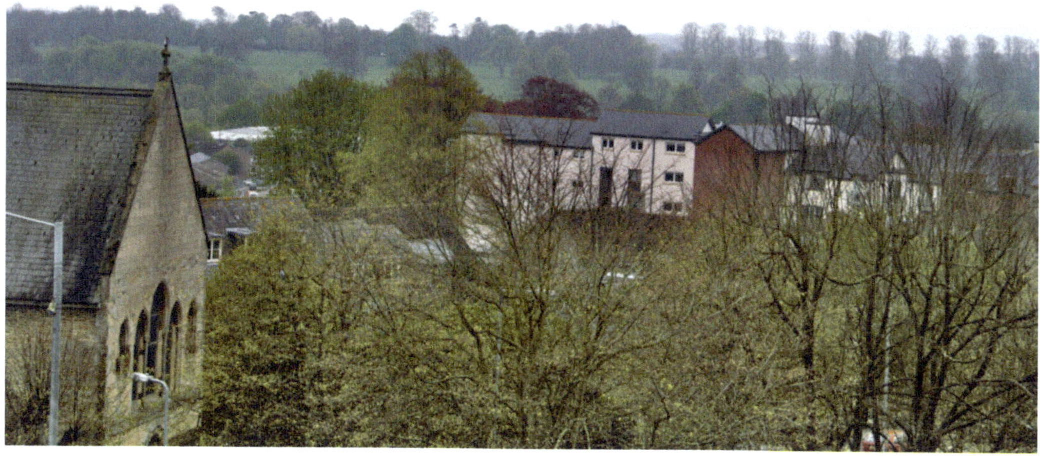

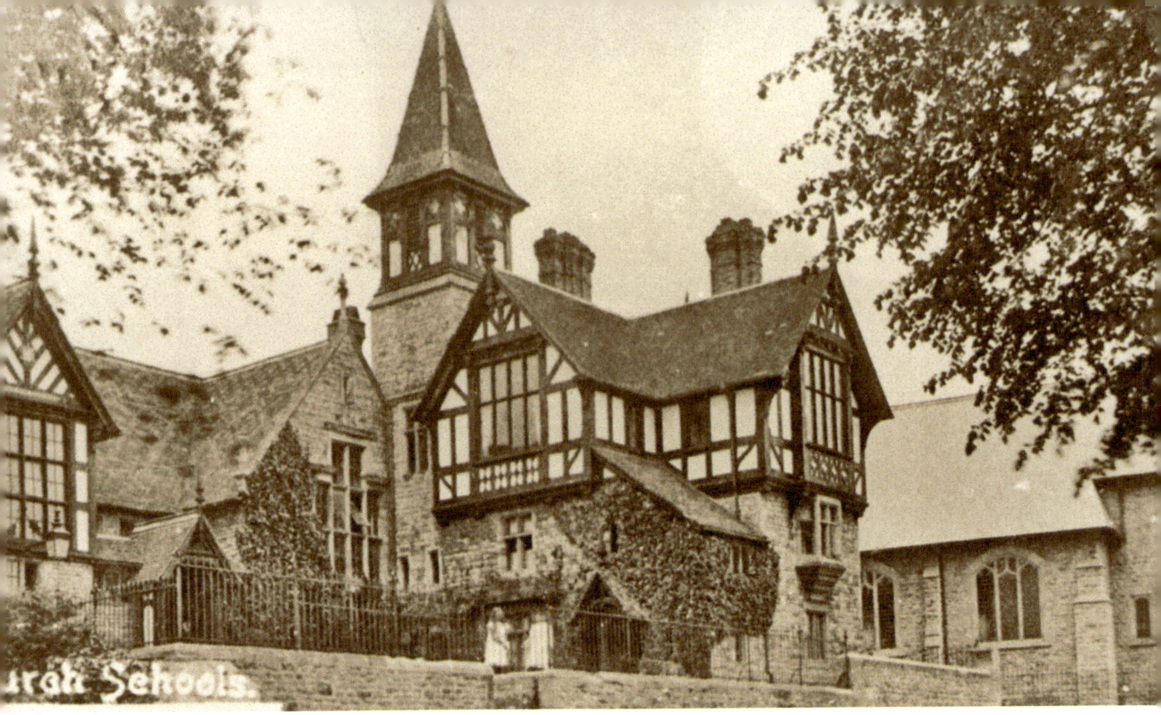

Near the Masters House, *c.* 1900–10

The photographs are taken outside the master's house by the traffic lights looking across the road. It was the home of the master of Magdalen College School (and the boys' boarding house). It is also known as Northgate House. The head teacher of the school is still known as the master. This is thought to be linked to the time in the sixteenth century when between eight and ten boys only had one teacher, the master. The first master was Thomas Goodwin. In 1740, a horrible murder took place at this house. The Revd Dr Littleton Burton lived in the house, chaplain to Prince Frederick and the Rector of Credenwell. He dismissed a young serving man called Henry Kerwood for being 'saucy', but the servant then hid in a loft. When he was discovered, he was again told to leave. At this, Kerwood picked up a pitchfork and struck the reverend on the head, killing him. He fled the scene and, despite the offer of a 10 guinea reward, he was never caught. The memorial to Revd Burton is in the college chapel.

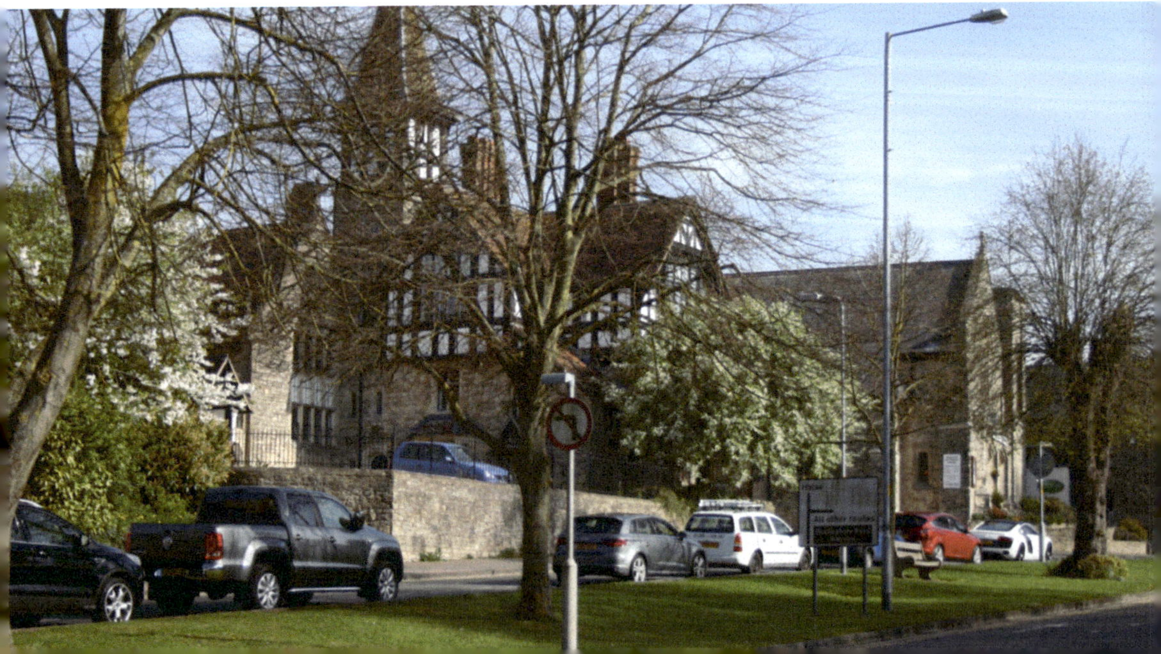

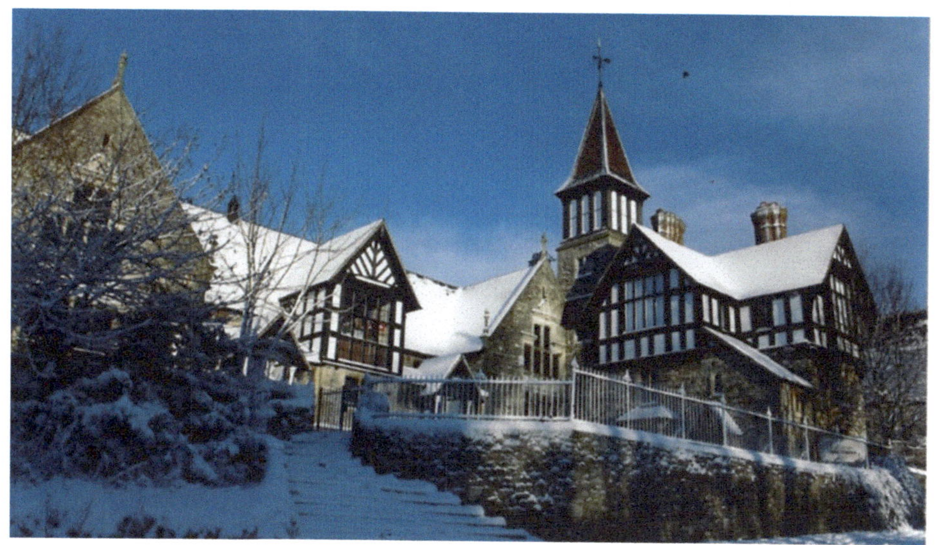

Bell Tower

This building was a Church of England infant and primary school. In the late 1960s, it was converted into a nightclub. In the early 1970s, the building was called the Bell Tower. The school was established in December 1817 when the great and good of Brackley held a meeting at The Crown to set up a school for the education of the poor of Brackley and the surrounding area. After being housed in different buildings, it was finally established in this building in 1870. 'Feed my lambs' is the local name for the Church of England Primary School, due to the carving of these words on the lintel. It had separate entrances for boys and girls, as was the norm in those days. It remained a junior school until 1968, and many older residents remember having school dinners in the small hall that used to stand at the other end of Hill Street. The Tudor look reflects Brackley's association with the Egerton family's home area of Chester and of the Puritan religious background of Elizabeth I. The Anglicans had refused to work with the Methodists in the building of this new school, and were determined to undermine the influence of the earlier but smaller Methodist school. The entrance to the school was a hole in the wall. It has recently been converted into apartments that have some of the best views in town.

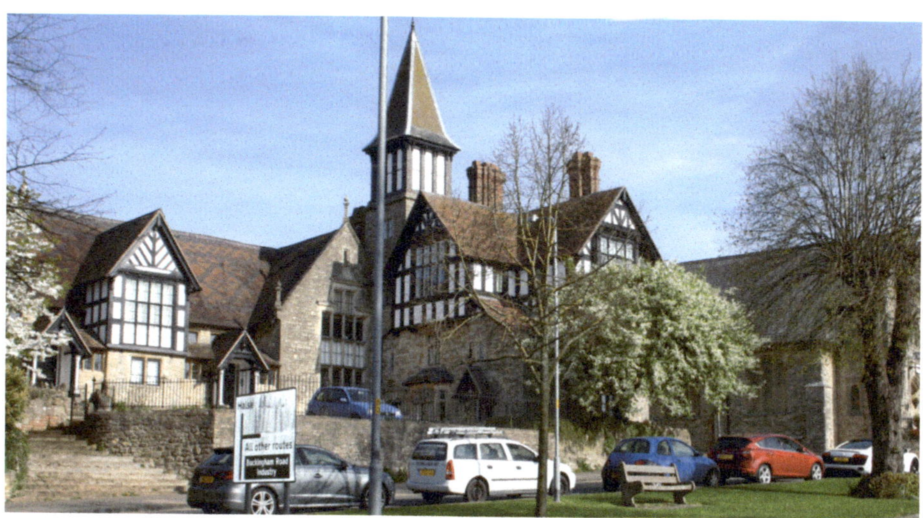

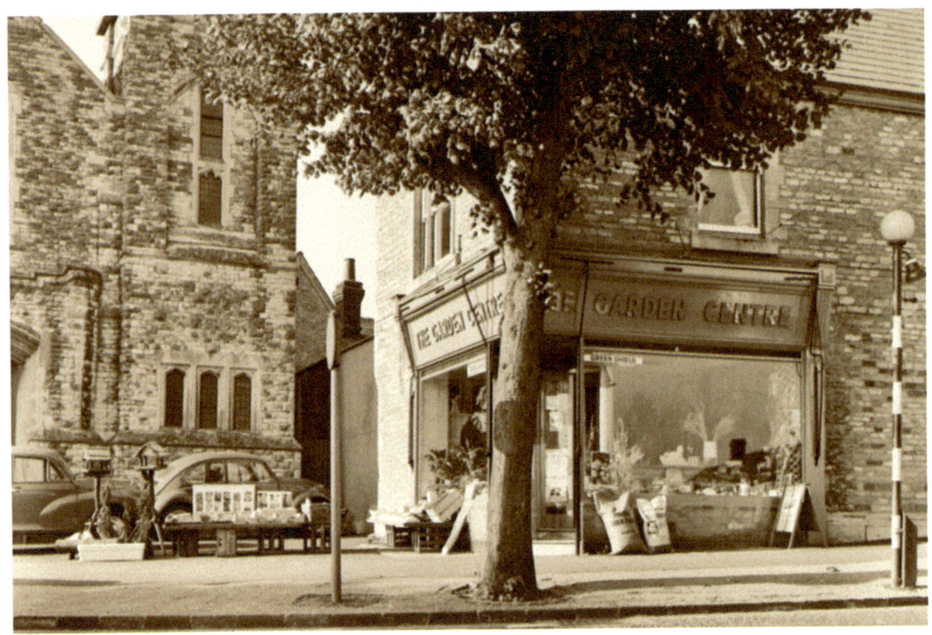

The Garden Centre, Previously International Stores

For many years, this was a brightly coloured landmark at the top of the High Street with bunches of flowers arrayed outside. Note the Methodist church next door. John Wesley preached in the town in 1784 and described the crowd's reaction as 'understanding me no more than if I had been talking Greek'. There was already a small society of Methodists established at that time. The year before, a former curate of Brackley, John Moore, had become Archbishop of Canterbury. The first Methodist church building was opened in 1804, less than 100 yards from the present building. The remains of the entrance door and two windows can still be seen in the garden wall of Chapel Cottage. The present building at the junction of High Street and Hill Street was opened in 1905. The growth of the population has helped to reestablish an important presence in the town.

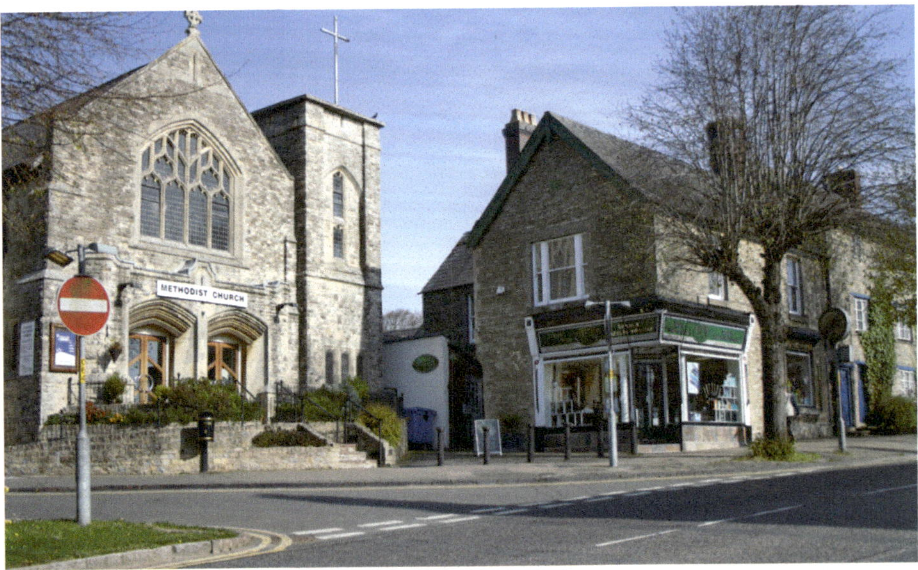

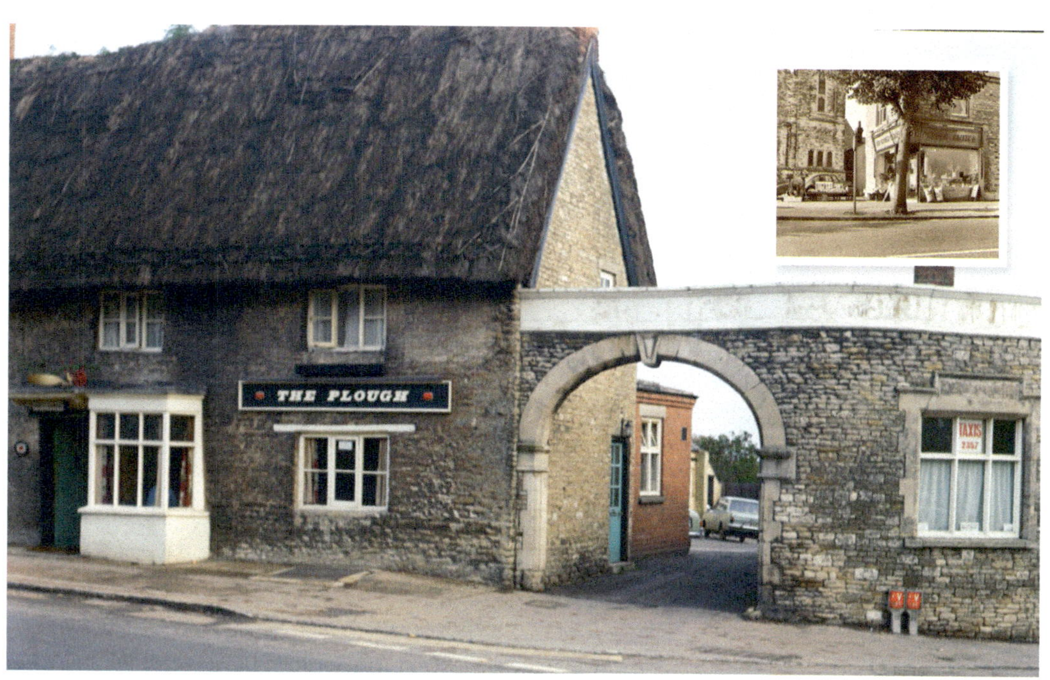

The Plough, *c.* 1960

If you are young and energetic, The Plough is the place to watch sport on Sky television today. Irene Freeman speaks about how she spent all her youth in The Plough: 'I met my husband in The Plough thirty years ago! The bar had been moved, I didn't stay long as it wasn't the good old Plough I remembered my misspent youth in. During the '70s it was always packed; everyone went to The Plough and then the Bell Tower. Good times!' Note the coach gate and stable block that now houses a body repair shop at the end belonging to Enotts, who have a long history at this site.

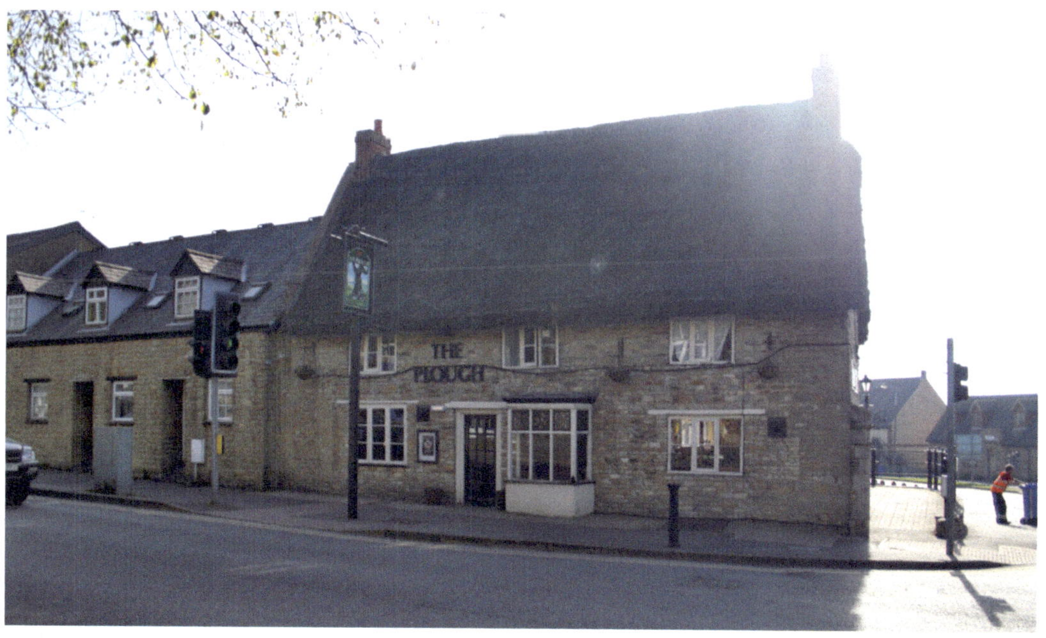

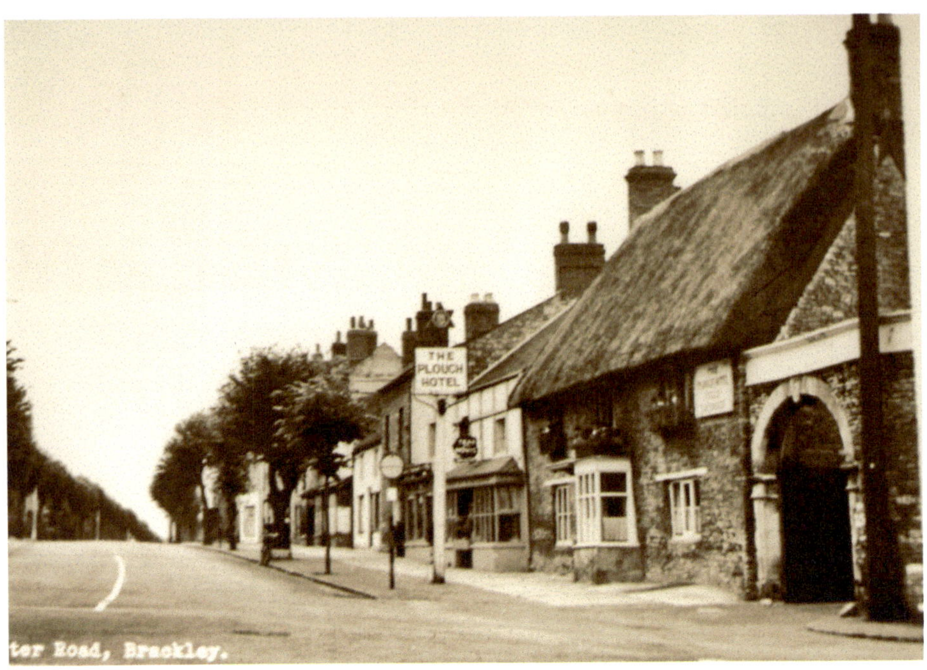

The Plough

Oak Cottage (next to the Plough) was George's café and at one stage was pulled down after a hole appeared in the floor. Plough Mews was built on the site. Mrs Merry's chemist was located next to the café until the 1960s. Nos 5 and 6 were pulled down in the 1980s. Peter North still lives in the three-storey house. What is now Milano pizzas was once Whites Classic House, selling cards and gifts. Mr White was on the town council and owned White's butchers (now Right Angle on Manor Road).

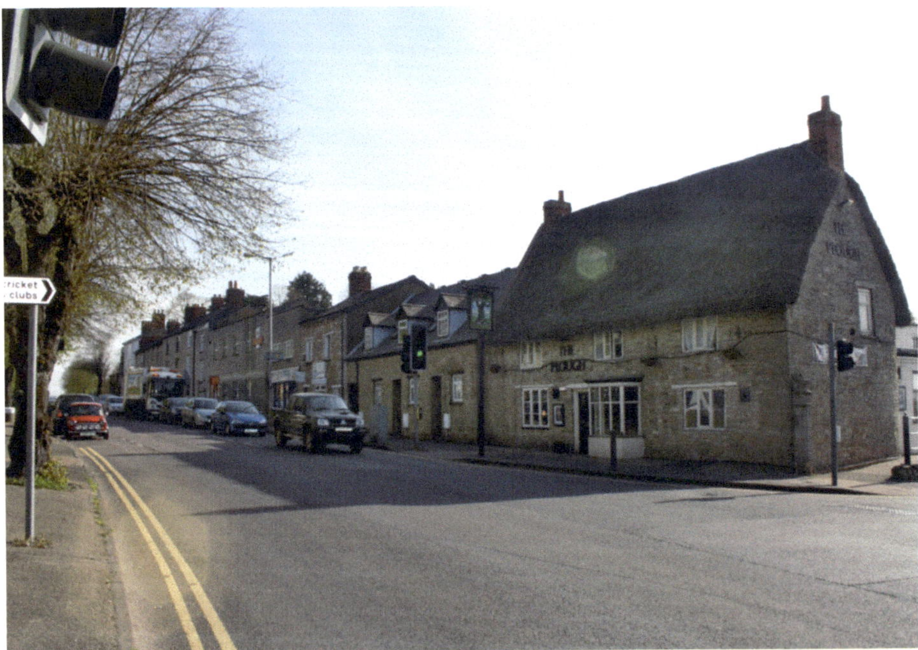

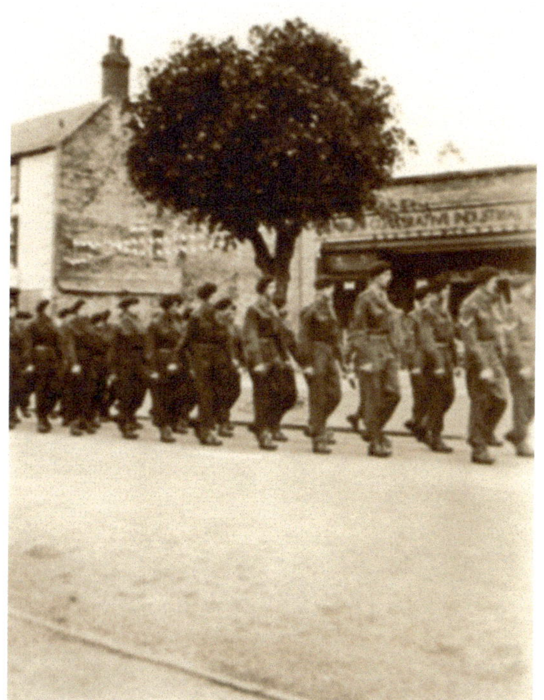

Coronation Celebrations, 1953

Soldiers marching in the High Street near the current post office. The sorting office is on the opposite side of the road. The buildings in this area are a mixture of residential and commercial properties, which has been the case for some time. A funeral director has been on this site for many years.

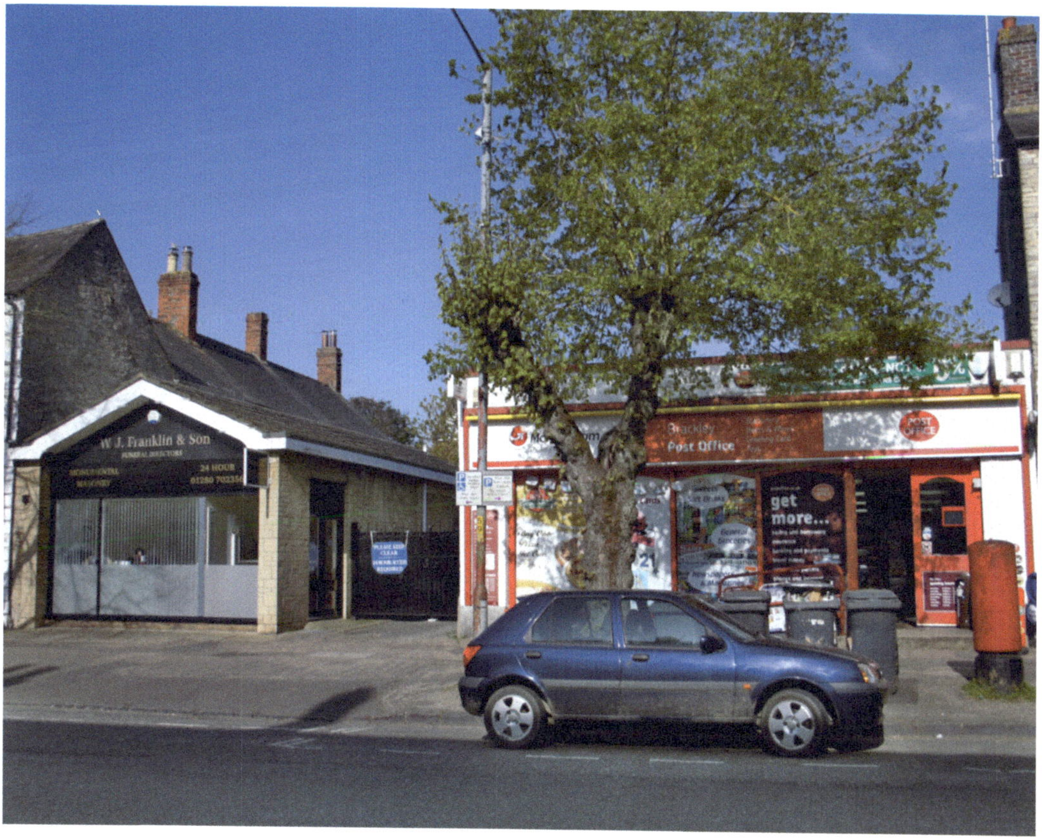

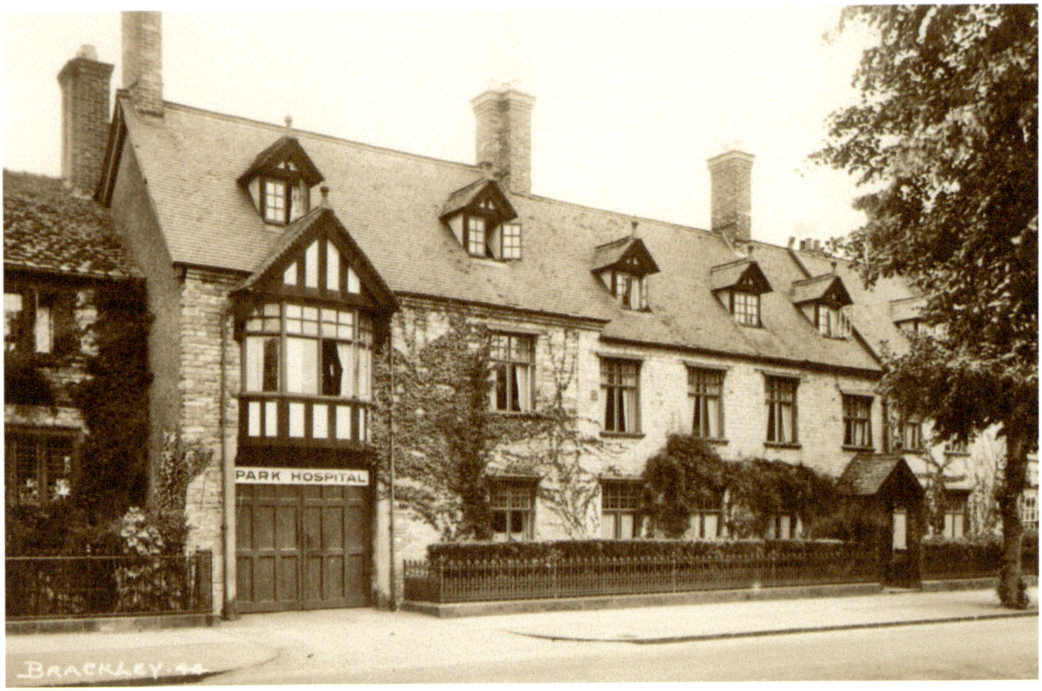

Park Hospital

Park Hospital was situated at what is now called 'Sutton Hundreds' opposite Brackley Park. At some time, pre-NHS, one of the local doctors had an issue with the local Cottage Hospital and therefore chose to open his own hospital. He is believed to be a Dr Stathers, who was still a doctor in 1950s and whose practice eventually grew and morphed into Springfield Surgery. Prior to Dr Stathers, Dr Sowden used the facilities there. Today it is a private house.

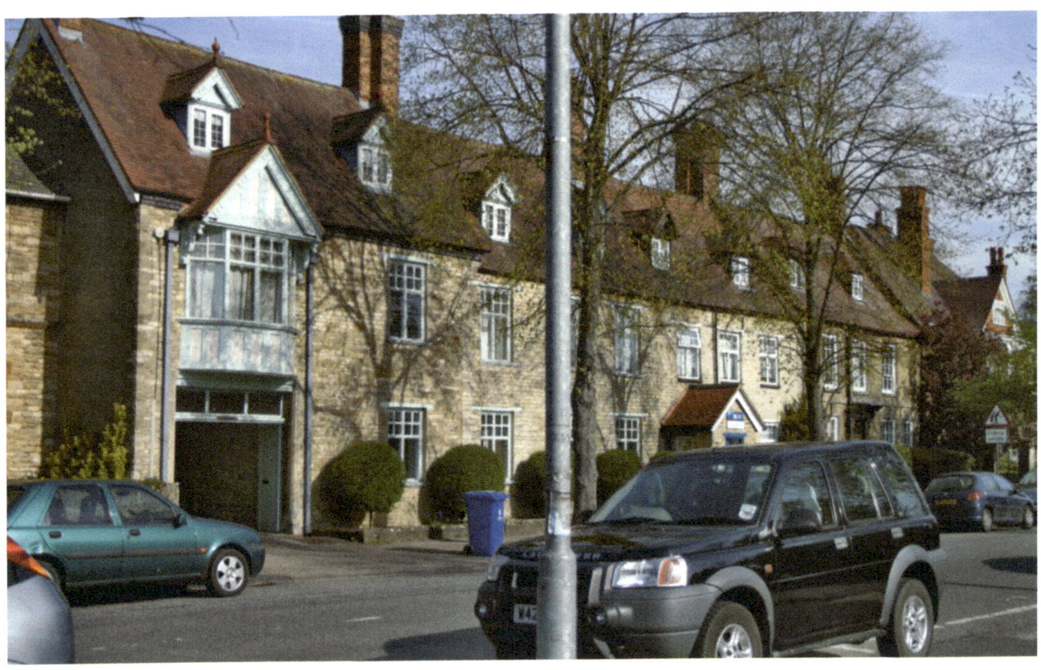

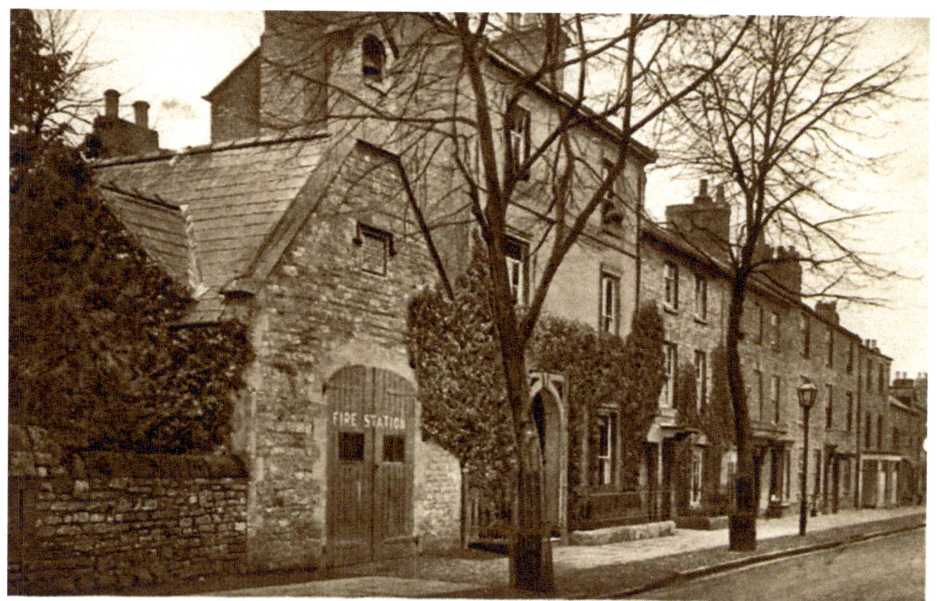

Brackley Old Fire Station

This building is situated next to Brackley Park. The old photograph shows the fire station in 1885. The adapted building dates to 1887 and is Grade II listed. It was bought by the town council from the National Trust in 2013 after the fire service moved into a new station on Bridge Street. The move took place in 2010 and was opened by the Duke of York. The old station had been in use for 123 years, run by volunteers (retained force). Its future, which is currently being decided, is likely to be a centre for community activities.

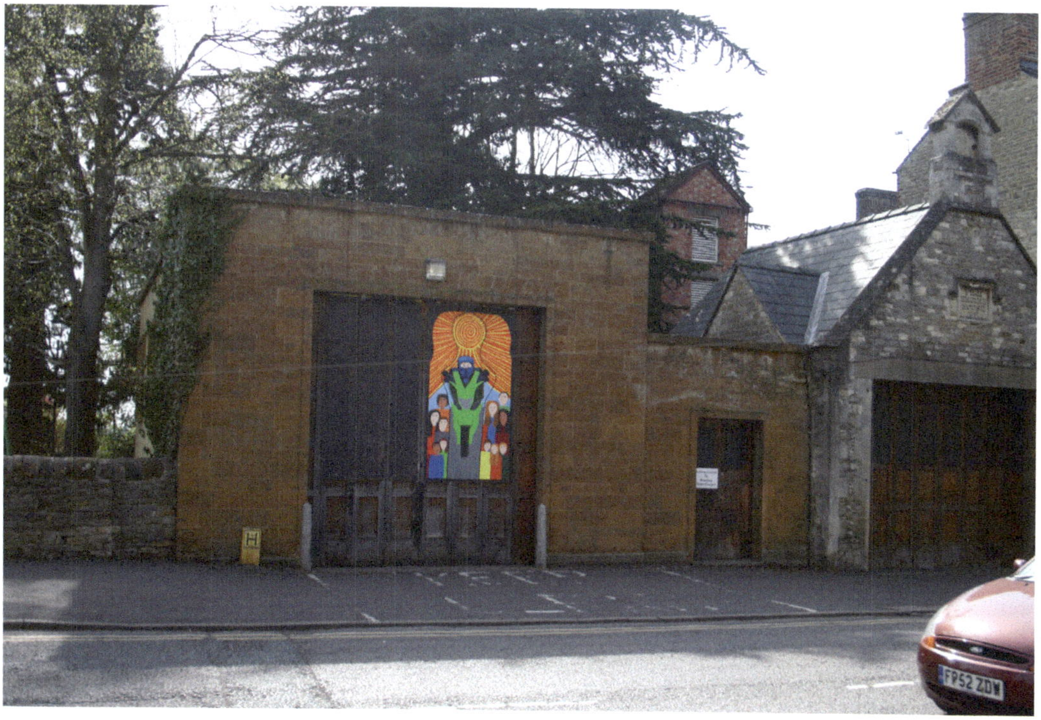

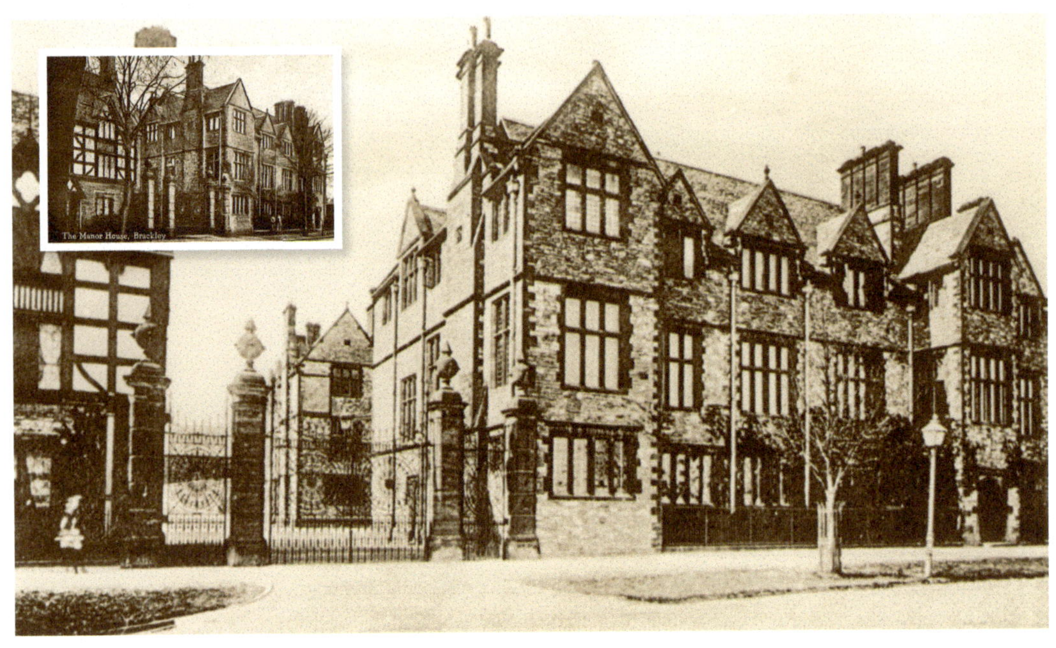

The Manor House (Winchester House School), Early 1900s

There was no known manor house in Brackley before this building, even though there were a number of important buildings occupied by powerful people. Previously, an old Tudor tithe house existed on the site, which originally had one storey plus attic dormer. In 1875–78, the Earl of Ellesmere had it rebuilt as a rather grand manor house in the same style, but retained the doorway and one window of the original building, which can still be seen today. It is now Grade II listed. The chapel is on the right, and there used to be a door into it off the street. The building now houses Winchester House independent preparatory school for children aged three to thirteen. The school moved to its present site in 1922 and became co-educational in 1976. The main house at Winchester House was built in the early 1800s.

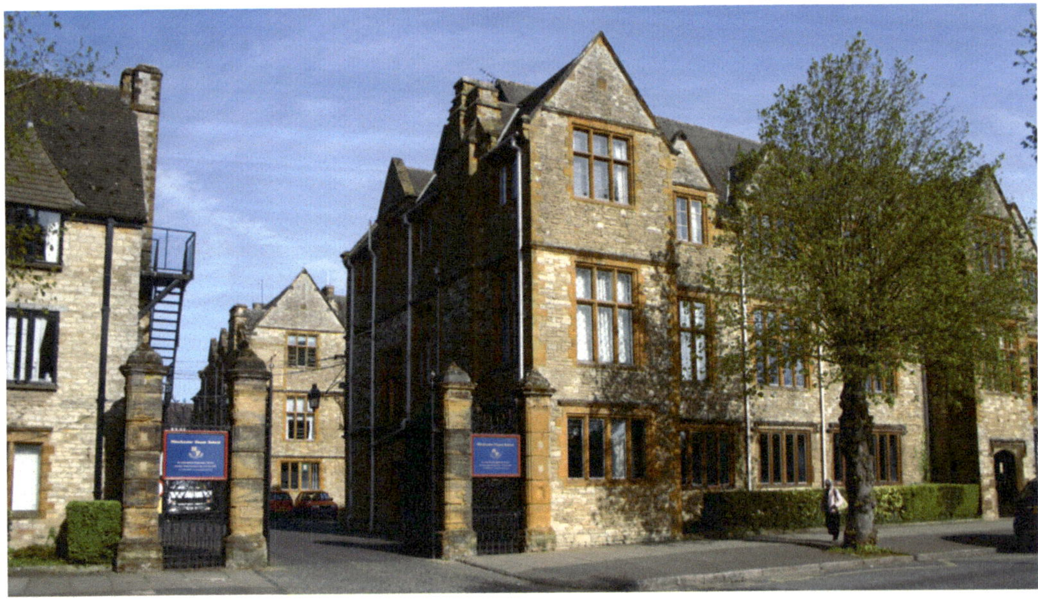

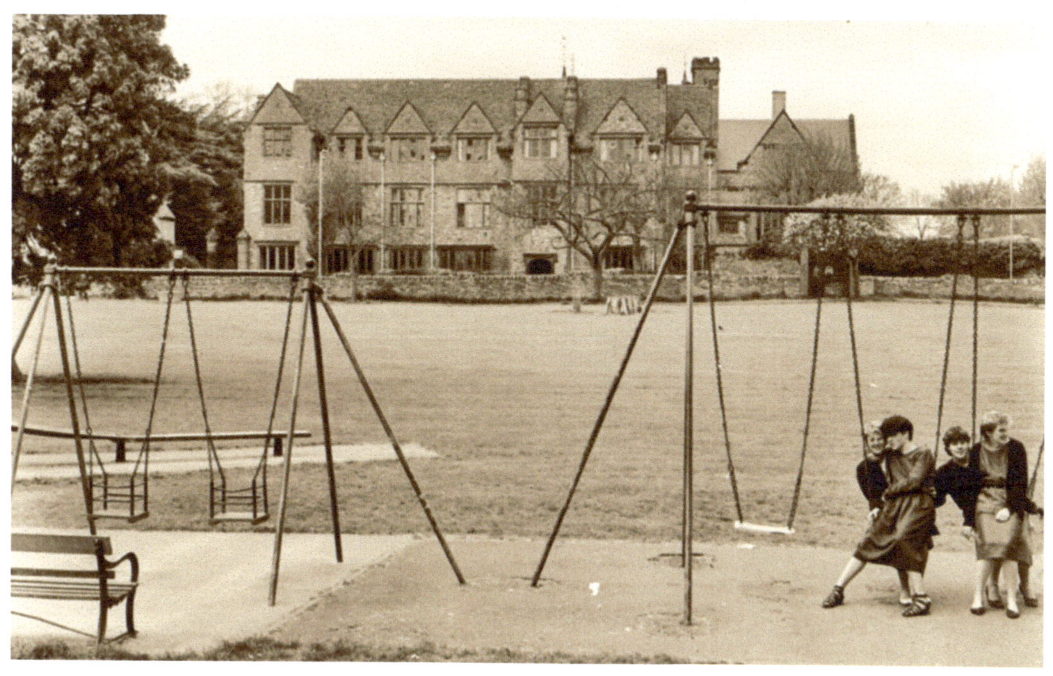

Winchester House School from Brackley Park, c. 1960

The town boasts a large number of parks and green areas, which give a feeling of spaciousness to the town. Situated opposite the manor house is Brackley Park, surrounded by many large, imposing trees, including a number of cedars. The town council ensures good play facilities for young children, and it is also a convenient enclosed space to host some of the festivals that take place in the town. The annual Beer Festival takes place here, for instance – an event not be missed in the town, in addition to relaxed summer music events in the park.

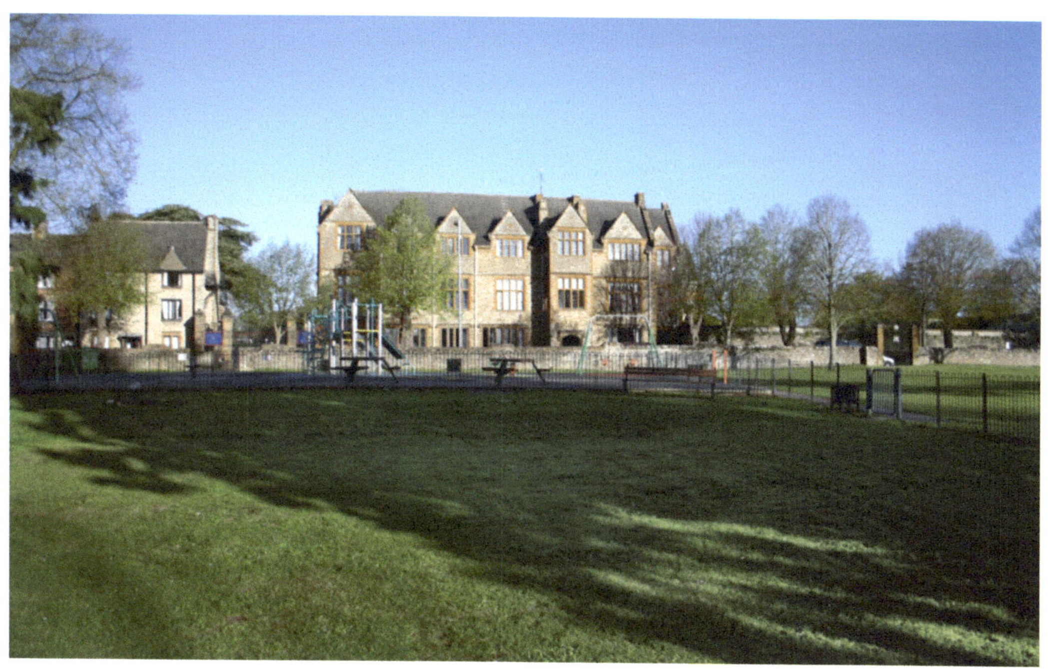

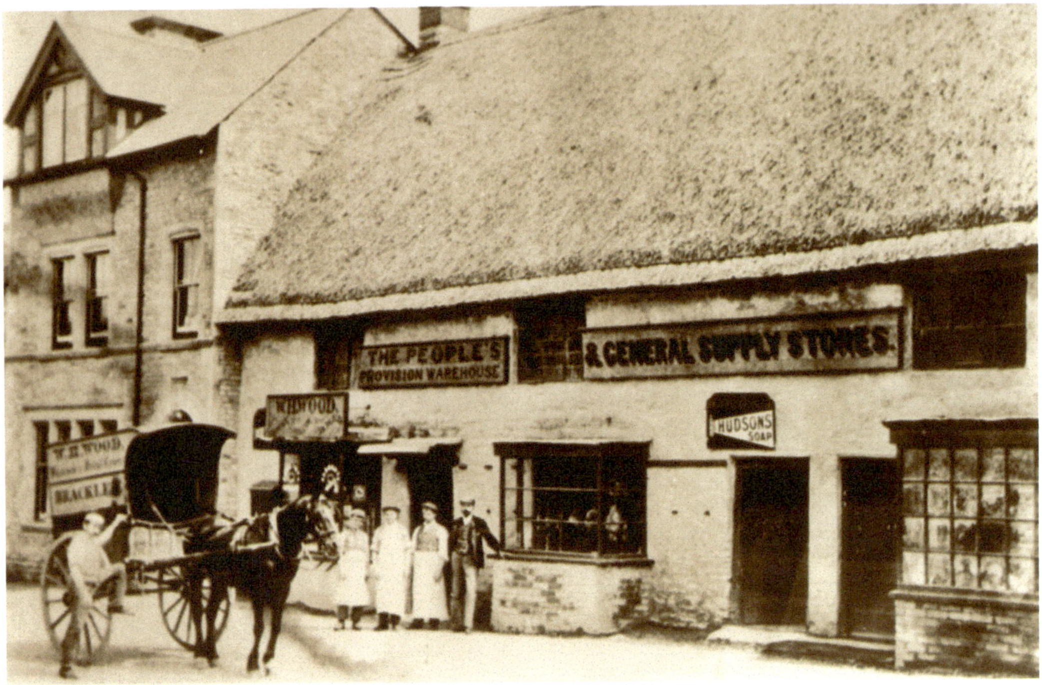

No. 83 High Street, *c.* 1900

A wonderful photograph of No. 83 High Streeet, with thatched roofing in keeping with local style of the period. It is near to what is now the Kushboo Restaurant, one of five Indian-style restaurants currently to be found in Brackley. It was bought by Walter Parish for £3,300 in 1970. No. 85 High Street is on the left of the photograph.

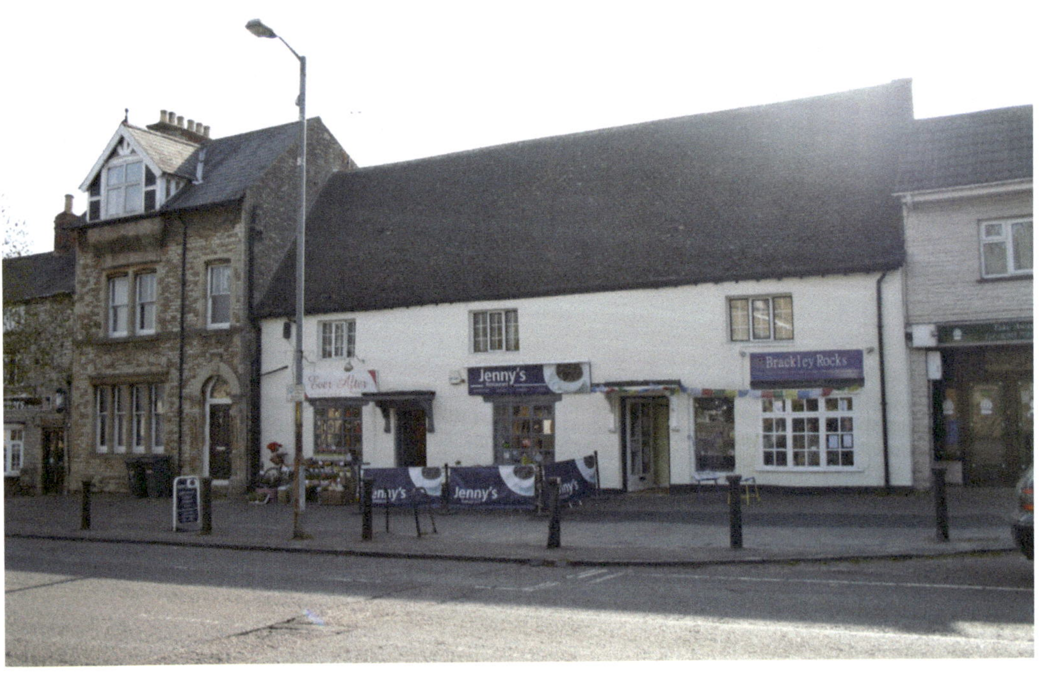

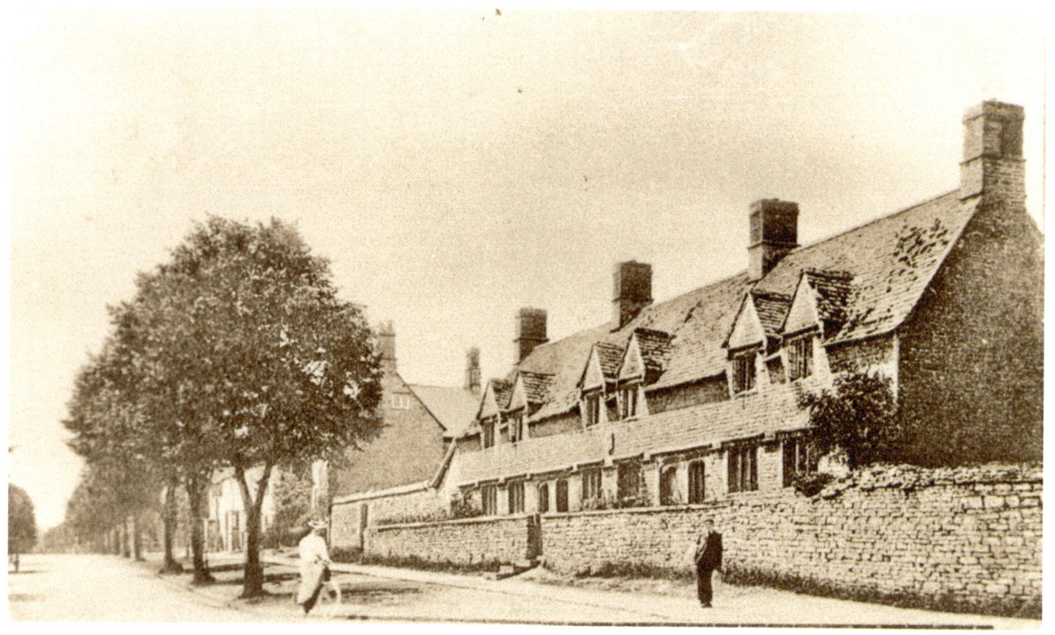

Almshouses, 1909

The Almshouses were founded in 1633 for six poor people (women) of the parish by Sir Thomas Crewe (speaker of the House of Commons, 1623–25), who eventually became Baron Crewe of Steane. Eligibility for occupation now extends to gentlemen and younger women. They are managed by the Sir Thomas Crewe Almshouses Trust and maintenance rates are currently around £50 per week. They each have one storey plus attic dormers. They were endowed with a rent of £24, which was increased in 1721 by his descendant Lord Crewe, Bishop of Durham, to £36. The poor law union of Brackley comprises thirty parishes or places, of which twenty-five are in the county of Northampton, three in Buckingham, and two in Oxford, and contains a population of 13,508. The inset shows the dedication plaque.

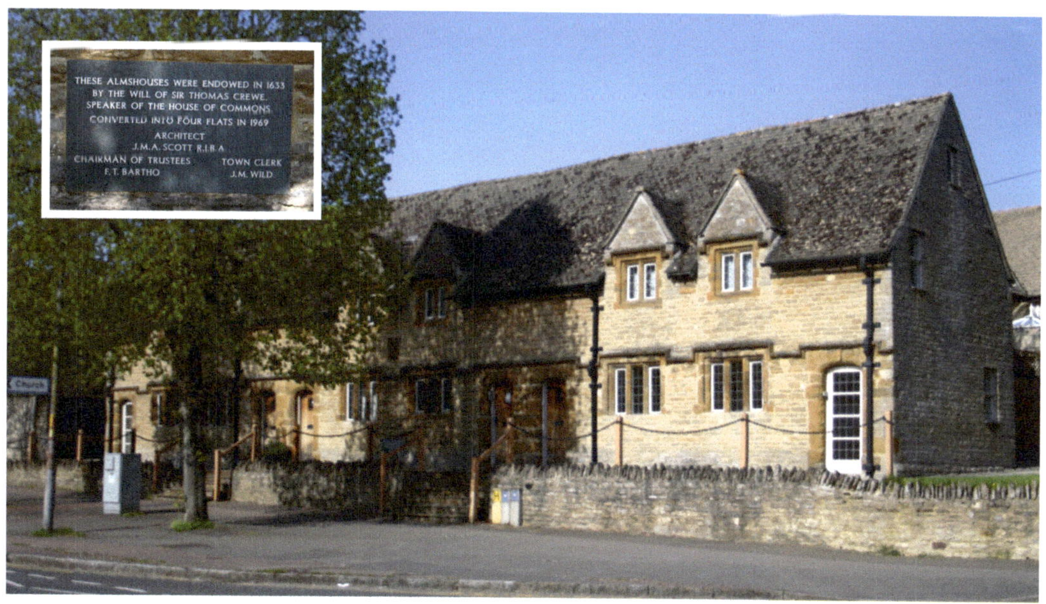

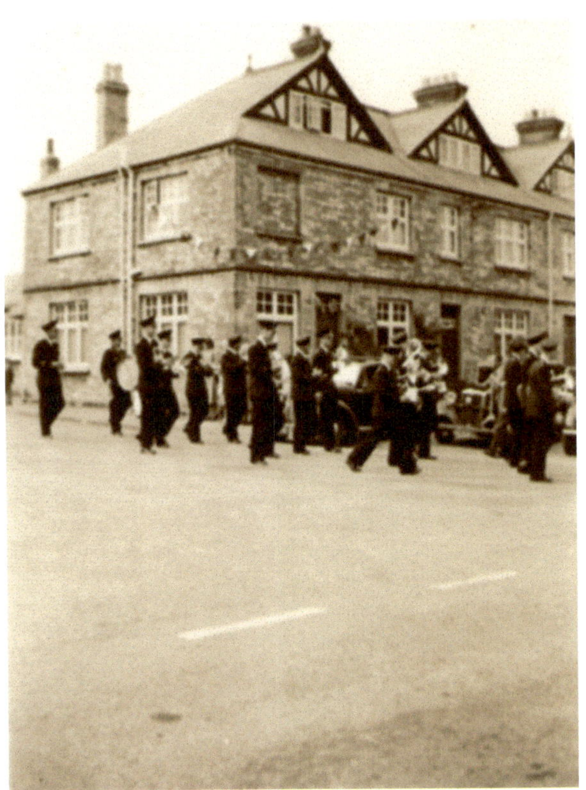

Marching Band, 1960

Exiting the Halse road onto the High Street, 1960. Brackley has a strong tradition of successful brass bands. Brackley & District Band was formed in the mid-1970s when a group of young musicians finished their time at school but still wanted to enjoy playing in a brass band. Soon after this, a junior band was also started. For over thirty years, it has been based in the Band Club in the centre of Brackley. Some players still remain from the early days. The band has competed at all levels over the years, competing against some of the top bands in the country. The inset shows the entrance to the Band Club in Drayman's Walk.

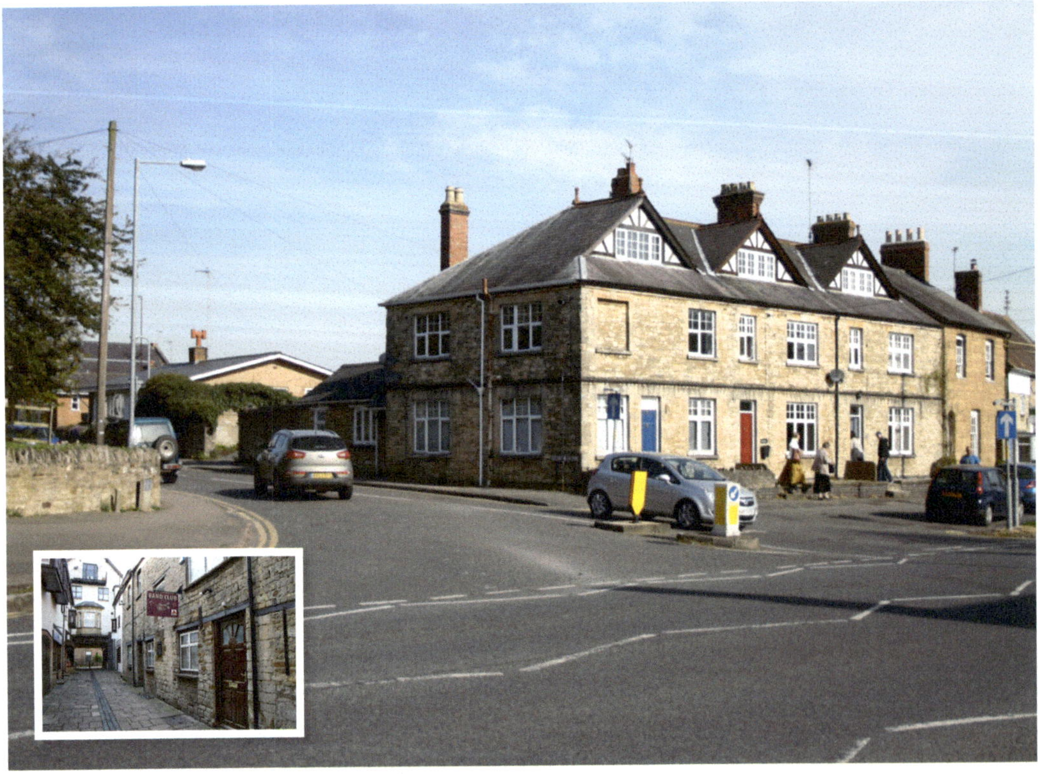

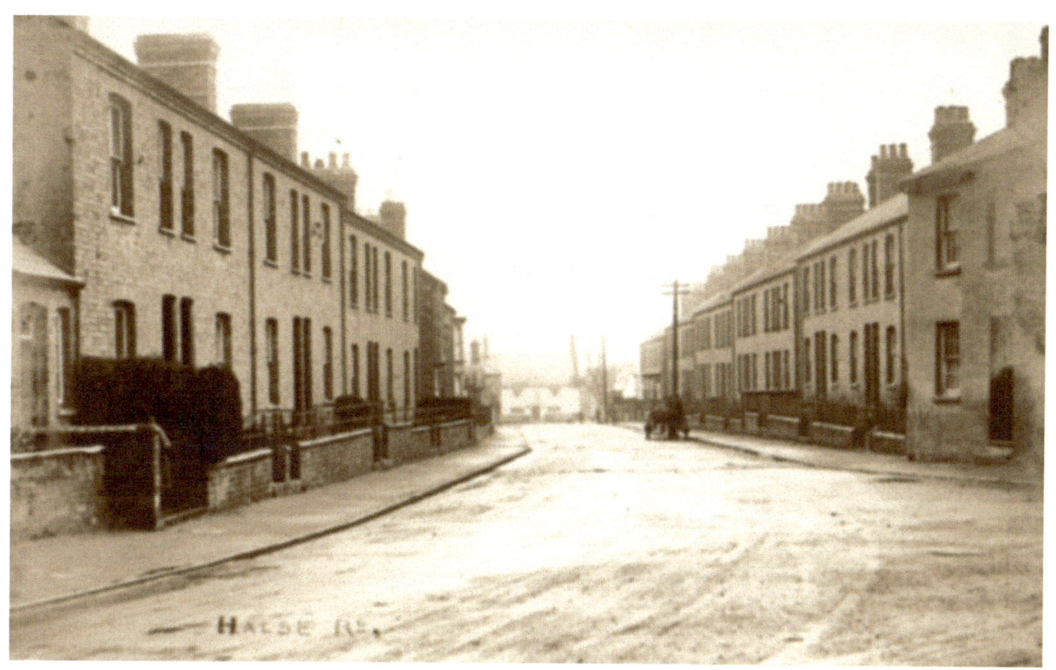

Halse Road, Manor Road Junction, *c.* 1950

Now a busy road cluttered with cars as traffic makes its way towards the Halse Road housing estate, Brackley Health Centre and Washington House surgeries. The Greyhound and Bell pubs are both popular near the junction, and for many years the Brackley Fish Bar has served the community with delicious fish and chips.

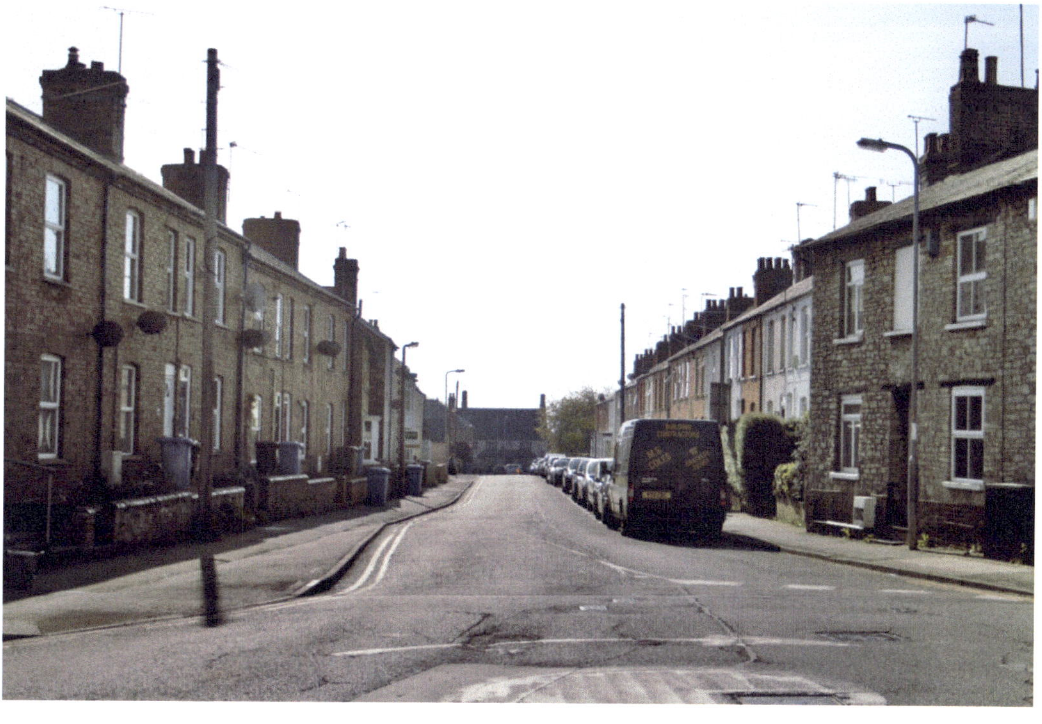

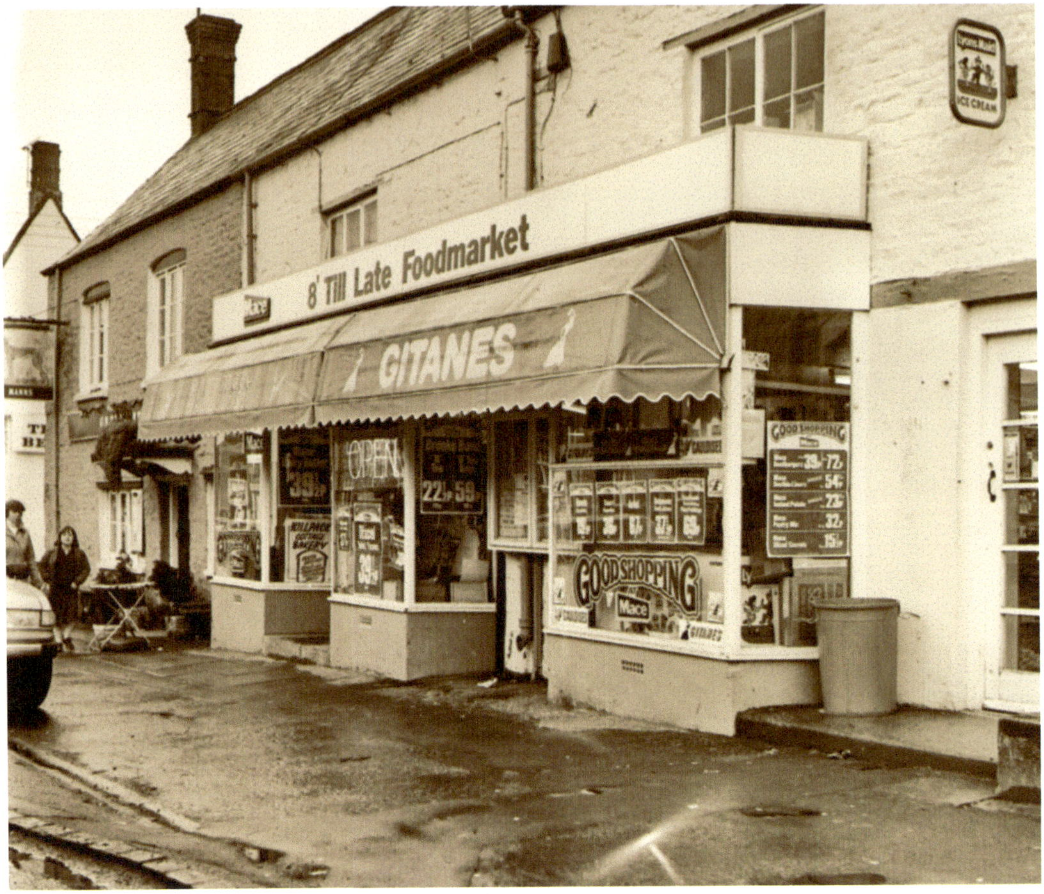

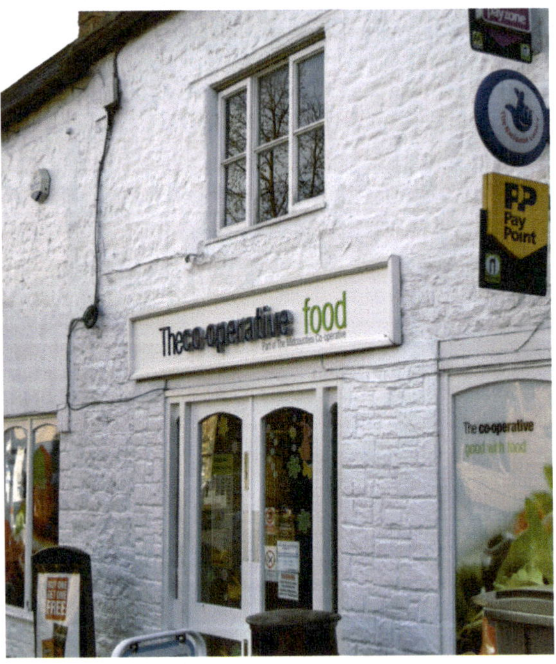

Eight 'til Late

Another one of Brad's ventures, situated next door to the Greyhound public house opposite the Halse Road junction. It sold all manner of household items and, as the name suggests, was open from early until very late. It became a godsend to many late workers who had forgotten items of shopping. People also came from surrounding villages, knowing that the shop was always open. Today it is the Midland Co-operative, still plying the same trade with a more limited range of goods and more restricted hours.

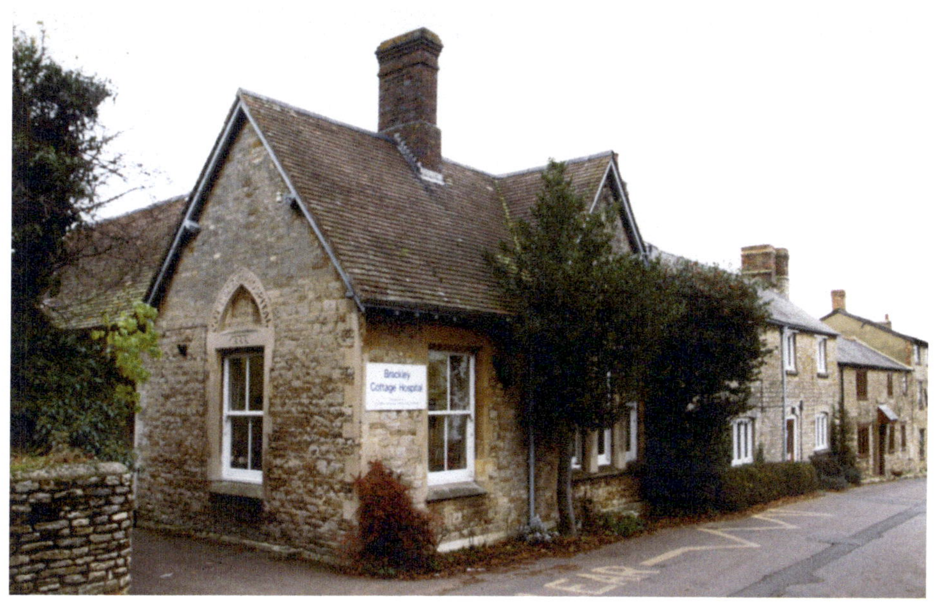

Old Town: Cottage Hospital

Situated on Pebble Lane on the edge of the historic Old Town area. A public meeting on 12 October 1876 resolved that a trained hospital nurse should be provided for the sick of the neighbourhood, and a committee was appointed to draw up a prospectus and receive subscriptions. The Cottage Hospital became part of the NHS in 1948. Since 1991, the hospital has been run by a private trust and ceased to be part of the NHS. Through recent decades, it has served Brackley town and surrounding villages, acting as a local emergency centre, a registered care home with a small number of beds for the elderly and a number of other medical services. For twenty-three years, the hospital has been under threat and local committees have fought to renovate/replace/upgrade the facility. As a new development plan for the future of Brackley is currently being composed, a new health facility is intended as part of the extensive plans.

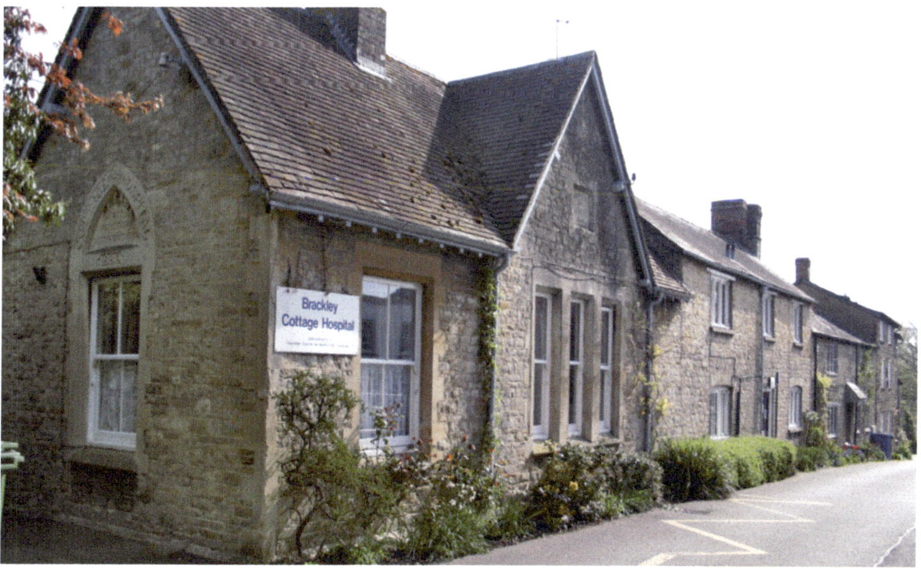

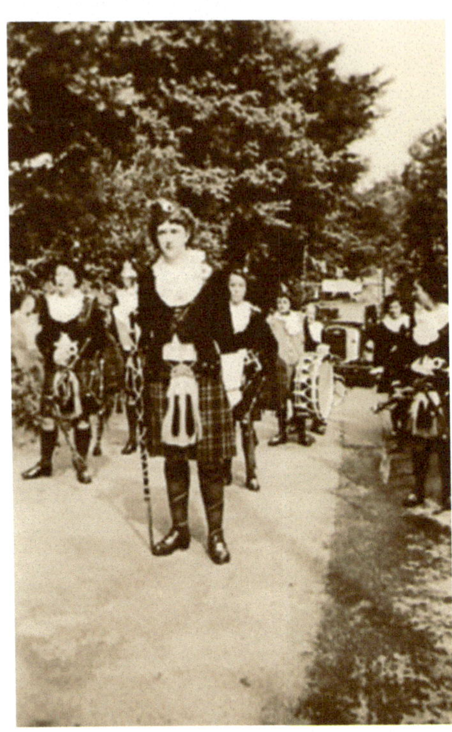

Dagenham Girl Pipers, Pebble Lane, Coronation Day, 1953

Pebble Lane is in Brackley Old Town, which is thought to have been occupied for more than 2,000 years. It is a significant architectural site in Brackley with Saxon and medieval associations, even though some developments in the latter half of the twentieth century had a negative impact on its historic character. It is a conservation area andis generally centred around St Peter's church.

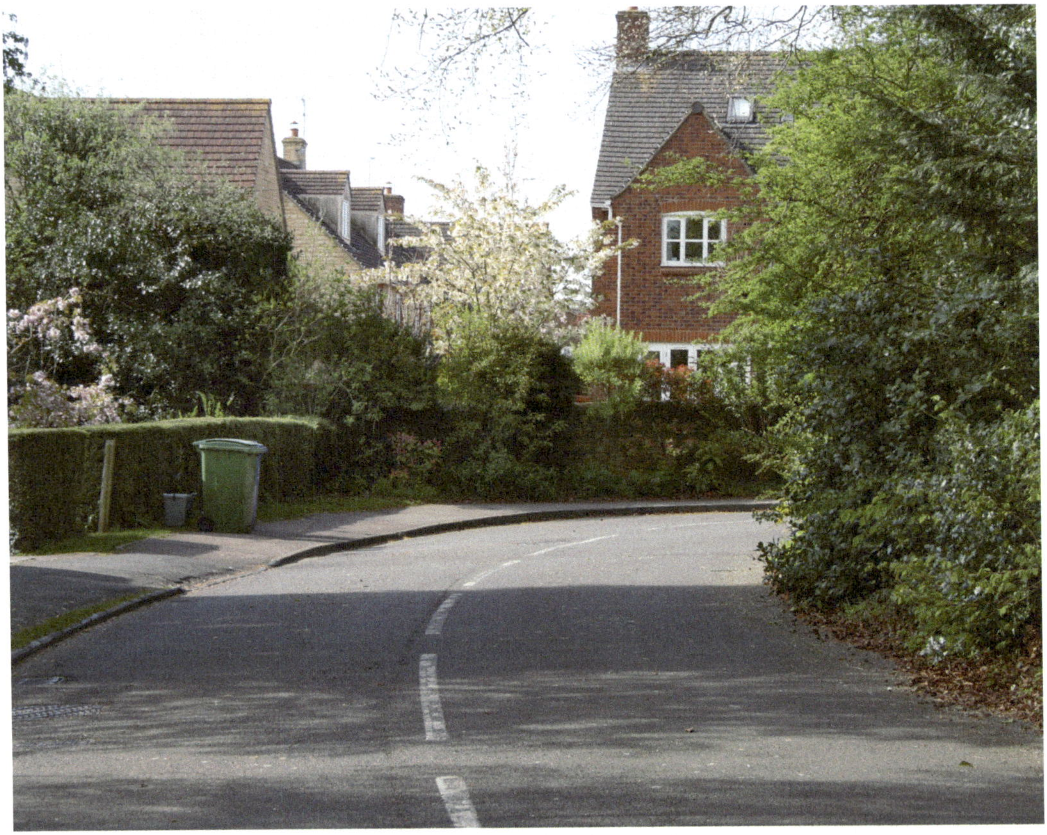

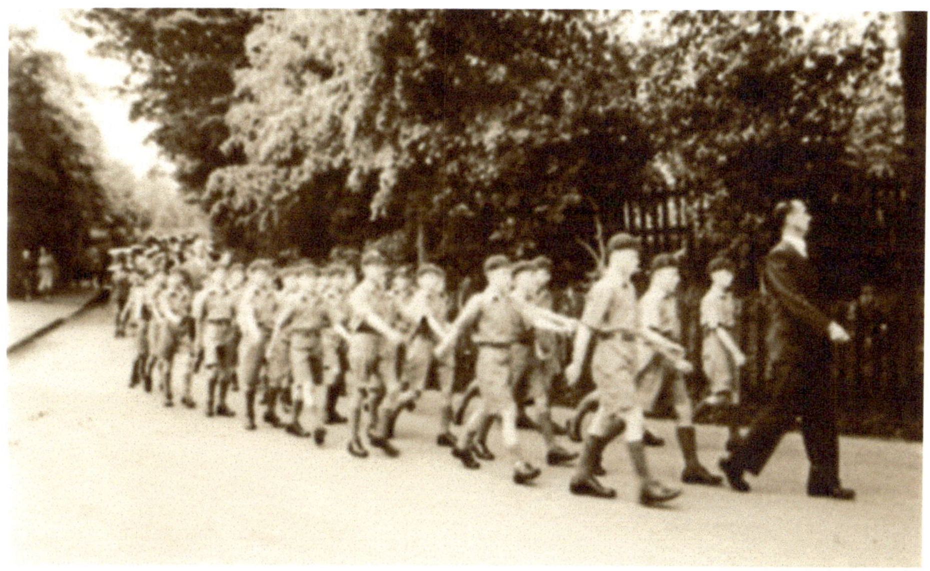

Scouts, Pebble Lane, 1953

There is a well head of the Golden Spring (*inset*) near the marching group as they move close to St Peter's church. It is thought to date back to the thirteenth century, but many old and interesting buildings and limestone walls mark out the area as attractive and historic. Scouting has been strong in Brackley and has been part of community life for many years. Nowadays, only the 5th Scout Group survives. 1st Brackley was registered in 1917 as an open Wolf Cub pack with one leader and twelve Cubs meeting at an address in the Banbury Road. In 1991, the Brackley District ceased to exist and became a part of the newly formed Hazelborough Scout District by amalgamating with Towcester District. In 2005, the Scout District changed once again, with Hazelborough joining with parts of the Northampton District to form a South Northamptonshire District called the Grafton Scout District.

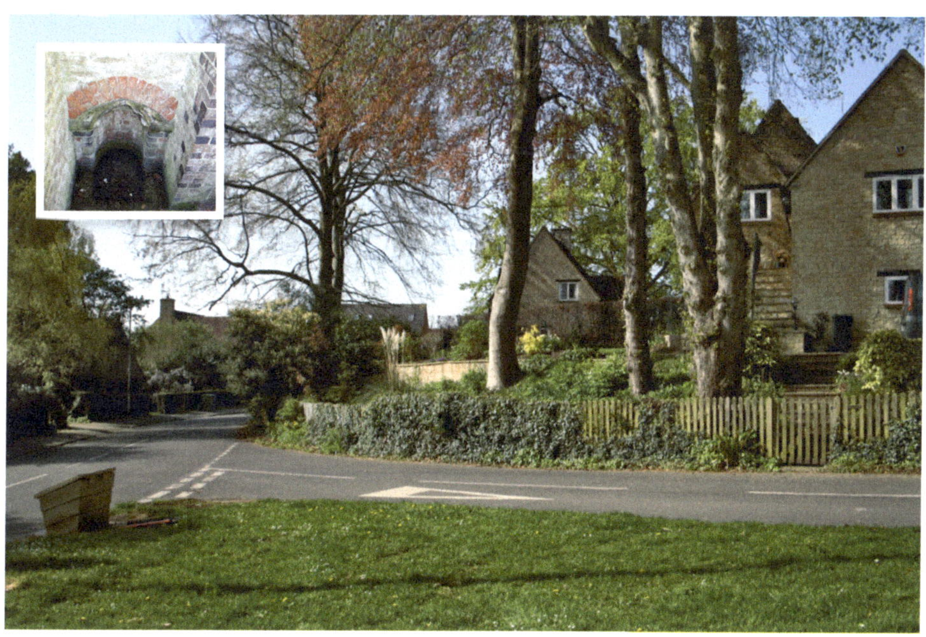

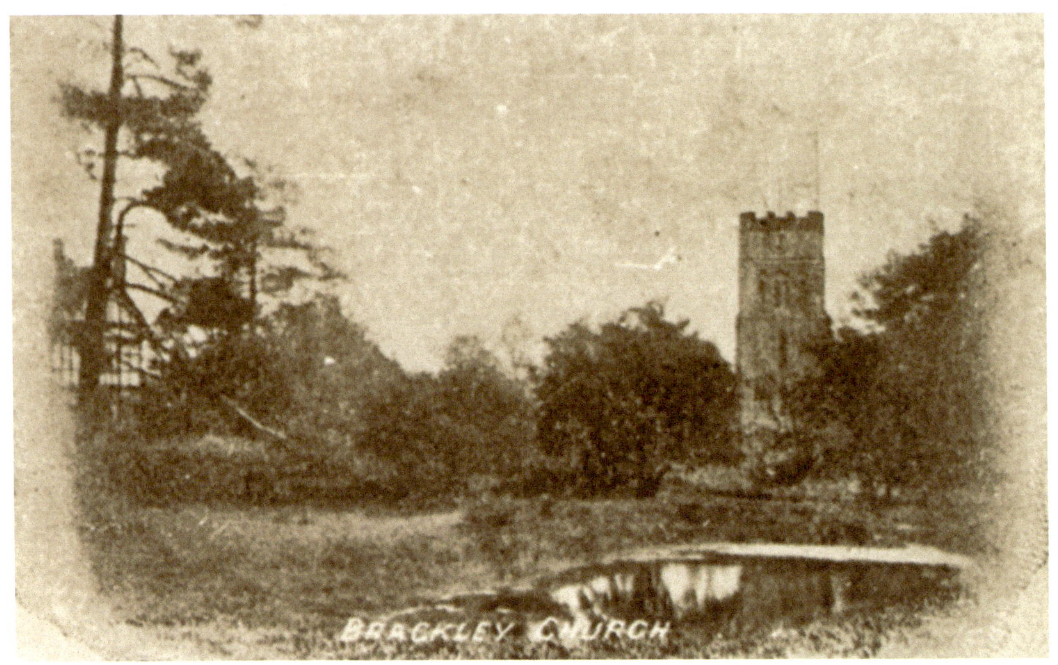

St Peters Church, 1979

The church of St Peter is an ancient building, with a low embattled tower, and contains a strange Norman font. St James's, formerly a parochial church, is now a chapel of ease and there is a place of worship for Wesleyans. The church forms the heart of the Old Town area. In 1066, Brackley consisted of a pattern of lanes around this church. The village pond, fed by Golden Spring, was on Egerton House school playing field and this little triangle of grass at the end of Church Road is a remnant of the old village green.

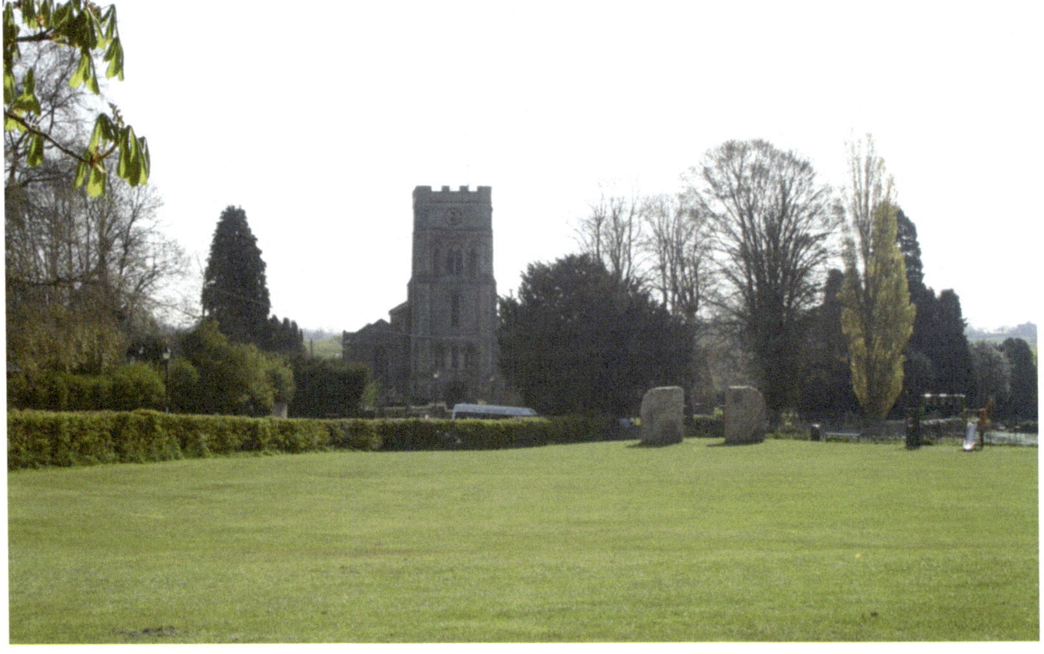

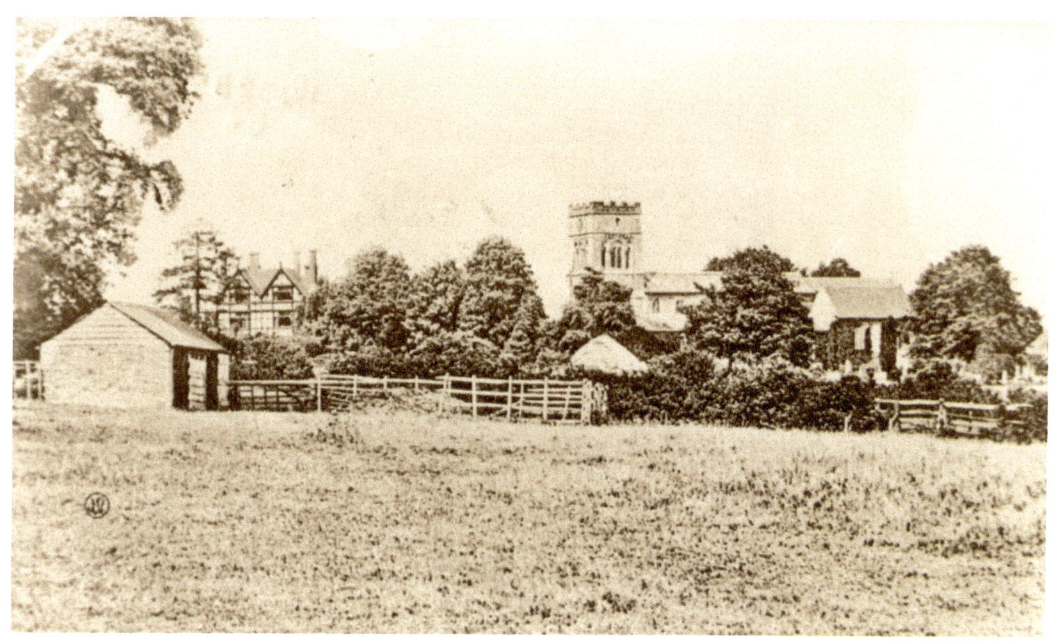

Glebe House, 1906

Glebe House was the Georgian house on the left, viewed across Glebe field, built by Francis Thicknesse, who was vicar from 1868–79. He also built the mock-Tudor vicarage, which later became Egerton House School. Thicknesse had plans to knock down the church and build a new one in the town centre, but these never materialised. Glebe House was a school for girls but surrendered its certificate of closure on 12 March 1948. It was reopened as a Junior Approved School for boys known as Egerton House. It continued to be an Approved School until the 1970s, when it was closed. This has now been demolished to make way for homes at the north-west end of the churchyard. Church View was built on the land fifteen years ago. Glebe Field (known as Egerton House Field) opposite, was bought by the council to maintain as open space.

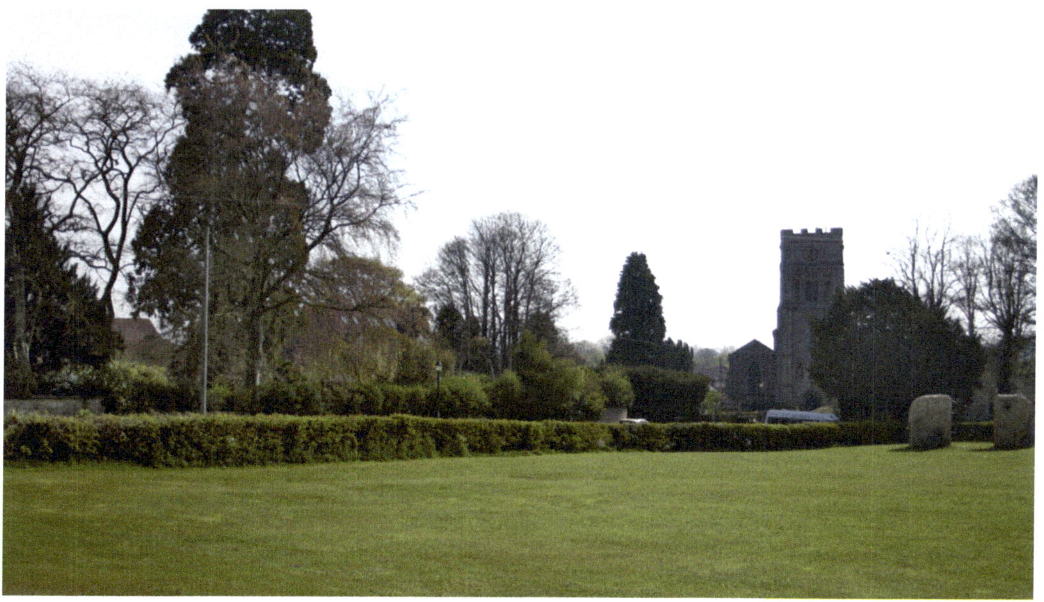

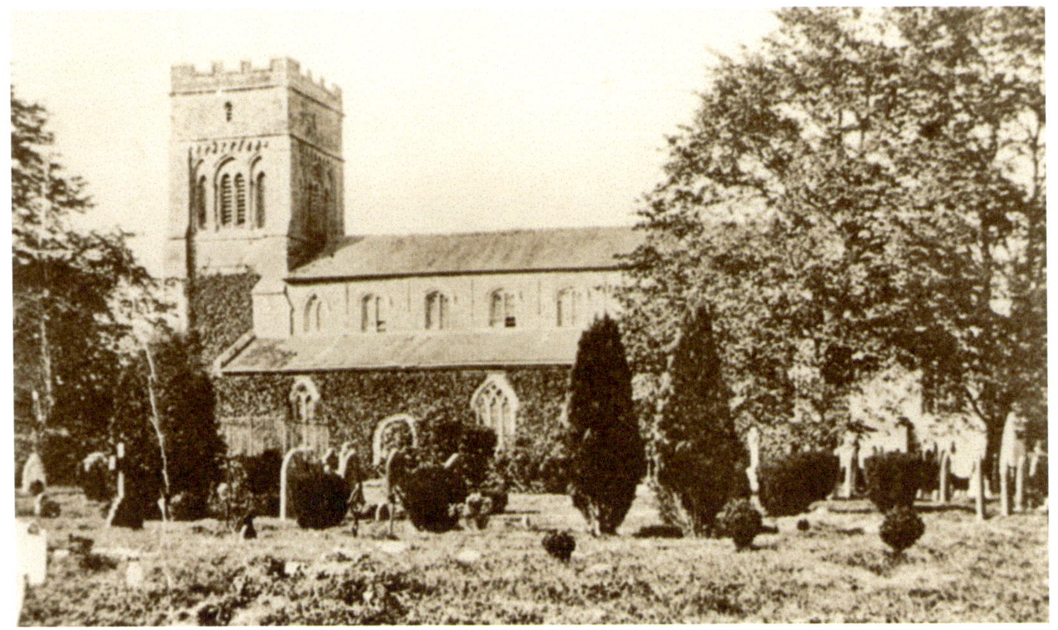

St Peters Church, 1911

There have been the usual developmental changes to the main body of the church over the centuries. Recently, a church extension was built on land to the south of the church. The extension was added to provide a church hall, kitchen and modern toilet facilities for the growing parish. It has become a well-used community hall. The oldest part of the church of St Peter at the eastern end of the town centre is an eleventh-century Norman south doorway. Both the four-bay arcade of the south aisle and the west tower with its niches containing seated statues were added in the thirteenth century. A similar view to the old photograph is now not possible as it was probably taken from the site of a recent housing estate. (*See inset for probable position where the old photograph was taken from.*)

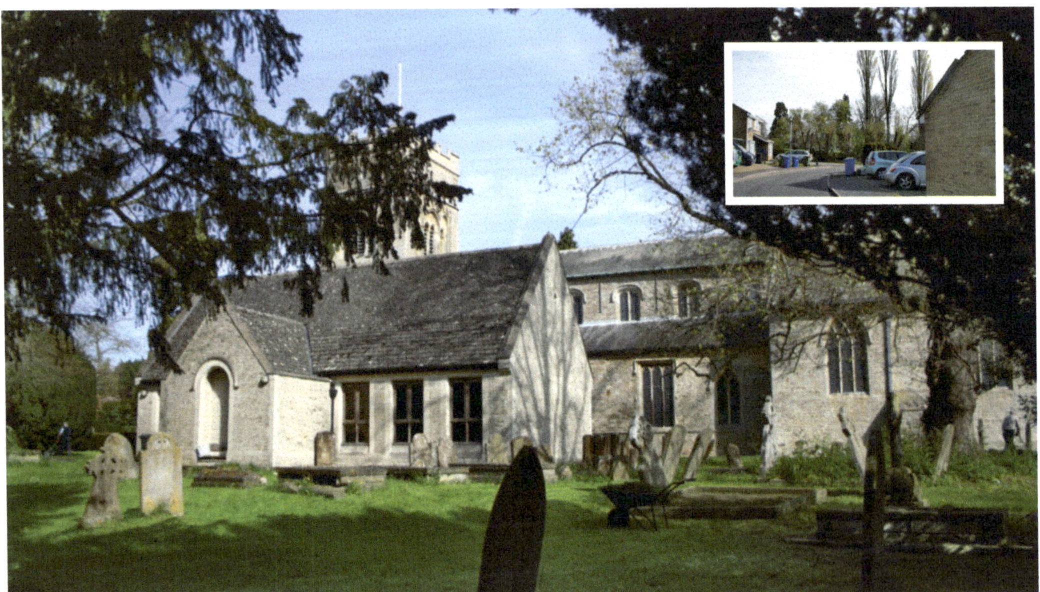

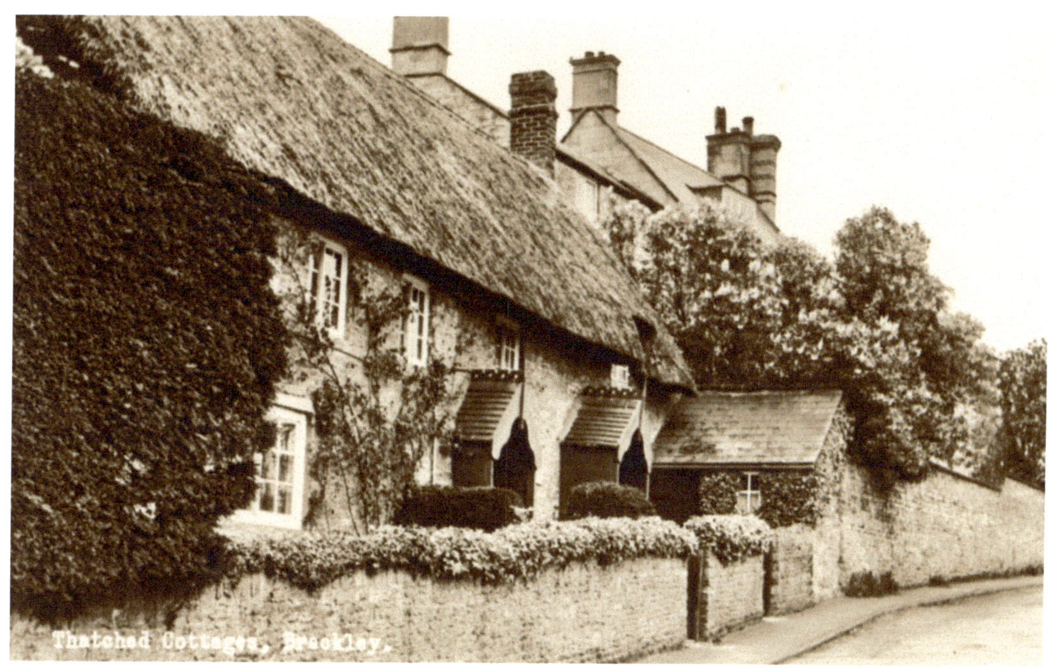

Church Road Cottages

These cottages illustrate clearly the beautiful old buildings that used to typify Old Town. There are few thatched cottages remaining in Brackley today, but these were reminiscent of nineteenth-century life. The local traditional form of thatch is long straw with a flush ridge created very simply. Stonework is generally limestone rubble, roughly dressed and laid in narrow courses. Welsh slate has replaced the thatch on many buildings in modern times. There is a survival of eighteenth- and nineteenth-century windows in some buildings. Nowadays, the old buildings are mixed in with the new.

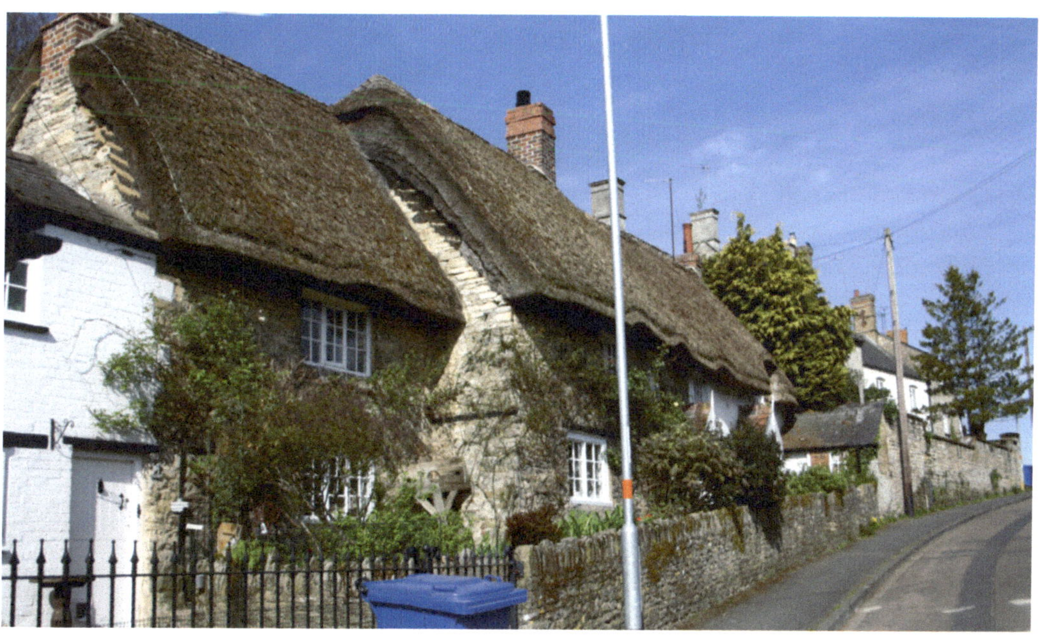

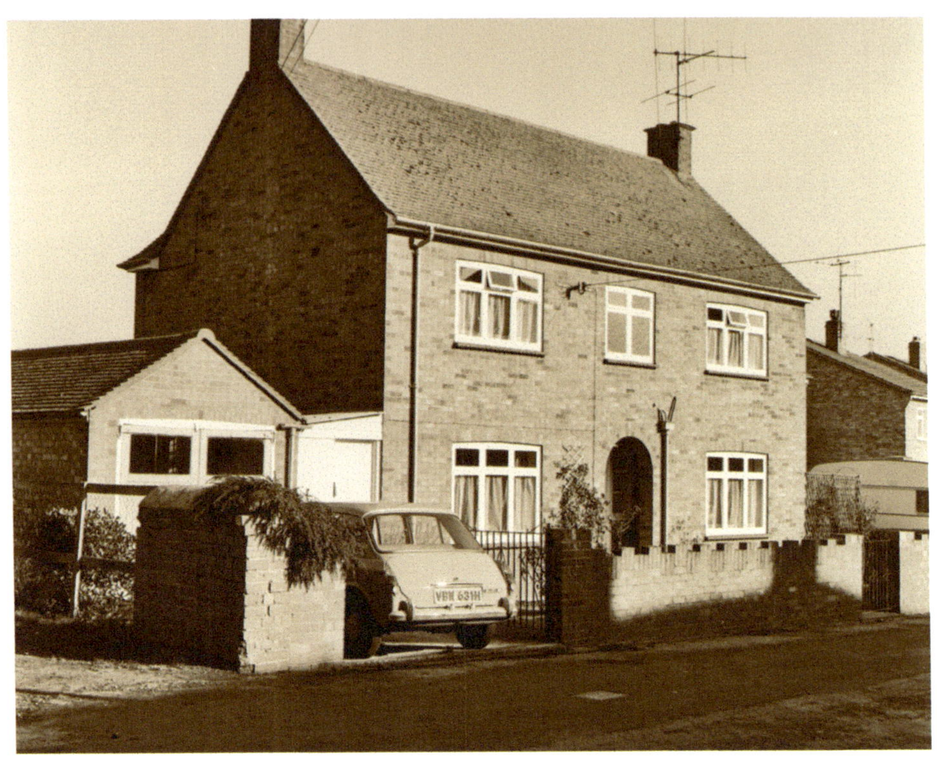

No. 18 St Peters Road, *c.* 1960

This area of Brackley verges on Old Town and consists of mixed generation housing. Some old cottages may be found here, with post-war up to modern twenty-first-century housing interspersed. The road is narrow and very much in keeping with the feel of Old Town.

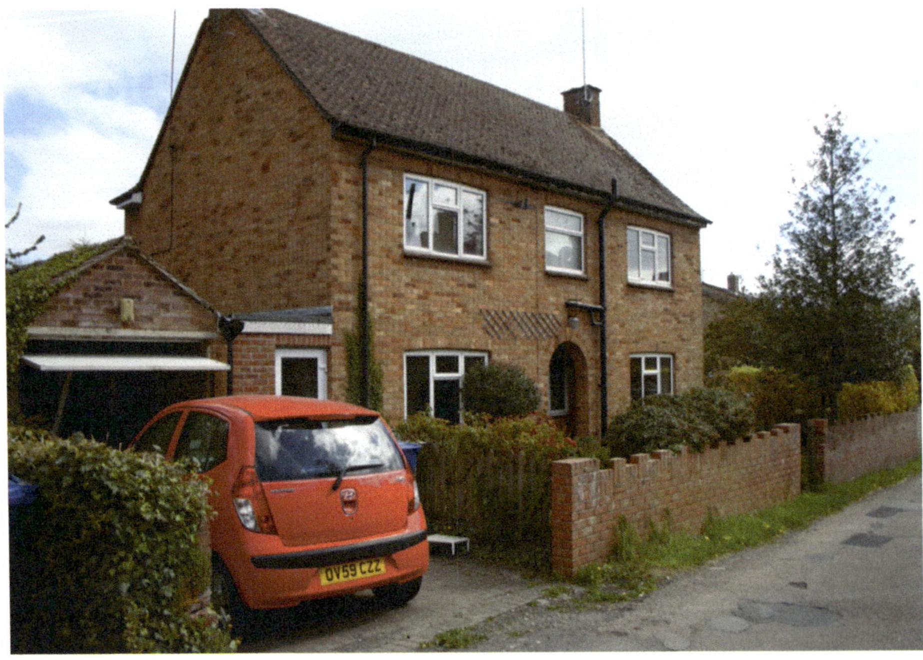

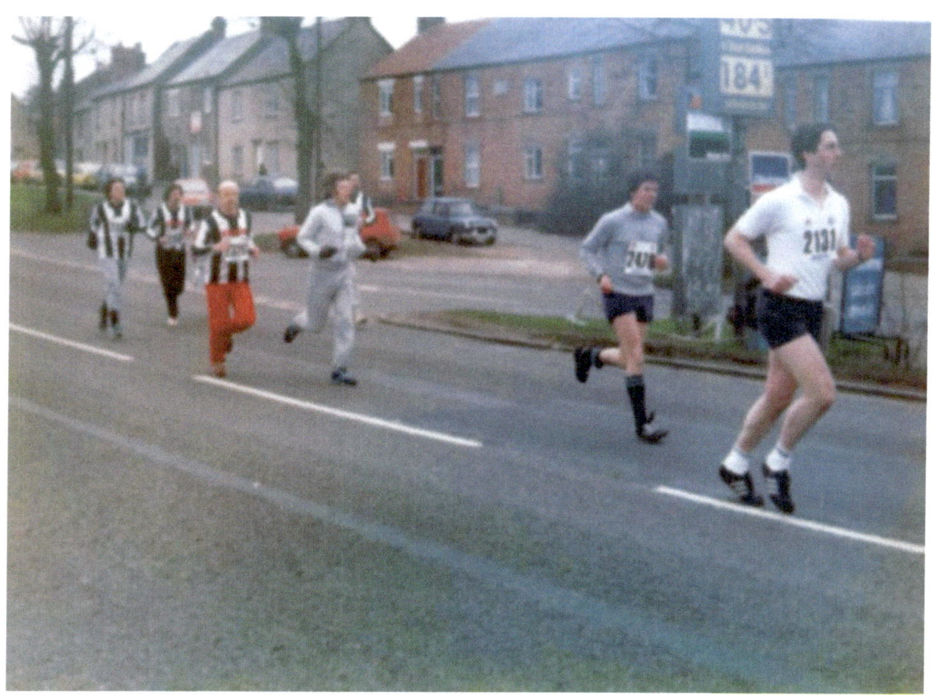

10,000-Metre Brackley Fun Run, 1984

This photograph was taken near the Valley Road junction with the High Street, north of the town centre. Early twentieth-century buildings line the western side of the road at this point, which are currently used for mixed residential and commercial purposes.

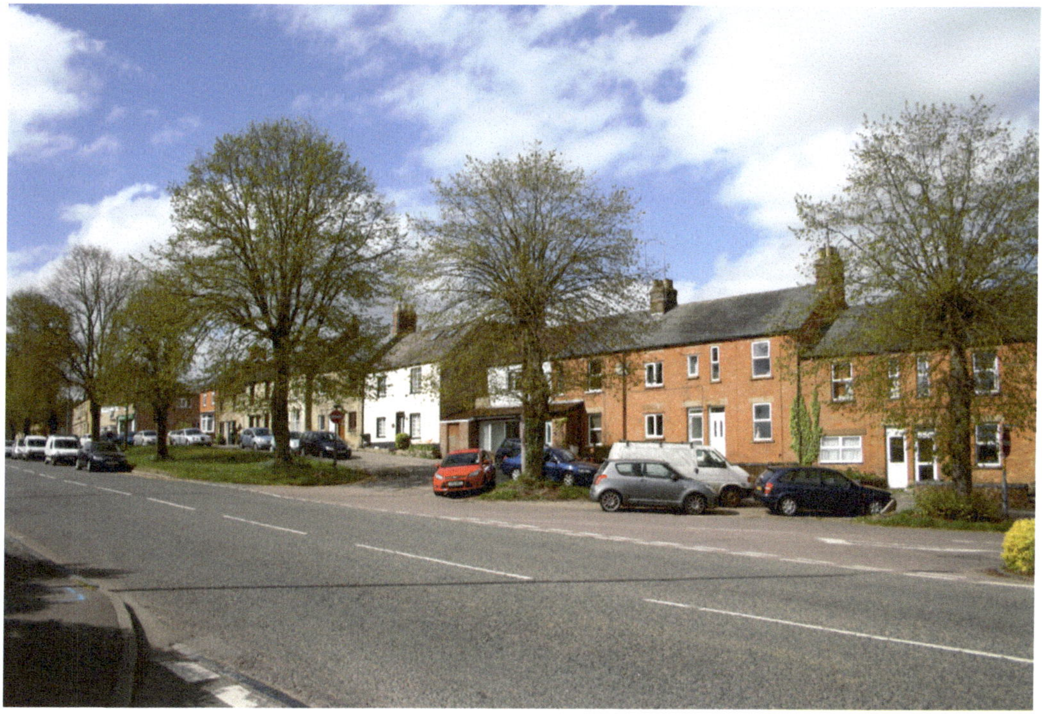

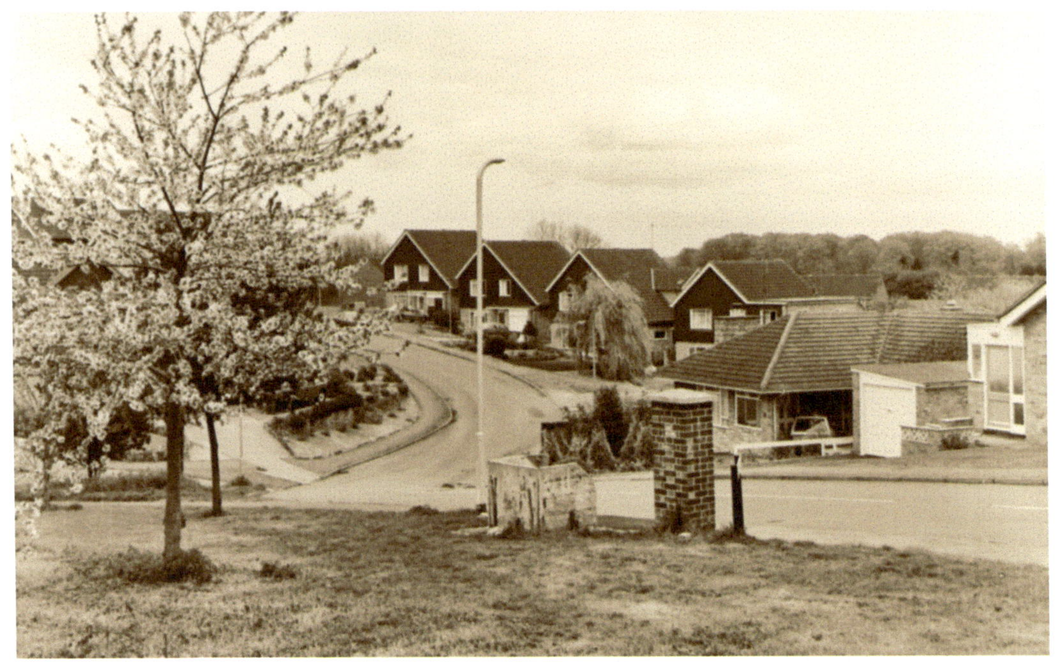

Valley Road Junction With High Street

This area was originally a farm belonging to Freddie Fricker, who sold it to the council in 1964. A rabbit warren existed in this area and a stream was piped underground close to where the photograph was taken. Close by on the Burwell Hill side was a neighbouring pig farm. The Valley Road housing is one of the earlier modern housing developments in Brackley, situated between the old top station and Old Town. The estates – Valley Road and Valley Rise – were adjacent to land belonging to the railway company and housed railway-related infrastructure. The houses are varied in nature with pleasant aspects.

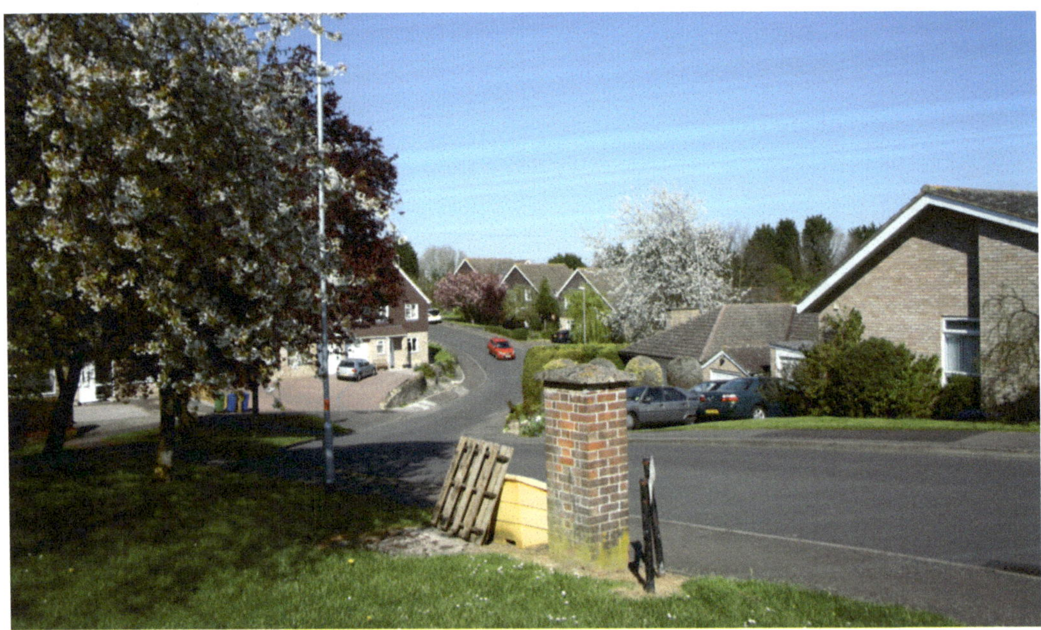

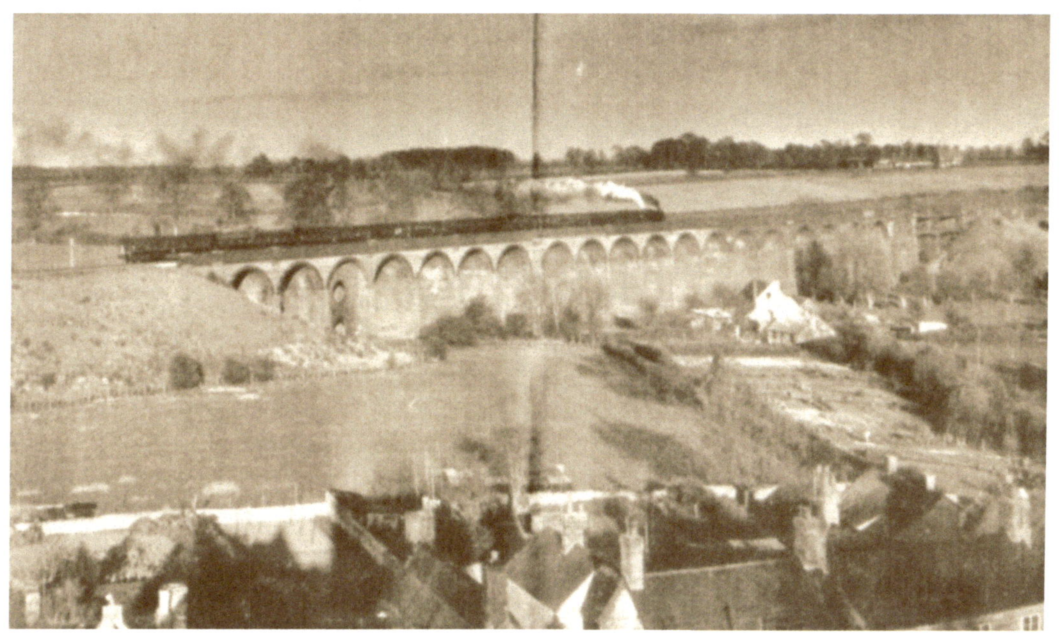

Brackley Central (Top Station) With Train, 1966

The station opened with the line on 15 March 1899 and was closed to all traffic on 5 September 1966. It was one of two working railway stations before Dr Beeching's report of 1963. The photograph shows the 5.15 p.m. from Nottingham on the Brackley viaduct on a summer evening in 1966, taken from the top of the parish church tower. The railway came to Brackley in 1850 and wealthy families would travel by train to enjoy hunting. They built themselves hunting lodges in the High Street with large stables at the rear. Even now, many of the doorways have curved red bricks lining the sides; they were originally the doors to each horse's stall and the bricks were smoothed and curved to prevent any damage to a horse going in or out.

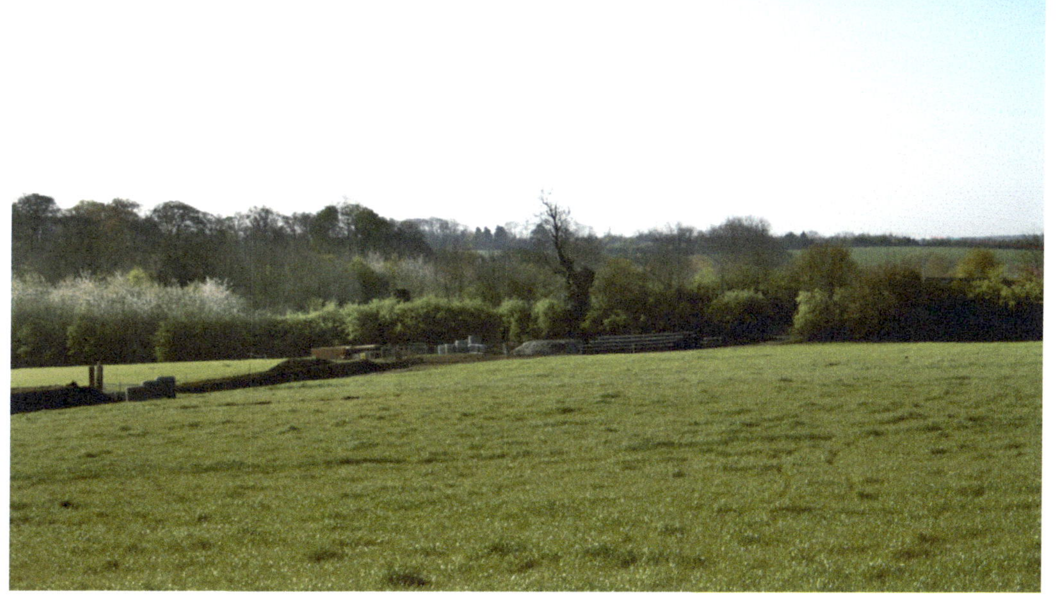

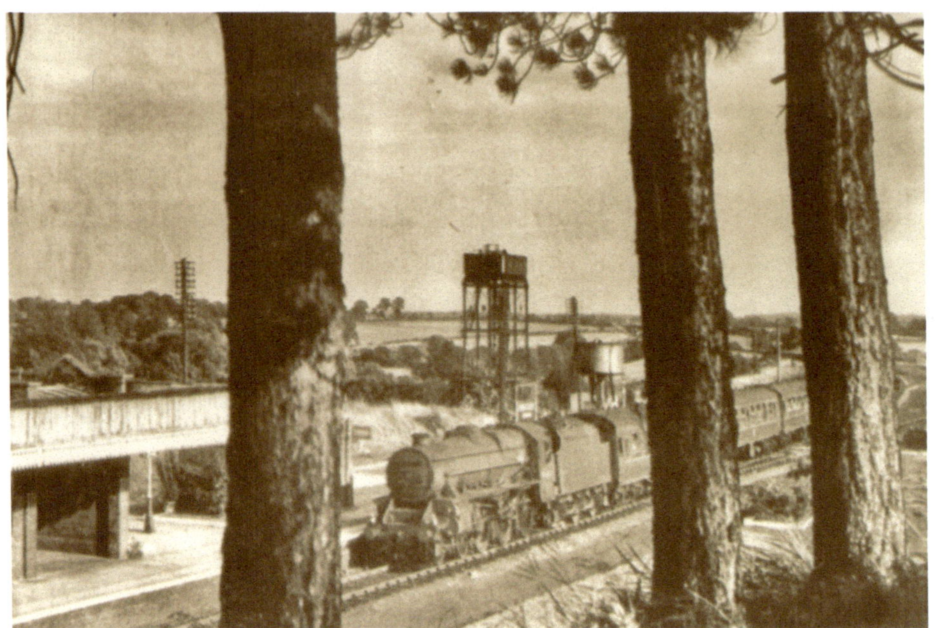

Brackley Central

Today, the entrance building at road level still stands and is occupied by the ATS Tyre Co. Down in the cutting, the platform and its buildings have gone. Improvements to the A43 following the line's closure meant that the bridge carrying the road over the line was demolished and the cutting partially filled in at that point. At the far (north) end of the building, the bricked up remains of the footbridge that led to the platform can be seen, while the grassy bank on the bottom left is a surviving remnant of the unfinished Northampton branch platform. The stationmaster's house has now also been demolished.

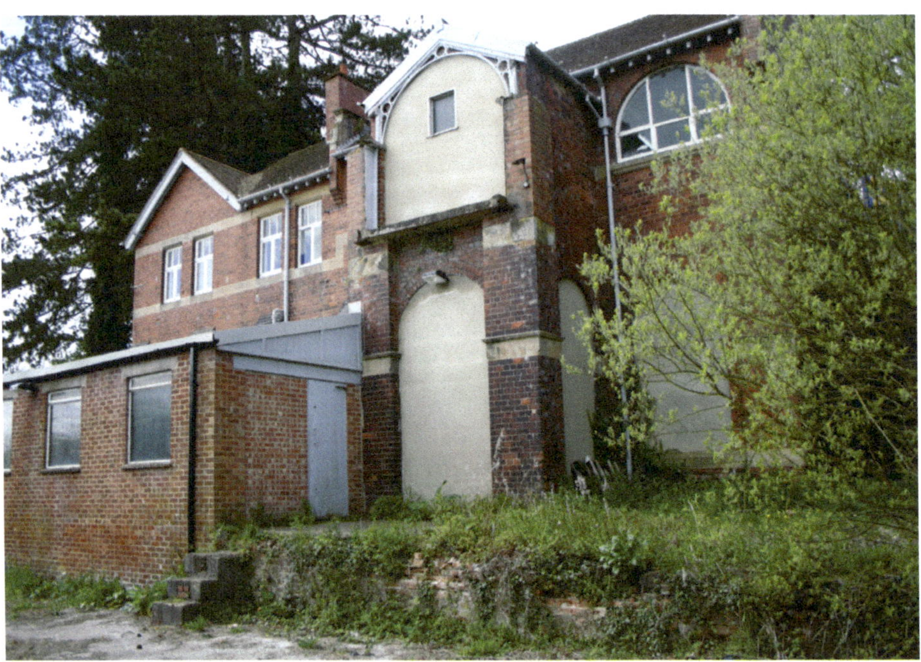

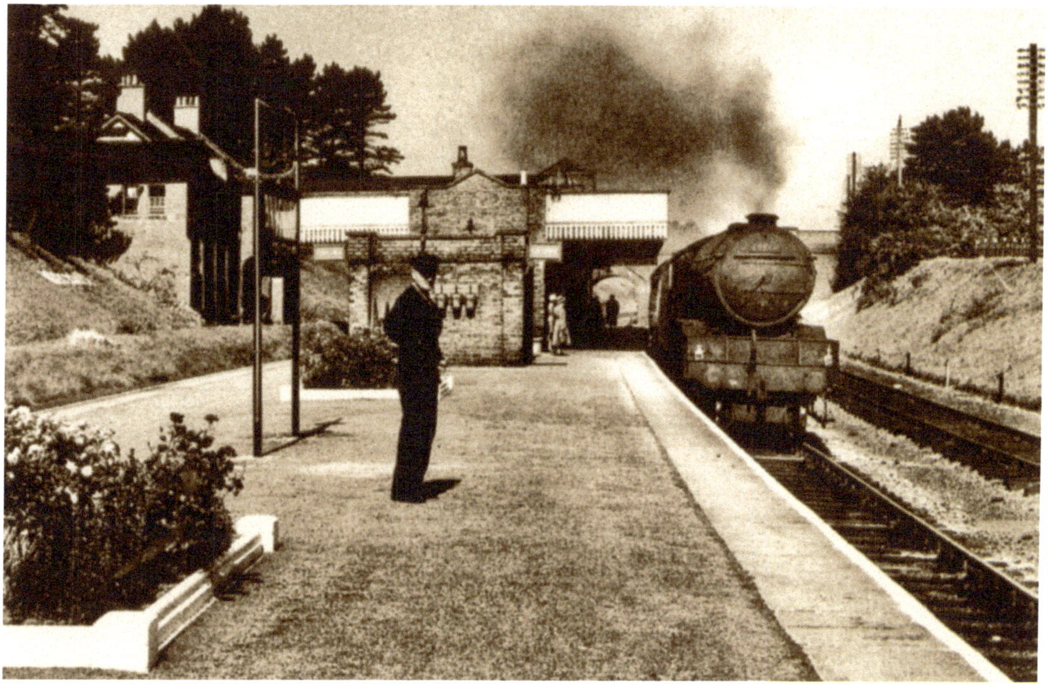

Top Station Train Heading To Yorkshire, *c.* 1950

The Master Cutler train went to Sheffield, even though most trains terminated at Leicester. The station and destinations served the woollen industry at the turn of the century. In the 1940s, it offered a fast train to London. A lot of traffic was taken by the Great Central. Note Brackley white pebbles in the old photograph. Soon, HS2 will be thundering past Brackley in the distance, going between London and Birmingham.

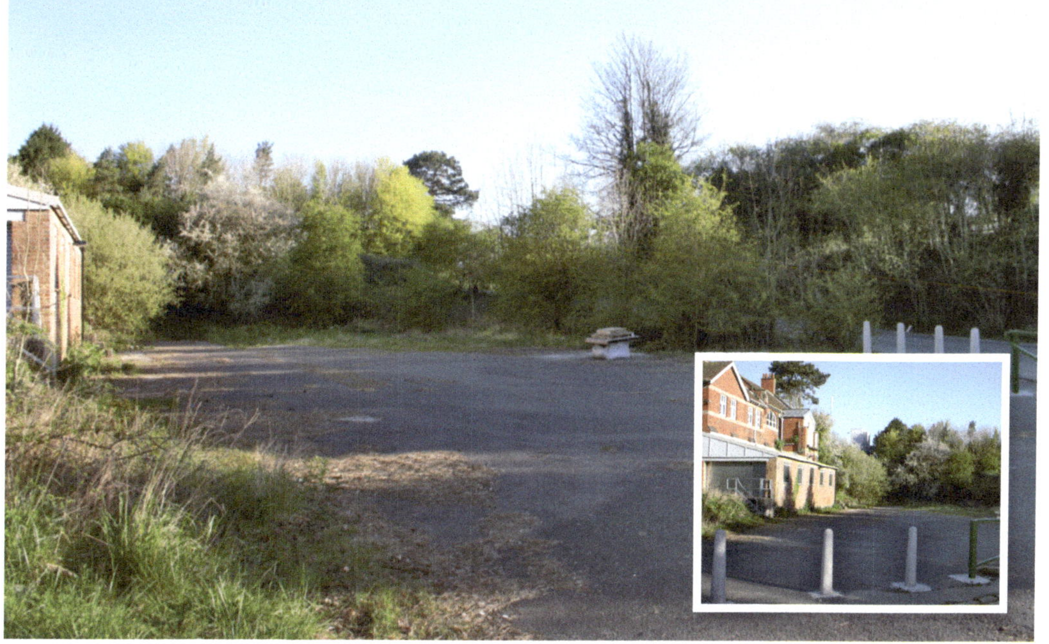

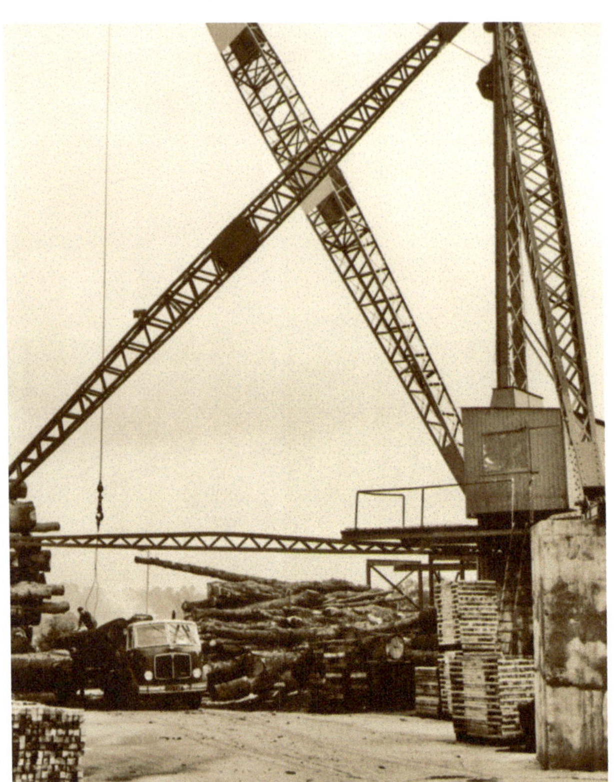

Brackley Sawmills, *c.* 1970
Brackley Sawmills was situated on the north side of the town where the High Street meets the Brackley bypass. Ralph Tempest was the managing director in the 1970s (a Rotarian). They ceased trading in 2007. The sawmills site had been in industrial use for many years and had a functional character, reflecting the processing of large-scale timber production enterprises, which includes large areas of hard-standing and large buildings. The majority of the site has been derelict for many years. In both visual and character terms, the sawmills site does not relate well to the surrounding area. A new residential development has been put forward by Providence Court Investments for 130 new homes, a play area and green infrastructure planting.

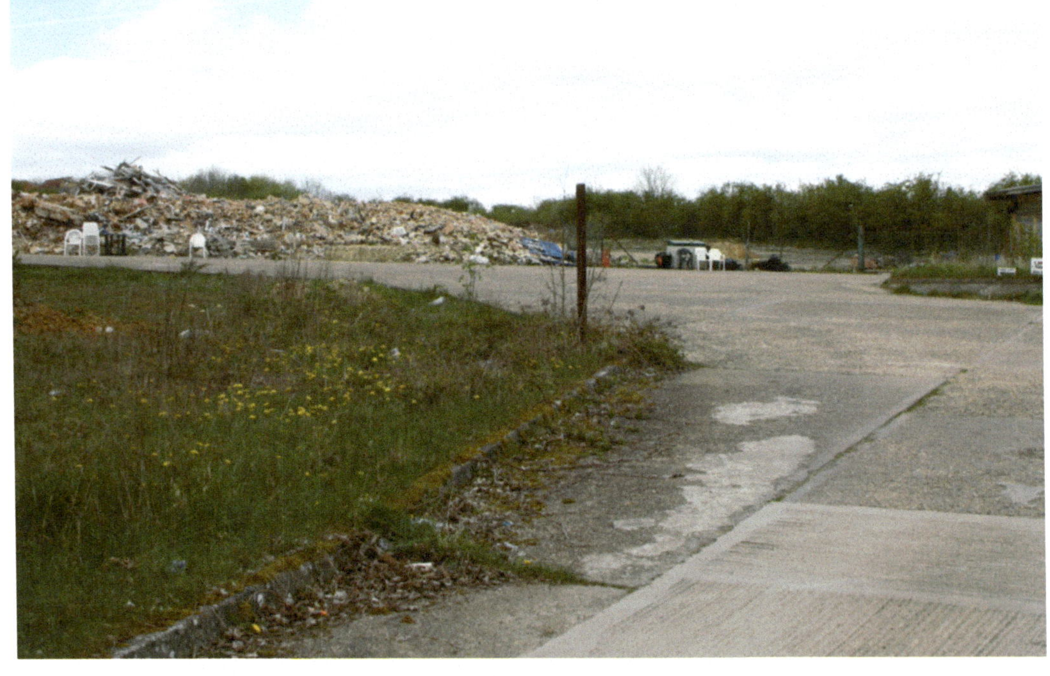

Part 2

A Journey from East to West

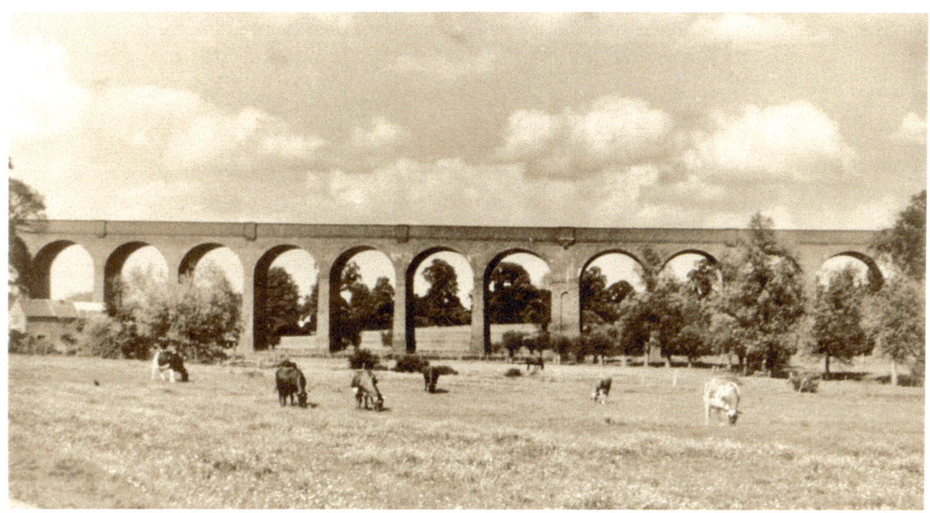

Brackley Viaduct, *c.* 1960

View taken from the Buckingham Road side (Mill House on the left). The modern photograph is taken from a convenient nearby site. A little way to the south, the ground level fell away rapidly so that the line found itself on a high embankment leading to Brackley Viaduct. This impressive structure started out with twenty-two blue brick arches, each of 34 feet 3 inches (10.44 metres). However, due to movement of clay beds beneath the south end of the structure when it was almost complete, cracks were noticed in the southernmost two arches. These were replaced by two girder spans, each of 35 feet (10.67 metres), while the third arch was filled with bricks to provide a massive buttress. Meanwhile, the third arch from the north end was walled up to provide extra bracing there. The structure was blown up in 1978.

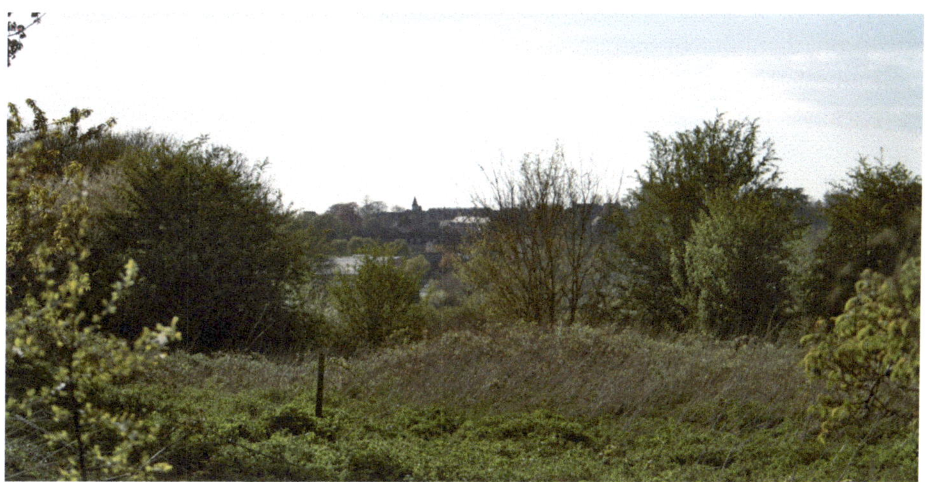

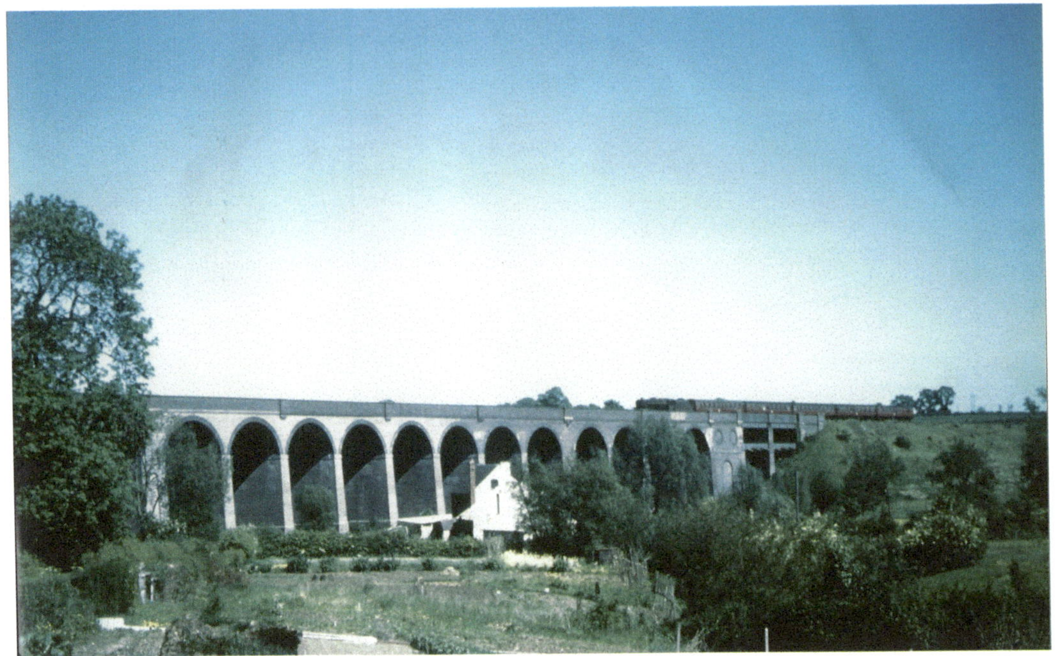

Brackley Viaduct, *c.* 1950

The old photograph was taken close to where Hawkins and Salmon used to operate from in recent years (now finished). These buildings formed part of the temporary accommodation that was erected by Walter Scott & Co. to house the navvies at work on Contract No. 5 of the Last Main Line (Woodford to Brackley). A contractor's yard is visible between the huts. Standing in the background as a testament to the navvies' labour, is the huge twenty-two arch viaduct that brought the London Extension across the Great Ouse river and flood plain. The inset shows an existing remnant of an arch.

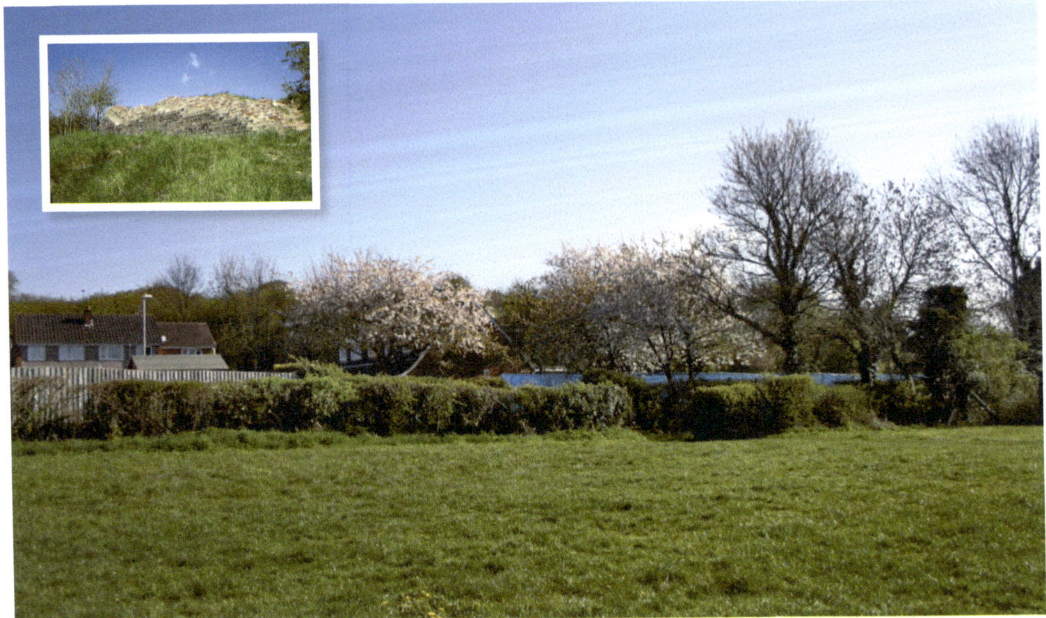

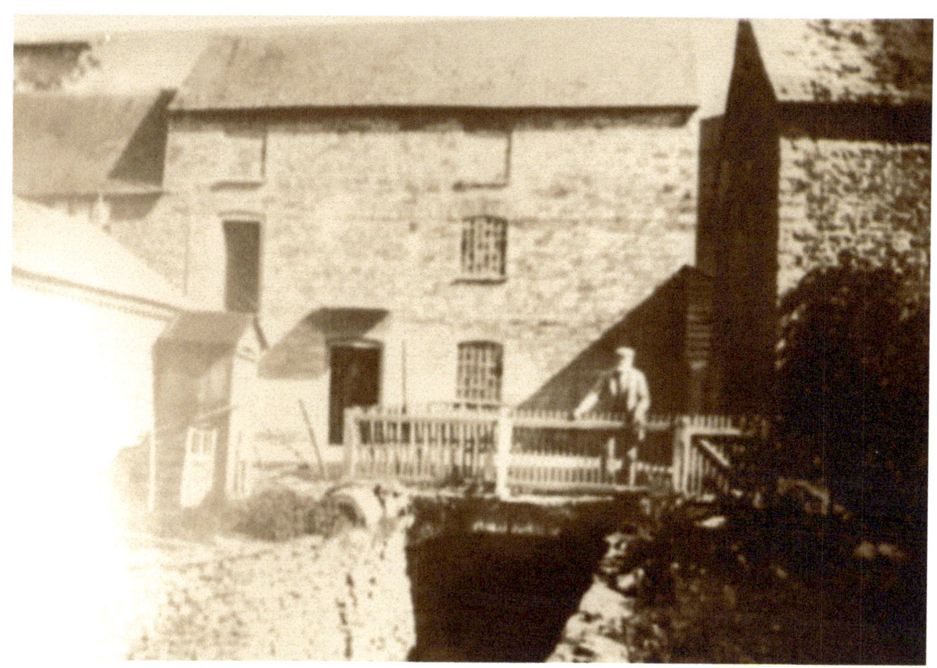

Brackley Water Mill, *c.* 1900

This was a corn or grain mill situated close to the viaduct. This photograph was taken of an elderly man posing in front of a watermill at Brackley. It was once owned by Fred Timms. The footpath towards the mill house and the river and the footpath connecting Water Lane and the Old Town Lane are part of the historic pattern of route ways. Another Mill House is situated off the Oxford Rd near St James's lake.

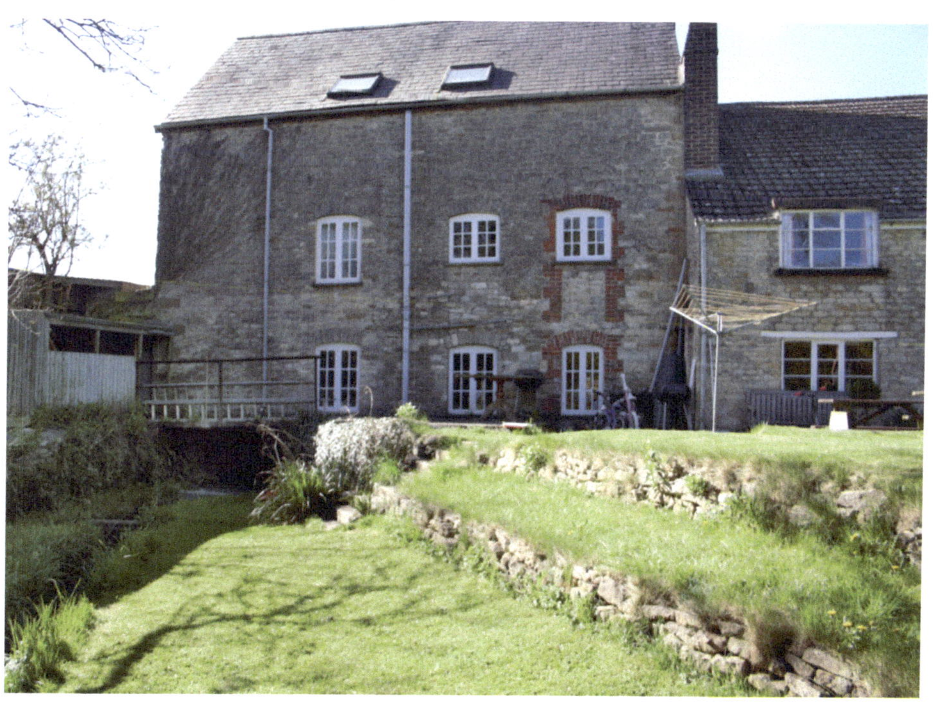

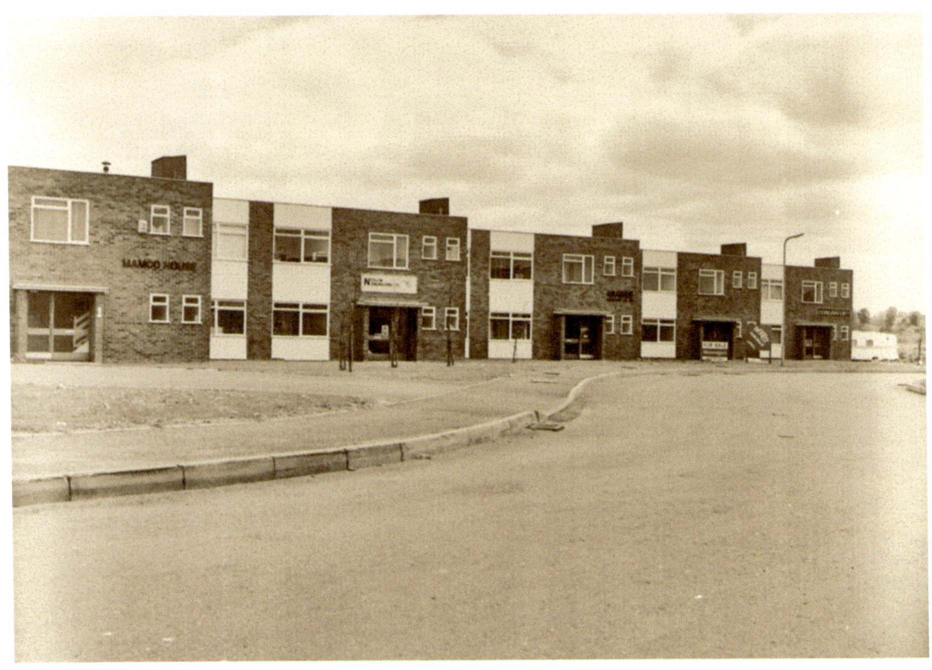

Buckingham Road Industrial Estate, *c.* 1970

In the south-east of Brackley, a large number of generally light industrial units are situated. Large units, such as Faccenda Group and De Boer Structures, have a long history. On the east outskirts of the town was H. Bronnley & Co., makers of handmade soaps, who held Royal Warrants of Appointment for supplying Queen Elizabeth and the Prince of Wales. Formula 1 racing's Mercedes AMG Petronas team (formerly Brawn GP, Honda and British American racing and Tyrrell) are based further west.

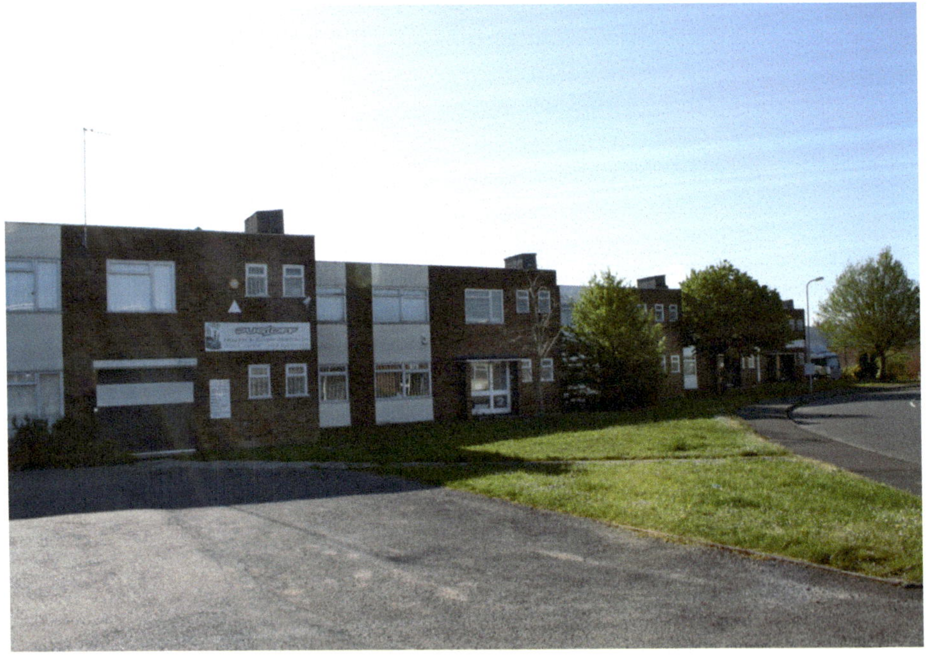

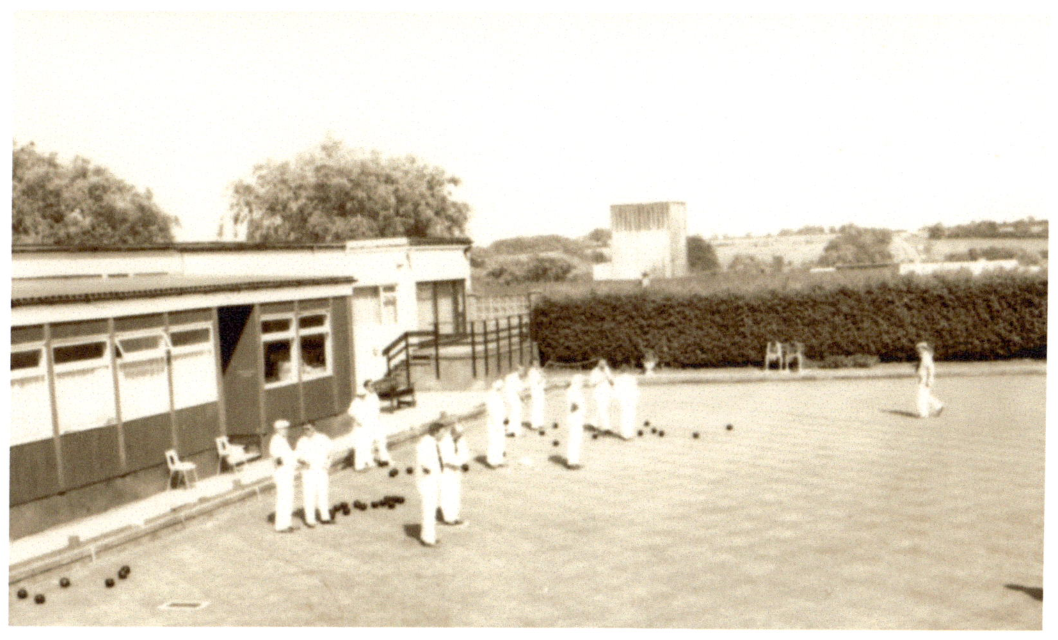

Brackley Bowls Club, *c.* 1950

Brackley & District Bowling Club started in 1921 when two rinks were set out in Pebble Lane, with a small wooden building serving as a pavilion. Members used the Conservative Club for meals. Later, members' wives would provide meals in the Church Institute in Manor Road. Subsequently, two more rinks were added, along with an extension to the pavilion, which provided a well-supported social side with bingo being a regular event in the bar. In 1974, the club moved to its present site in Westminster Road, with a green that can support seven rinks outdoors. In 1975, three indoor rinks were added. Two further rinks, a large function room and kitchen were added in 1992.

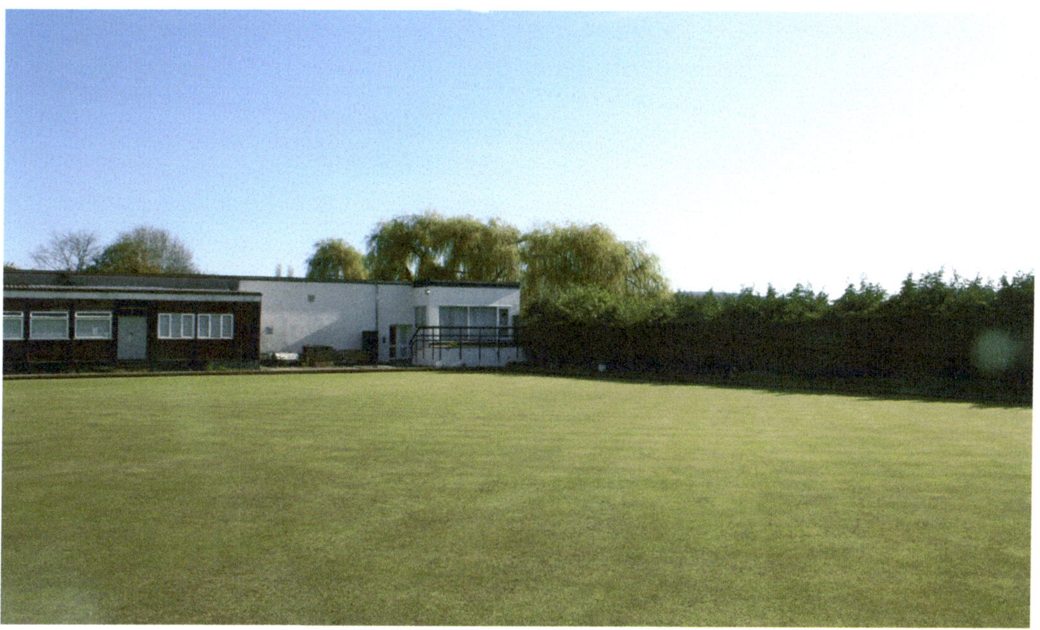

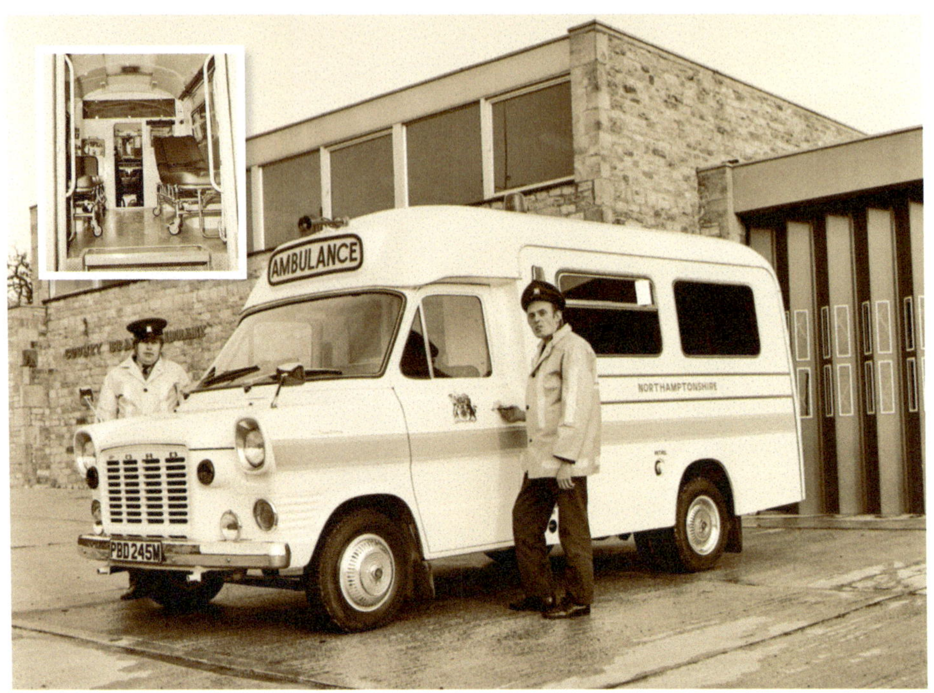

Ambulance Station, c. 1970

A short distance from the rear of Winchester House School, the area is generally residential, except for the town swimming pool. Local residents have been used to the service provided by the local ambulance station, given the rural location of Brackley and its distance from neighbouring towns, particularly in south Northamptonshire. With the continuous rethinks associated with medical services in the town in the 2000s, the ambulance station has been under threat for some time. In 2013, it was with great delight that town mayor Cllr Chris Cartmell announced that the station had been saved. The ambulance station is situated next to the very popular Brackley Library. Inset is the interior of a period ambulance.

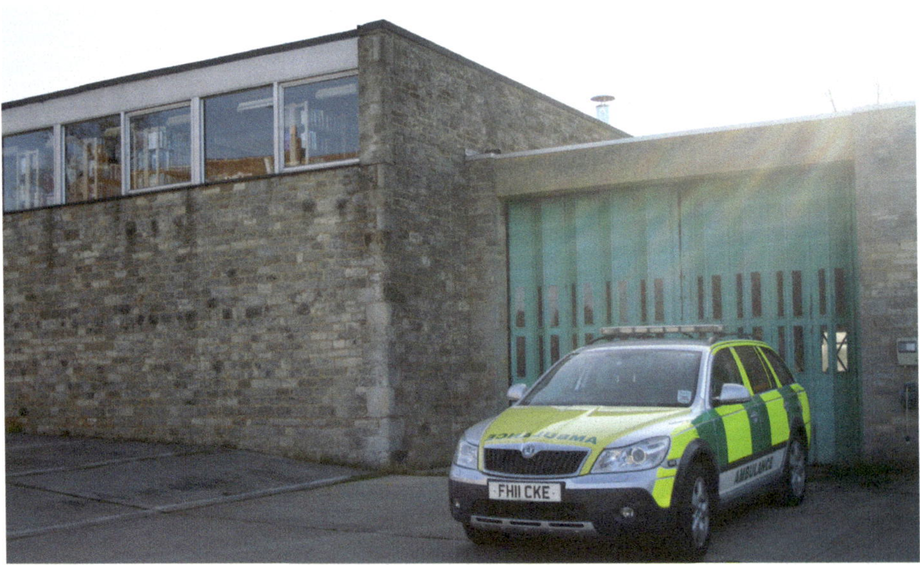

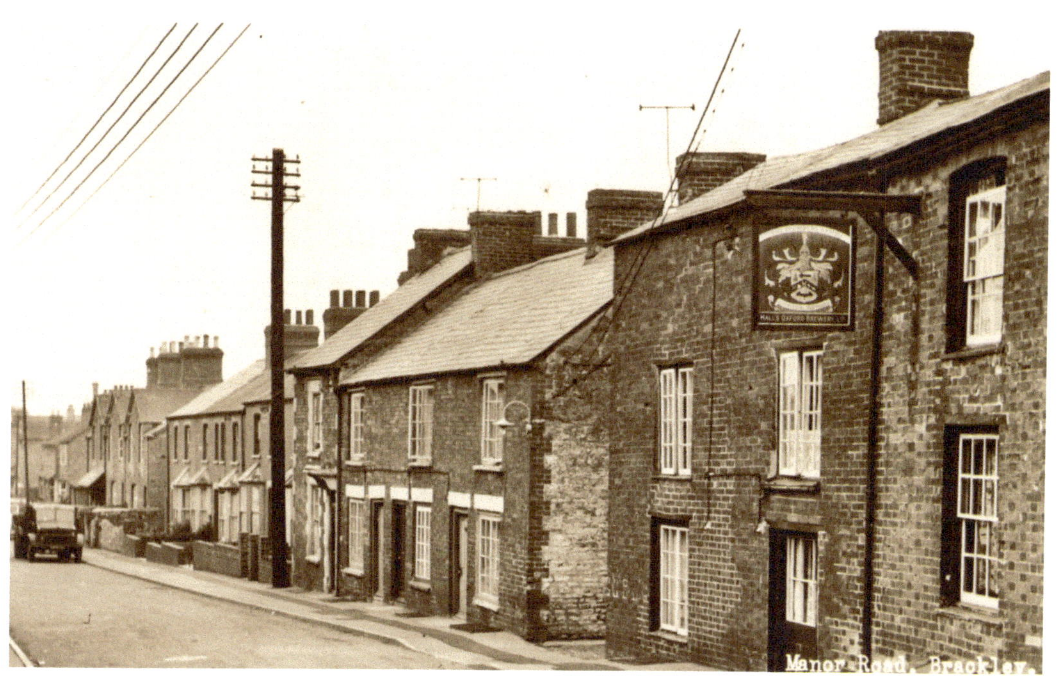

The Manor, Formerly the Plumbers Arms, *c.* 1960

A traditional whitewashed back-street pub with two bars. It has a large fish tank in the lounge. On the outside wall is a Halls Brewery mark, since the pub's history shows this as being one of the town's Blencowes brewery taps. They were subsequently taken over by Halls, itself falling under the Aylesbury Brewing Co. before being taken over by Ind Coope. In its former guise, it had an off-licence on entry, with doors leading to the two bars (as today). The mark is a square ceramic plaque made up of four tiles, an illustration of a hare and 'HALLS ... OXFORD AND WEST ... BREWERY COMPANY LIMITED'.

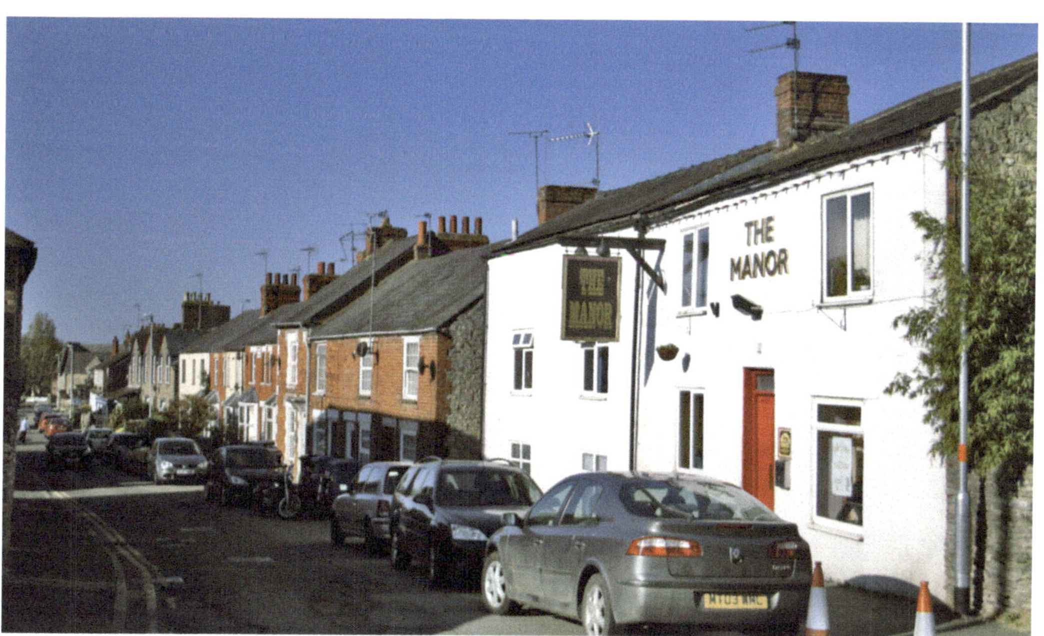

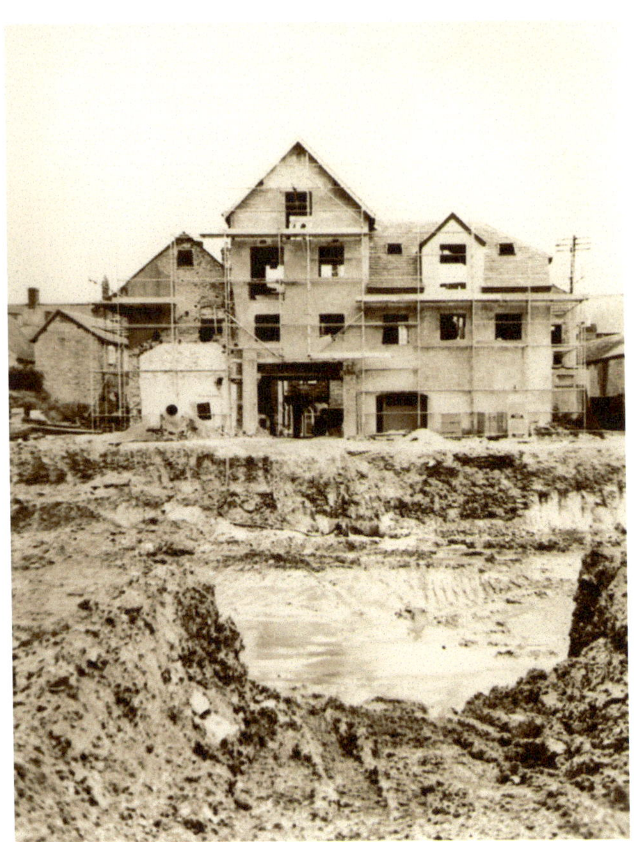

Manor Road Supermarket Site, Early 1990s

The site was originally occupied by cottages that made way for major commercial developments. Bronnley's (soaps) previously had a base on the site following demolition of some cottages. When the current development on the site was being planned, Budgens were going to house their national headquarters there, but they had a bad year and pulled out. The Co-op opened in 1993 (Blake Stimpson was mayor). Today the site is occupied by Waitrose (opened 17 July 2008) and a large, successful Antique Cellar (opened 2000). The building complex overall is viewed today as having a negative impact on the built environment, but the services offered by the organisations that occupy them are certainly appreciated by the residents.

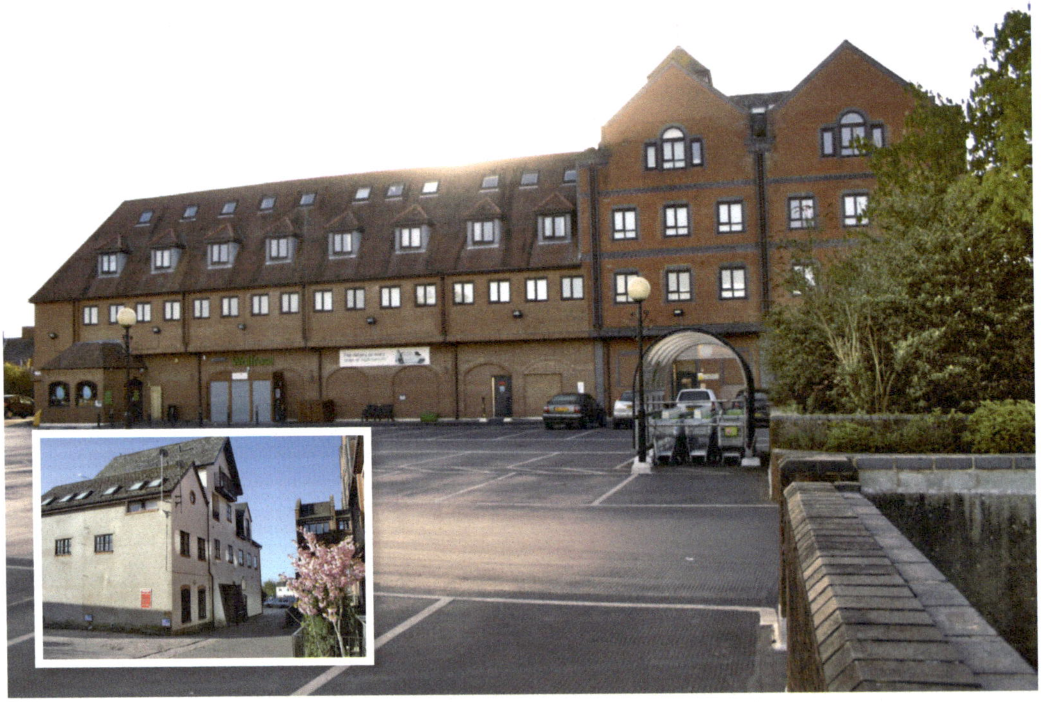

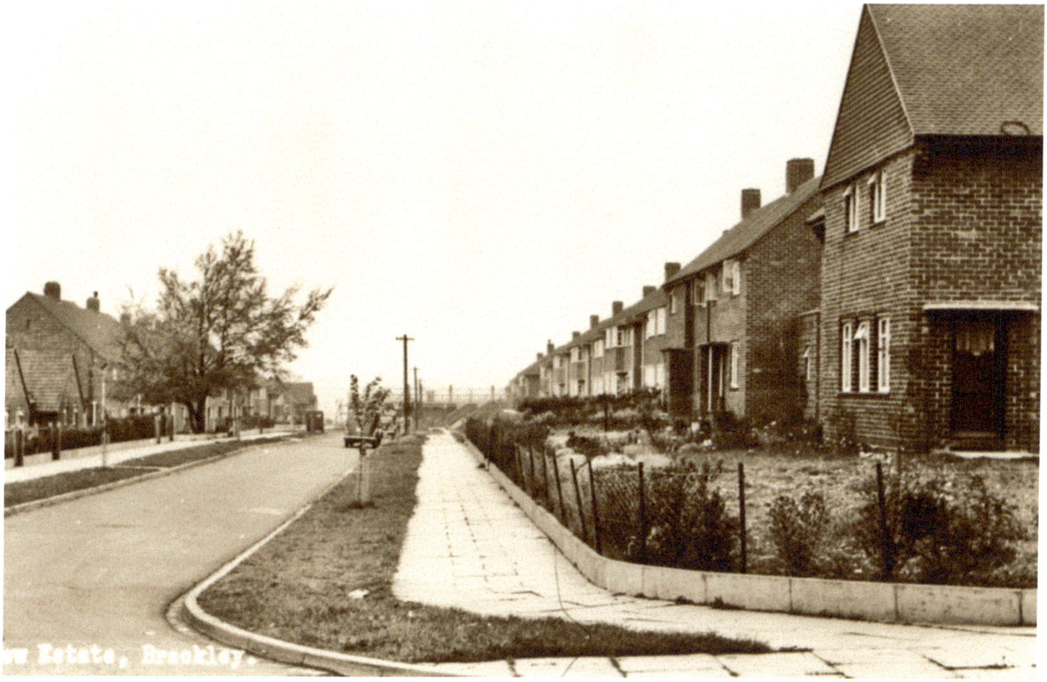

Beaument Crescent, *c.* 1960s

Beaumont Crescent is a post-war estate running adjacent to Waynflete Avenue and the Waynflete site of Magdalen College School. Until after the Second World War, the town was little larger than a large village, with a market place and 2,000–3,000 residents. The then Brackley Borough Council developed this estate and others as social housing after Second World War, when the pressure for residential and business expansion existed within Brackley.

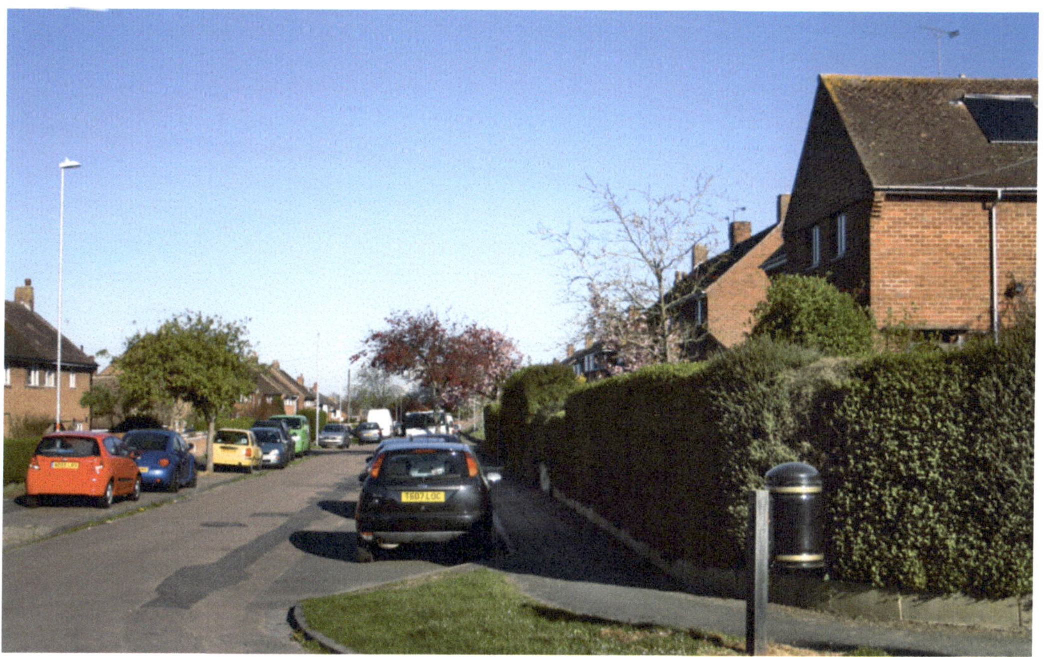

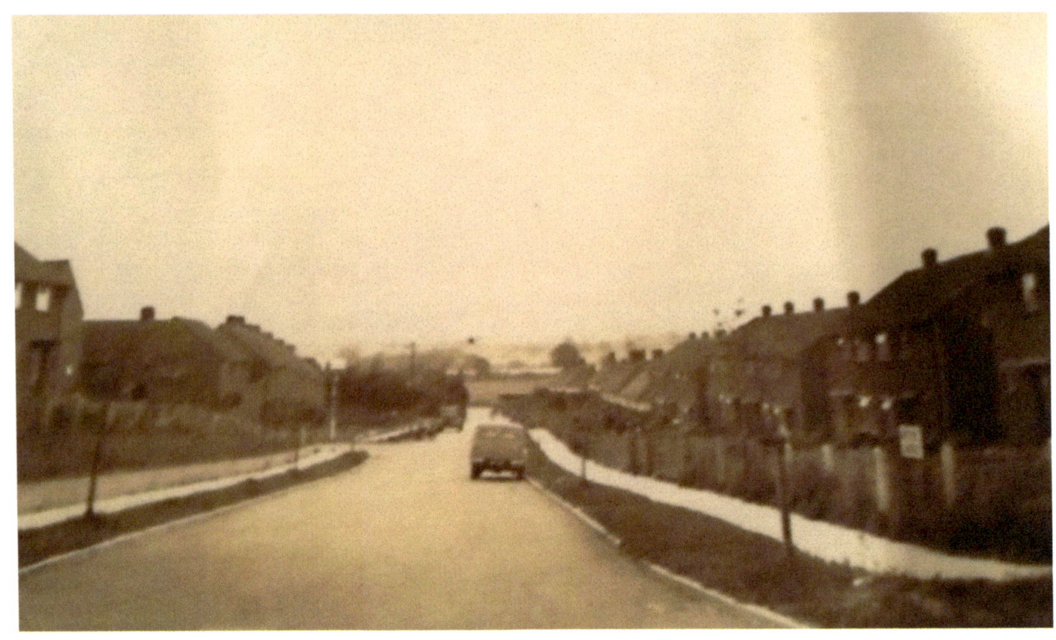

Westhill Avenue, *c.* 1960

As you look down Westhill Avenue towards the Banbury Road, this is where the Victorian workhouse was situated. The old wall at the bottom is protected, as it previously surrounded the workhouse. Nowadays, the whole area is developed with modern housing. The Brackley Poor Law Union Workhouse was established in 1835 and accommodated 200 people.

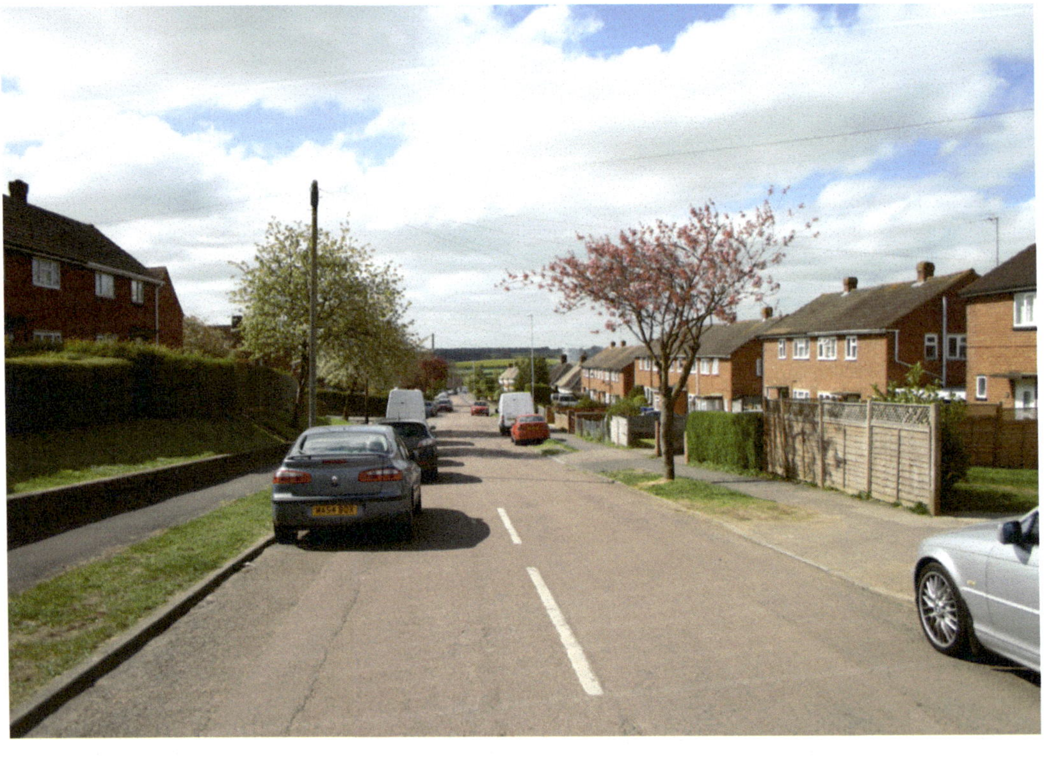

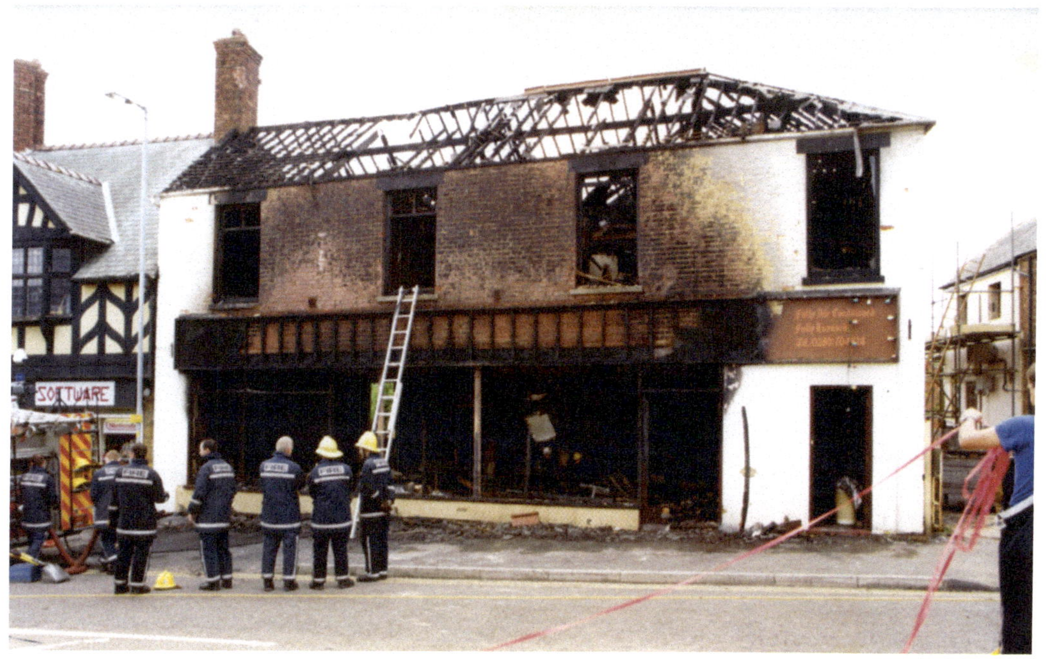

Fire at Jay Pur, Banbury Road, 1994

This was the very first Indian restaurant in Brackley. Since then, Brackley has become a centre for good Indian eating, with no less than five Indian restaurants, all of which are well-established and supported. A fire has occurred here not once but twice over recent decades. The restaurant is situated near the junction with High Street and Bridge Street and is now called the Chilli and Pepper. Charity shops have been popular next door for some time. The Katherine House Hospice shop now occupies premises there.

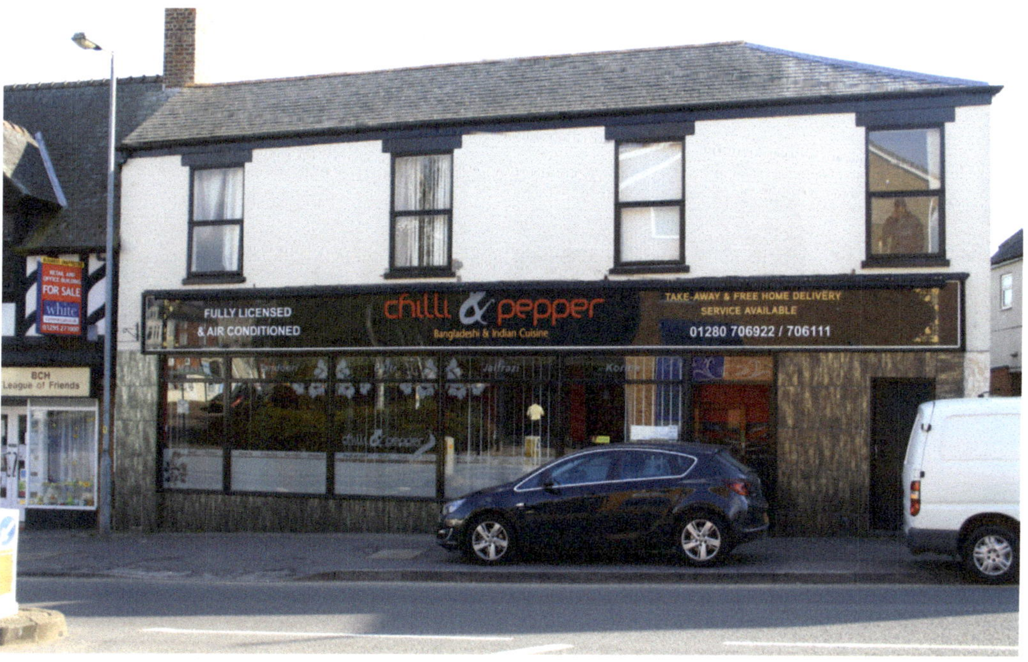

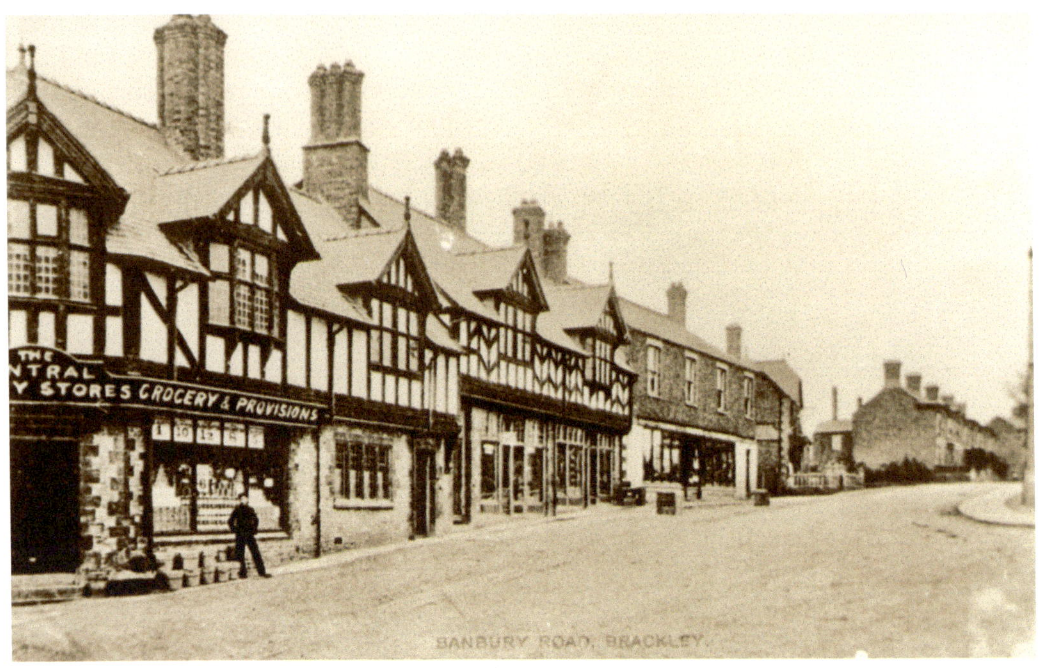

Banbury Road, 1905

This photograph shows the view along the beginning of the Banbury Road coming from Bridge Street. The third shop along used to be Kibbles department store (Nos 6 and 8), in the middle of the last century. The first building used to be a sweet shop, owned and run by Mrs Entichnap. Highfield Court is a new cul-de-sac with new housing to the left, one building after the Indian restaurant.

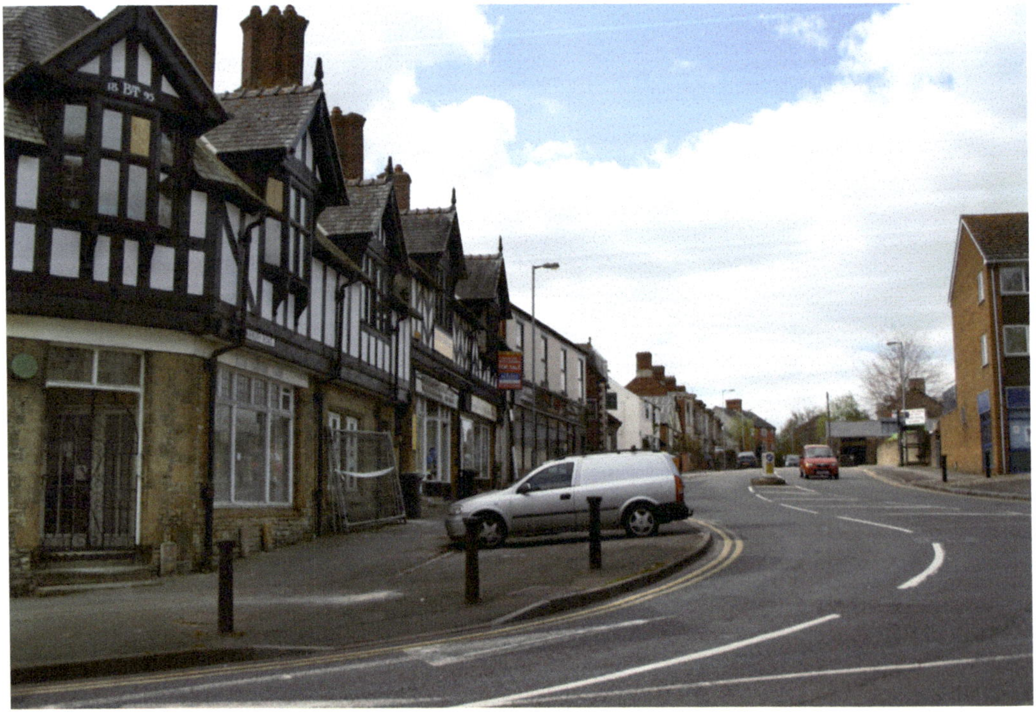

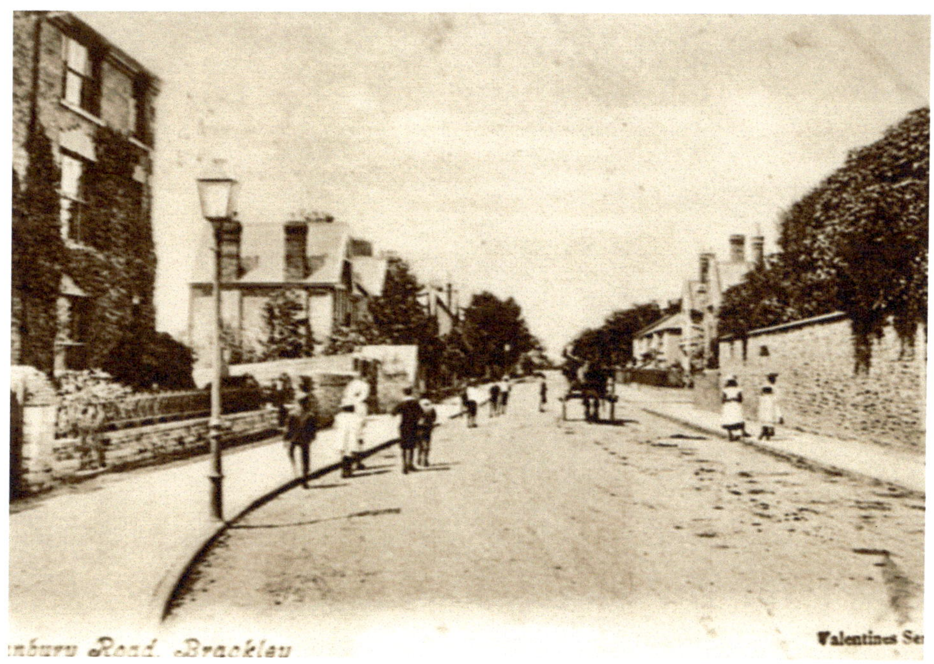

Banbury Road, *c.* 1930s

The photograph above was taken between Nos 32 and 34 approaching the Manor Road junction looking west, with the historic old police station on the corner, which used to house the police station, magistrates' court and two cells. The police station was in use until recent times. A girls' school used to exist just before junction with Manor Road on the left, which became Southfields School, now a state primary school. On the opposite side of the road used to be the girls' boarding house and canteen.

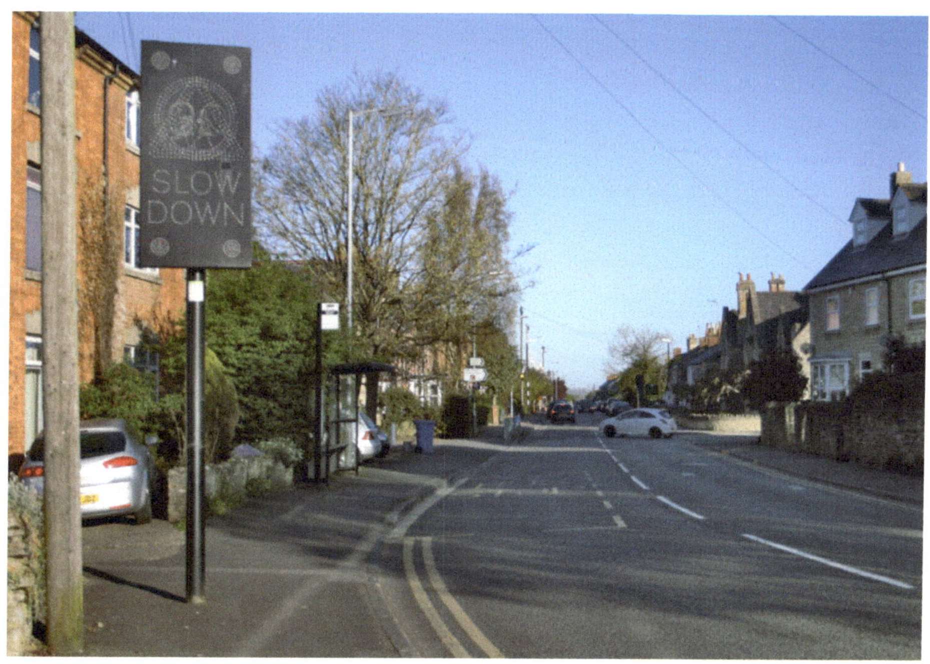

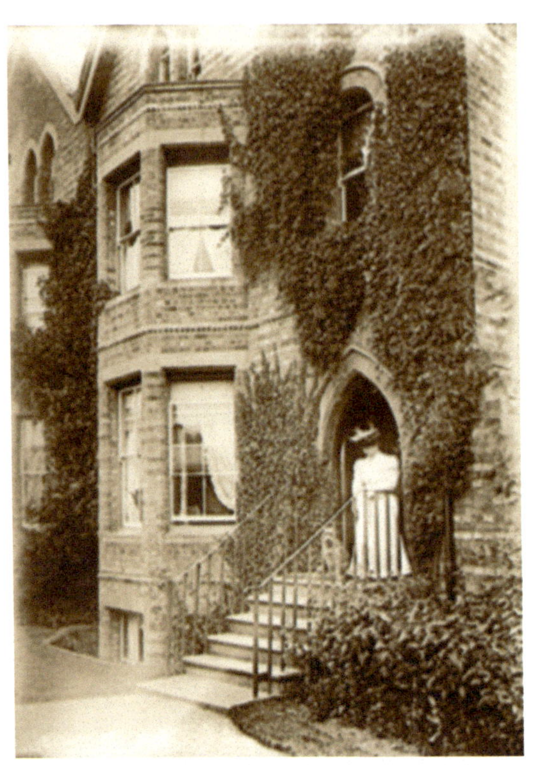

Warden House, Banbury Road, Brackley Lodge, *c.* 1900

A view from the road of a semi-detached gabled house in Brackley. At the eastern end of the Banbury Road, the houses are normally large, with extensive decorative detail, and were designed for prosperous people. The size and status of the homes generally diminishes as you move further away from the Market Place. Nowadays, the road is cluttered with parked cars for residents and for parents dropping children off for Southfields Primary School.

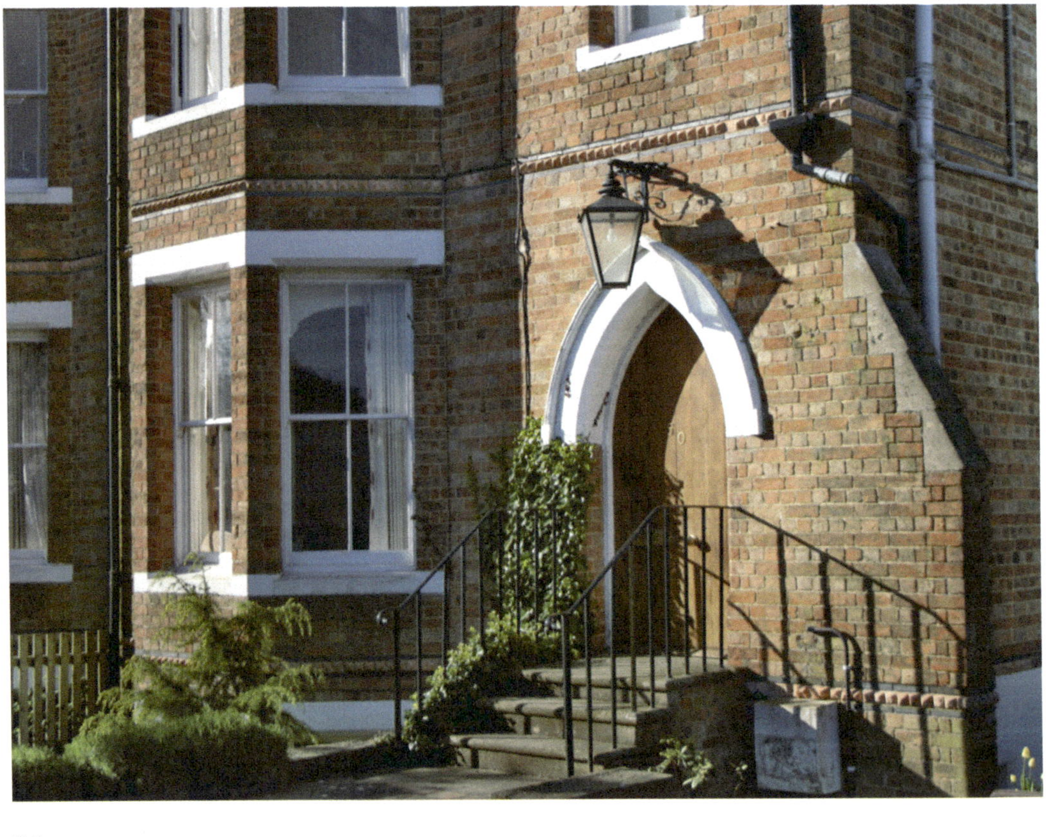

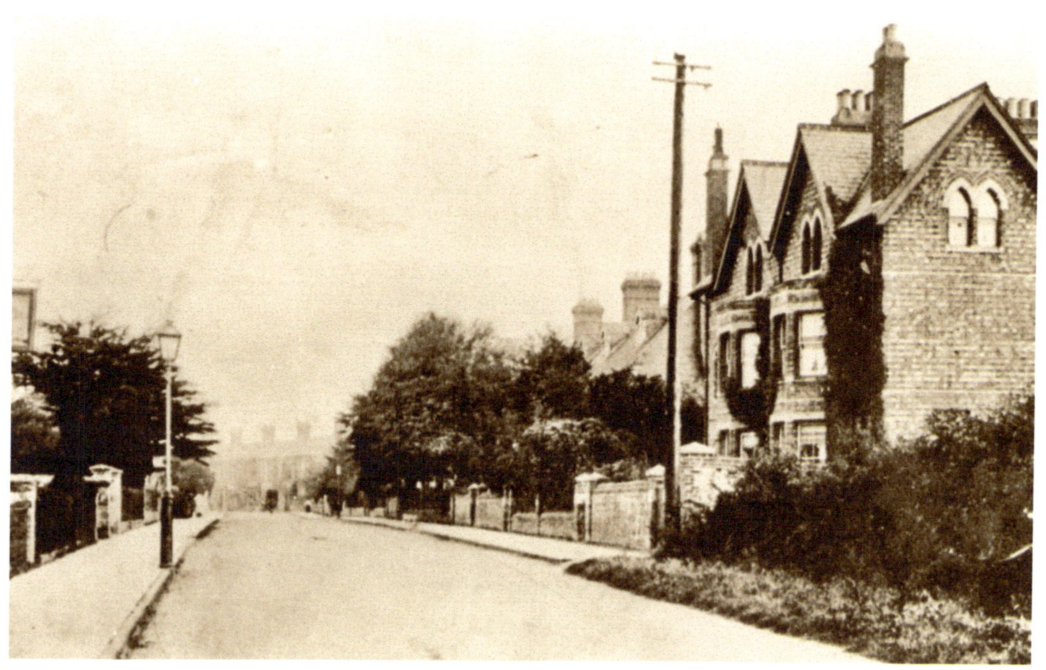

Banbury Road, Early 1900s

This is now a busy thoroughfare. The Victorian houses along the Banbury Road have the advantage of a lovely outlook from the back over St James's lake. Further west along the Banbury Road on the left is The Fox public house, near Nos 50–52 (you can just see the sign). It is now a one-room pub with a large bar area, with smoking facilities outside. It features an interior of mock black-and-white timber frames. The pub sign is now black and white and depicts a fox. Miss Draper once ran a private school in the first house on the right.

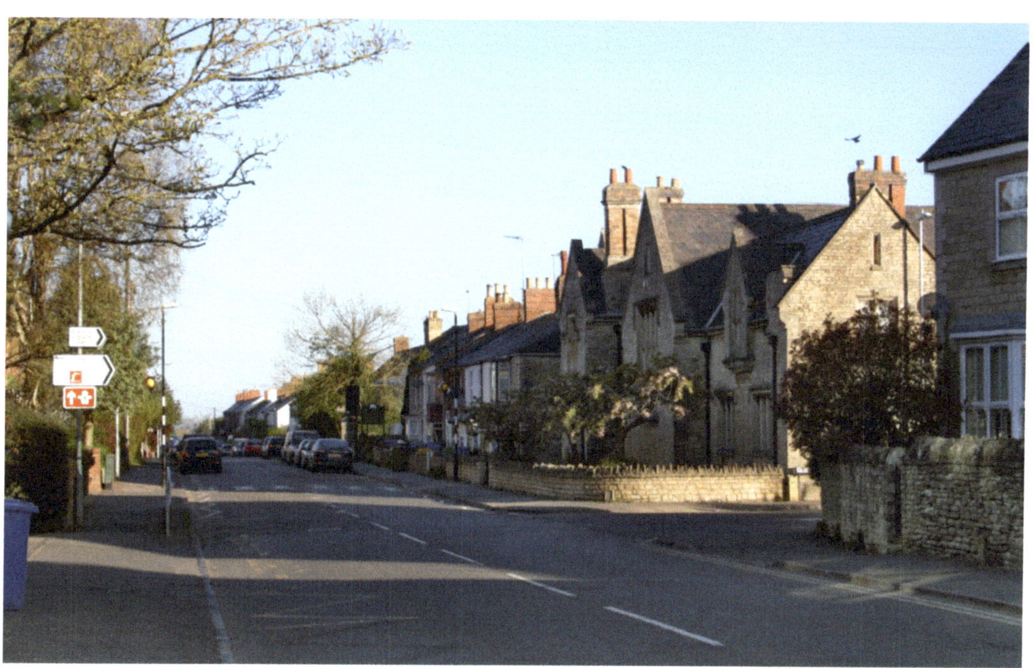

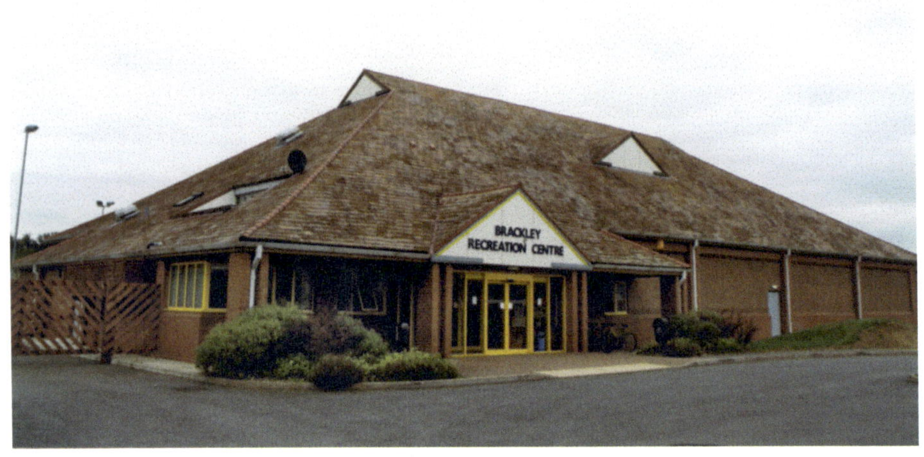

Brackley Leisure Centre, *c.* 1985

Brackley Leisure Centre is found on Springfield Way, part of the Pavillons Way 'French' estate (Pavillons Way is the backbone road running from south to north) – a recent addition to Brackley, opened in the 1990s. Previously open fields, the centre now brings a wide range of recreational opportunities to residents of Brackley and surrounding villages; it is an easy-to-reach location by foot or car. The centre is owned by South Northamptonshire Council and managed by SERCO. Walks to the west of Brackley, such as to Steane Park, are accessible from this area of town. In 2013, the South Northamptonshire Leisure Trust invested over £134,000 in improving Brackley Leisure Centre for local residents, ensuring the district continues to offer leisure facilities that are accessible and suitable for everyone, whether a casual visitor or fitness fanatic. A small shopping precinct exists nearby to serve the residents of Pavillons Way.

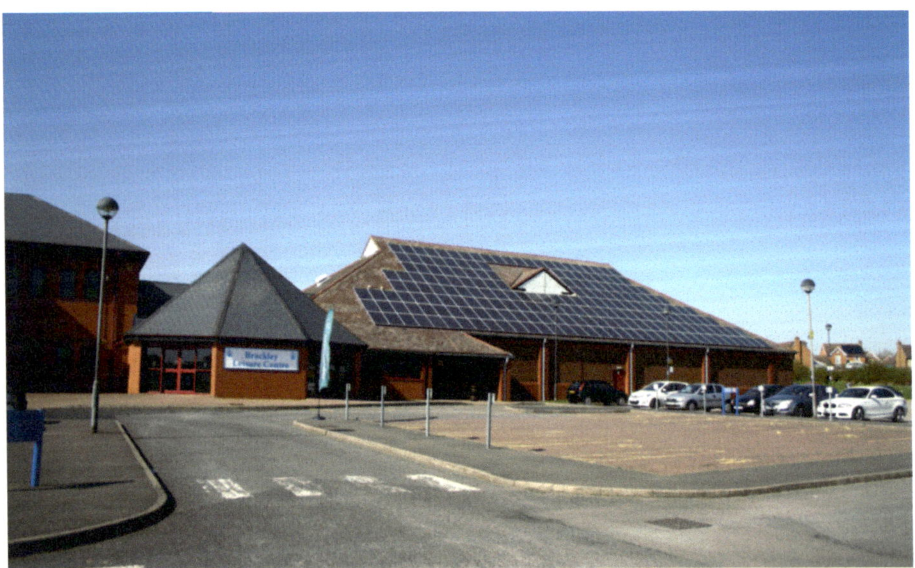

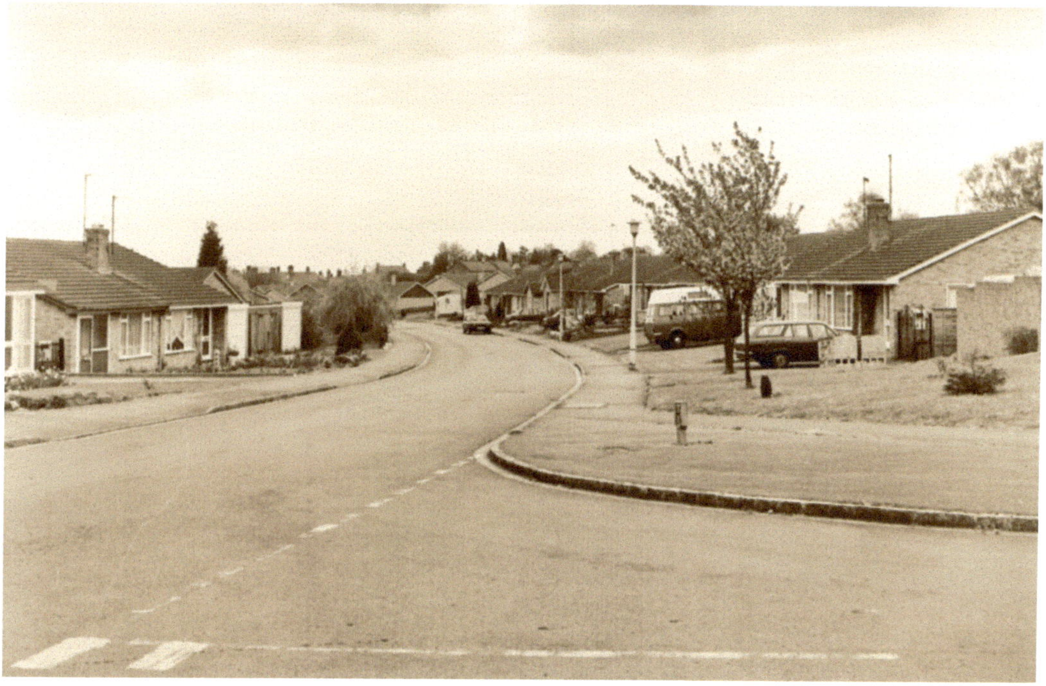

View Down Bridgewater Road From No. 57, *c.* 1970

The estate is in the north-east of Brackley, not far from where the top station used to be. It consists largely of bungalows. The road comes off Burwell Hill, where a Ford garage used to be called Burwell Hill Garage. Jarvis Court is now sited at the junction of High Street with Burwell Hill.

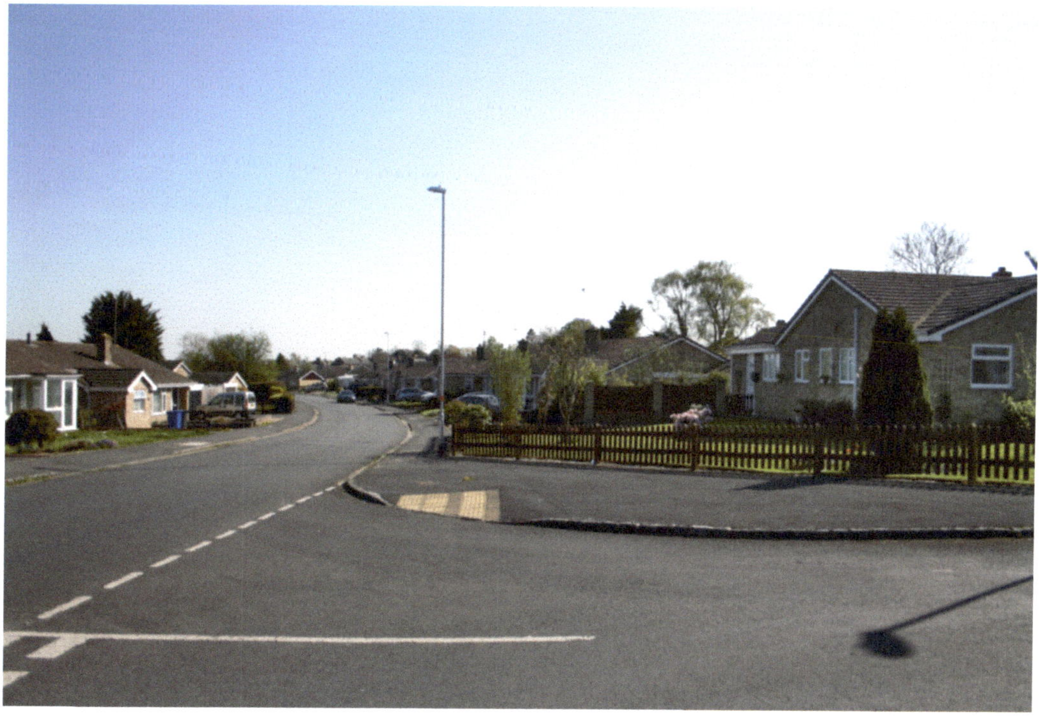

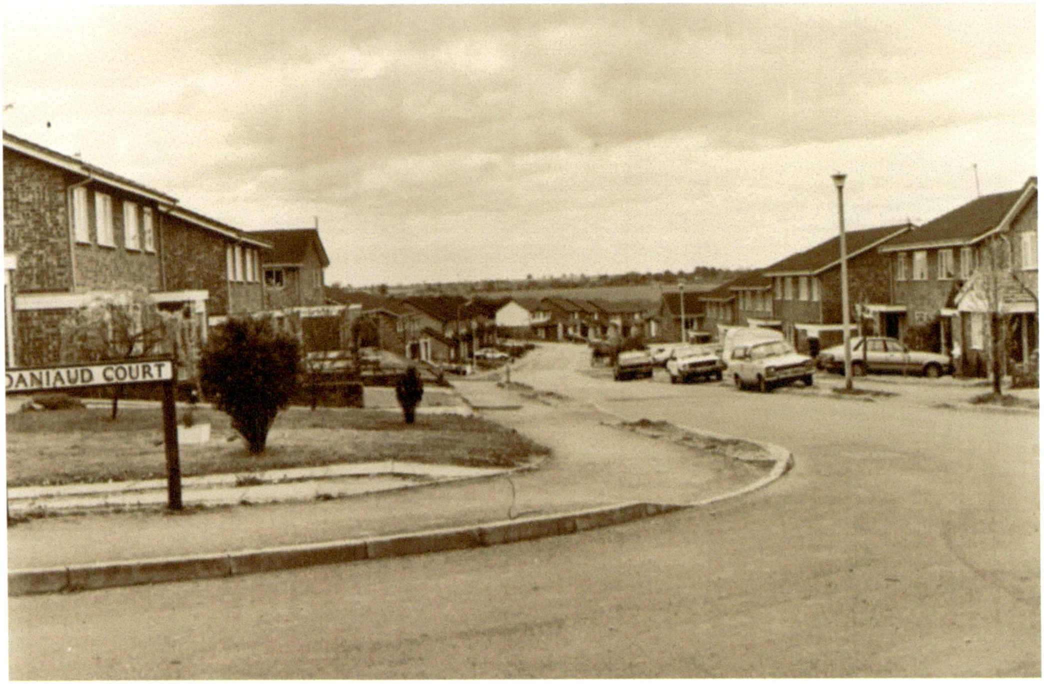

Martial Daire Boulevard, From Junction with Daniaud Court, *c.* 1970

Part of the western development expansion of Brackley at the end of the twentieth century. This road links Pavillons Way with the northern side of Brackley and consists largely of modern family homes.

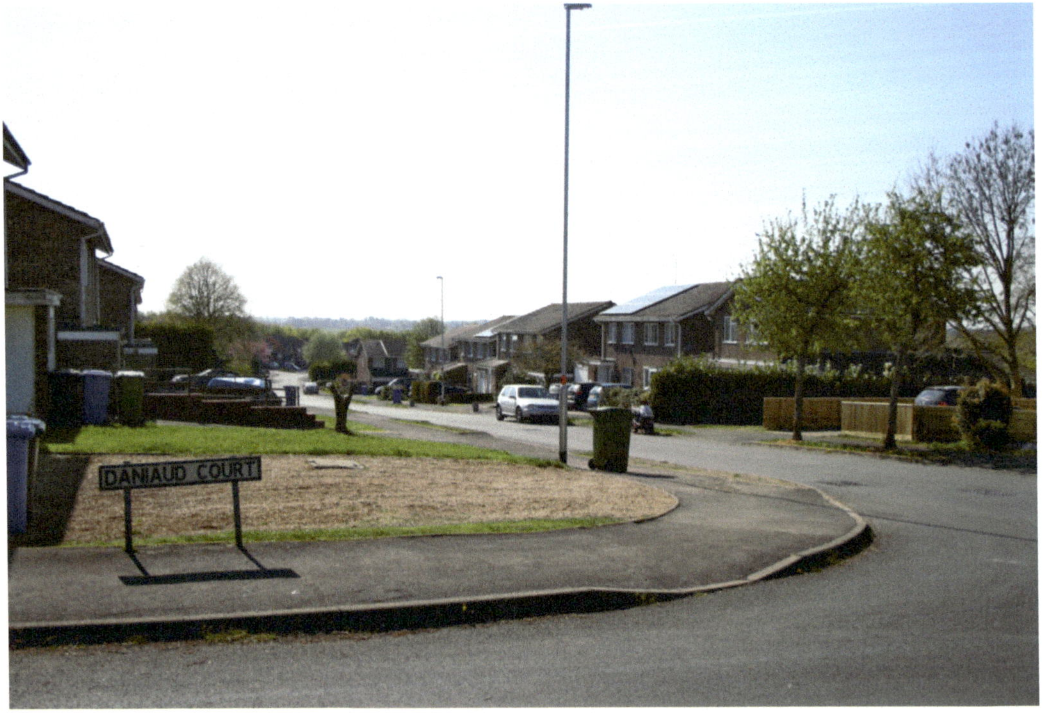

Part 3

Surrounding Villages

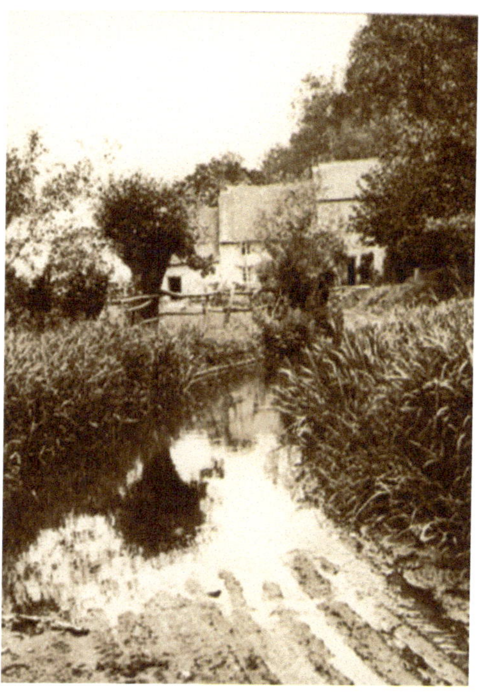

Turweston Watermill and Mill Stream, 1938
Near the Stratton Arms public house. Turweston is a stone village of great charm situated on a gentle slope down to the River Ouse. The river runs through the parkland of Turweston House, on a course to the west and parallel with the main village street. It is particularly attractive at the northern end of Turweston, where it enhances the approach to the village and provides a pleasant setting to Turweston Mill.

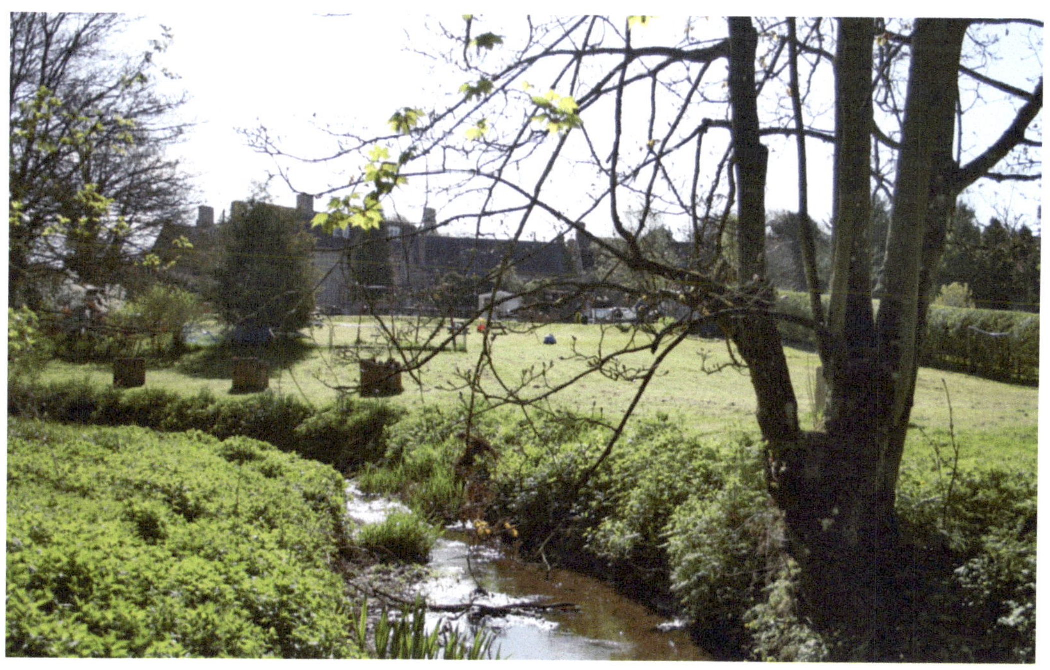

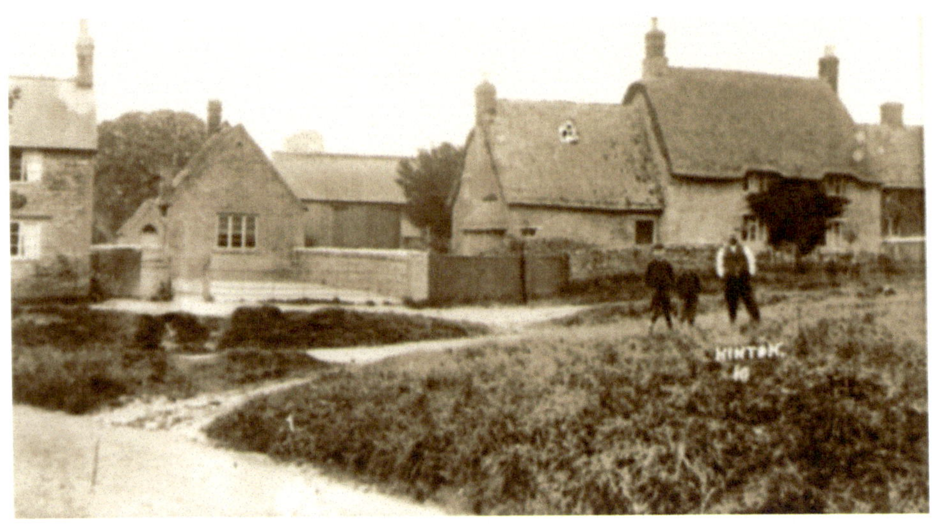

Hinton in the Hedges, Early Nineteenth Century

Hinton in the Hedges is a small village 2 miles due west of Brackley, and even today it has a distinctly rural and peaceful feel. The scene shown is in the centre of the village. There are a number of old and interesting buildings in the village. In the parish church, there are monuments to Sir William Hinton, the founder of the village. On the west side of the village is Hinton in the Hedges' private airfield. The land was bought by the Harrison family in 1924 and taken from them to build the Second World War airfield in 1939. It fell back into the hands of the Harrisons in 1963, and today is busy with gliding and a range of recreational flying activities.

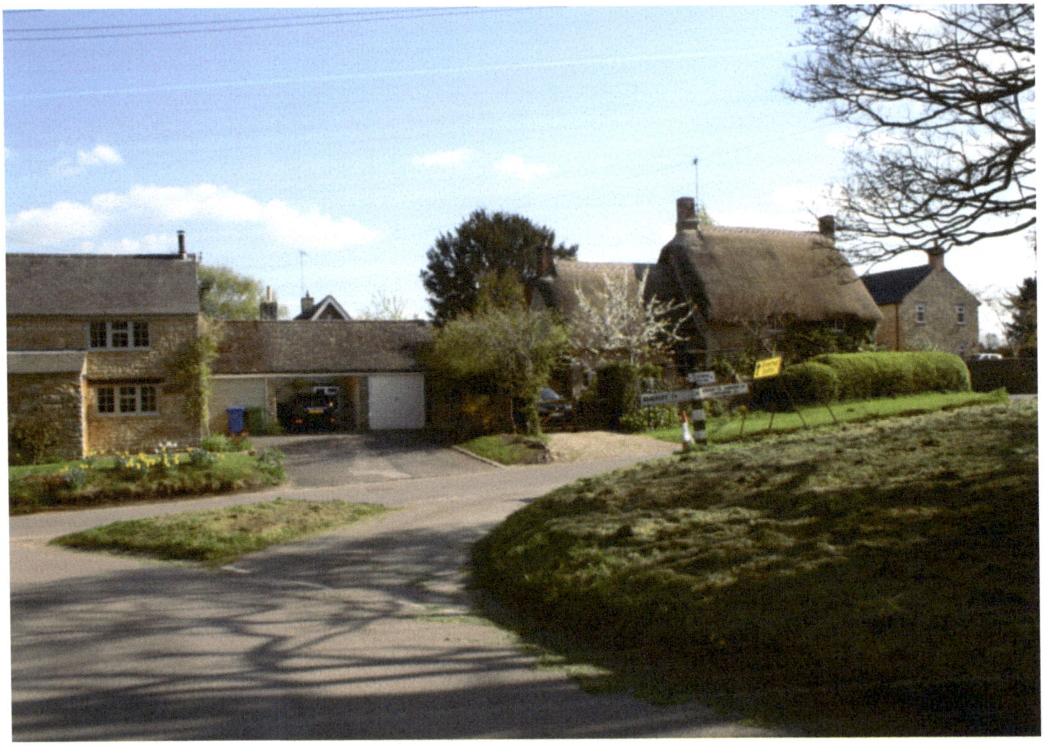

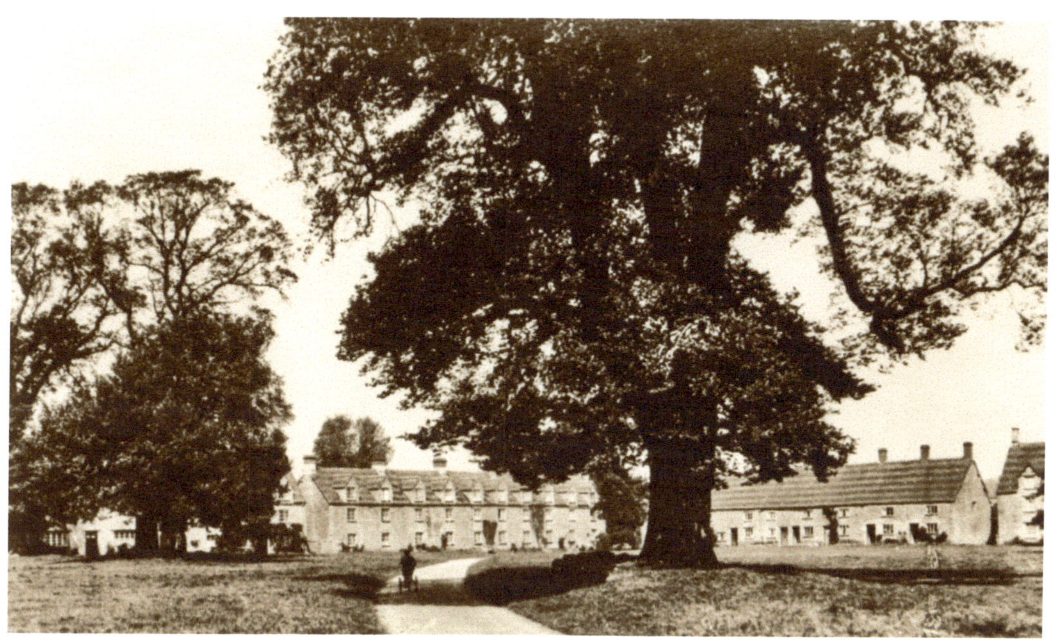

Evenley Green, *c.* 1930s

The parish of Evenley lies a mile to the south of Brackley. It is an ancient village with its roots in Roman times. It has an archetypical and idyllic village green, which has seen cricket matches through the centuries. The Green is surrounded by Grade II listed buildings. In the parish, the Georgian Evenley Hall, built in 1740 for Francis Bassett, was damaged by fire in 1897, and was run as a children's home during the latter part of last century. Evenley has a village shop and post office, as well as the popular Red Lion public house on the green. The parish church was built in 1535.

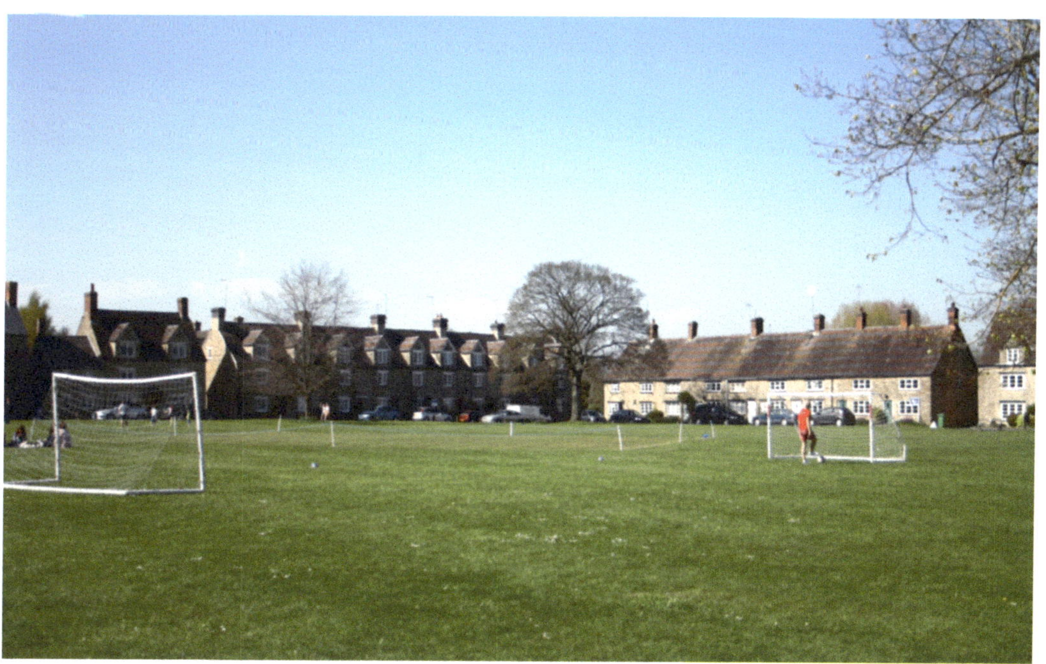

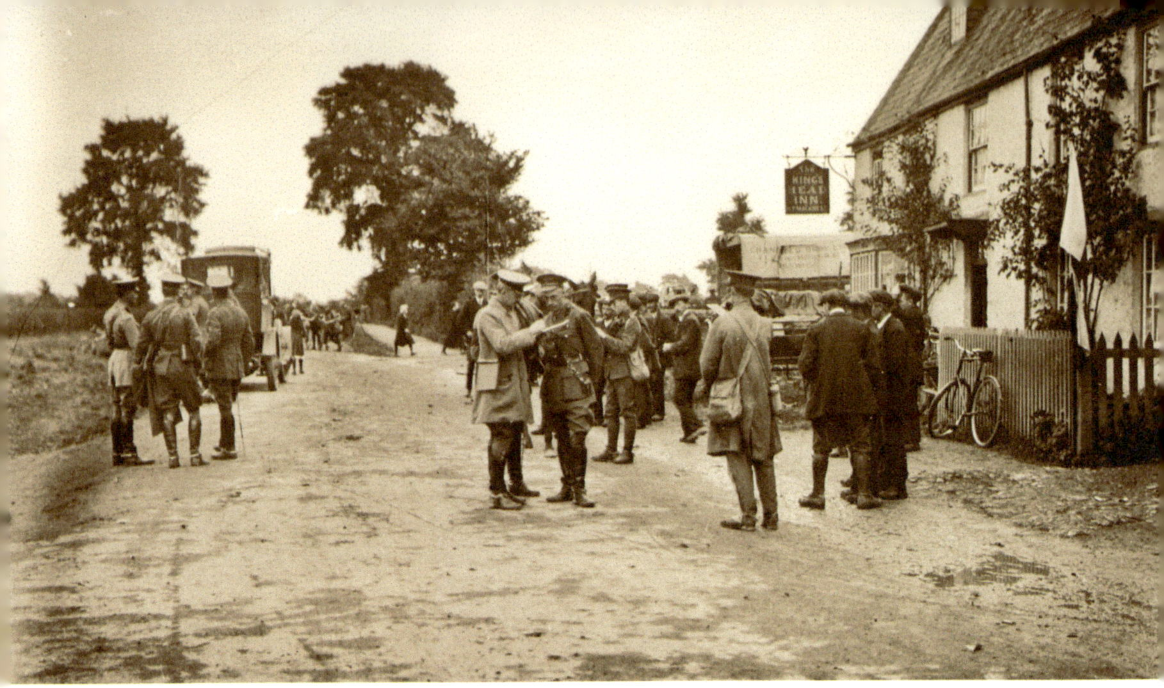

Army Manoeuvres, Syresham, Outside the Kings Head Inn, 1913

The parish of Syresham is a couple of miles to the north of Brackley. It is surrounded by ancient woodland, including Whistley Wood, Hazelborough Forest and Whittlewood Forest, the hunting grounds for several English kings, including Richard III. The Kings Head is a popular hotel today and does particularly well when racing takes place at the Silverstone circuit just up the road. Syresham has had direct connections to the livestock trade over many decades and several residents and village features relate directly back to the old cattle droving days. Good communications infrastructure means, as with most villages around Brackley, residents work away from their communities but enjoy good quality of life in their communities.

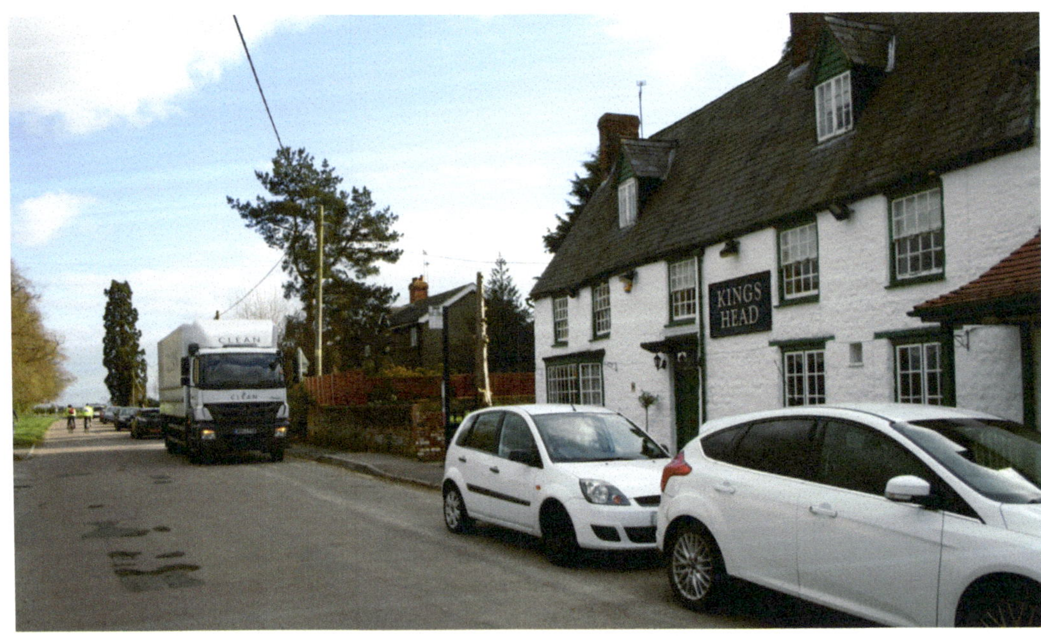

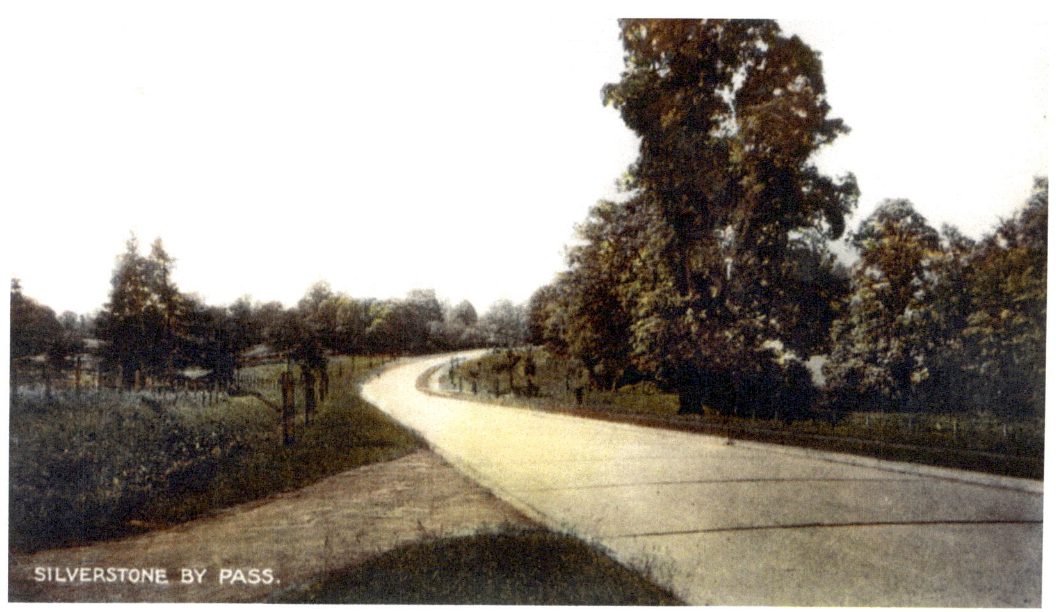

Silverstone

World famous for its Formula 1 circuit, much of the current economic strength of the whole Brackley area and beyond arises because of the circuit, and particularly the holding of the British Grand Prix there. The photograph above shows the main road that all northbound/southbound traffic followed in those days, which is very different to the current dual carriageway and routing of traffic around the area on race days. The village has a mention in the Domesday Book, and in the Middle Ages trade was mainly in timber and a woodyard still exists today. Silverstone Circuit was opened as a Second World War airfield in 1943. On 2 October 1948, amid straw bales and ropes, Silverstone's first event took place, the RAC Grand Prix. The winner of the inaugural race at the Silverstone circuit was Luigi Villoresi in a Maserati, who recorded an average speed of 72 mph to claim the first prize of £500.

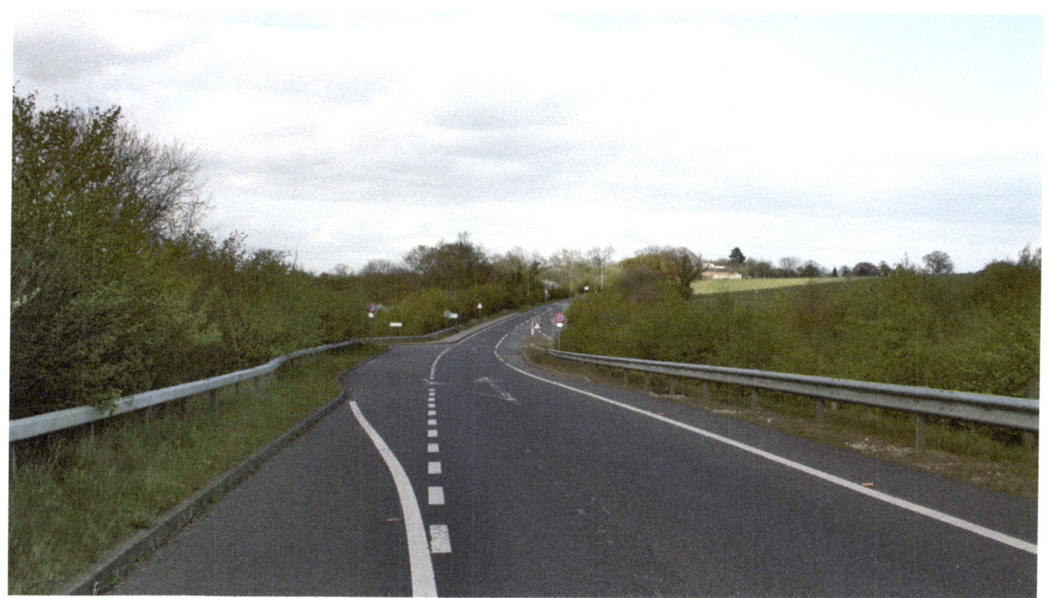

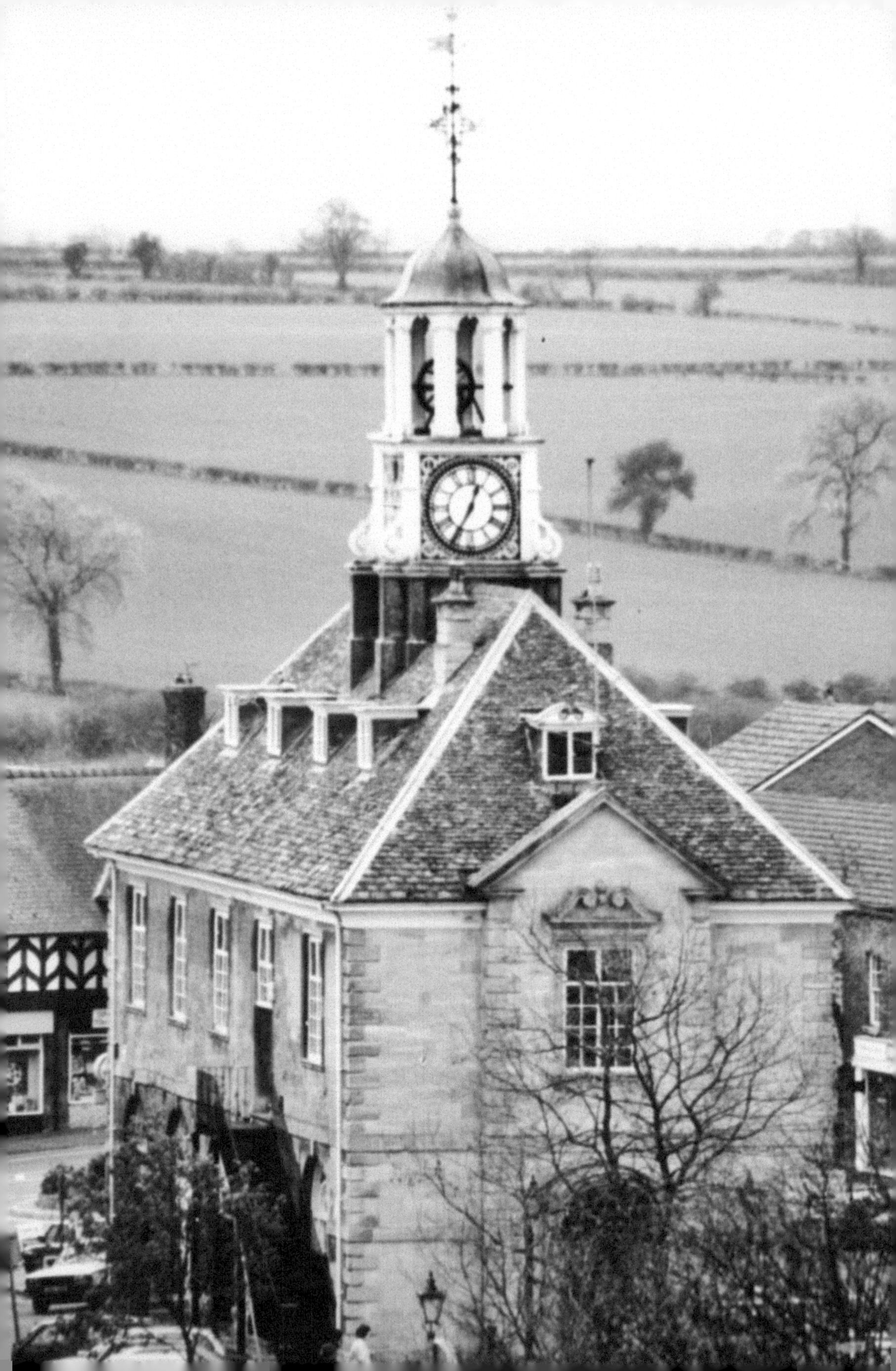

Printed and bound by CPI Group (UK) Ltd, Croydon, CR0 4YY

11/07/2026

02161070-0001